IN PRAISE OF
Home
Cooking

IN PRAISE OF
Home
Cooking

REASONS AND RECIPES

Liana Krissoff

Photographs by Chaunté Vaughn
Illustrations by Jenice Kim

Abrams, New York

Contents

Introduction

Managing an active home kitchen is little more than a balancing of abundance and scarcity. Use, preserve, and share when you can. Enjoy cooking with the best ingredients you can obtain, but know that pleasure and nourishment are not dependent on how much you can spend for them. Use the right tool for each task, but refrain from assembling a life overflowing with unnecessaries.

Community can be built around home cooking and larger food systems. Unless you're a professional cook, I don't think you have to "know your farmer" or "befriend your local butcher," but do try to know your neighbors and learn about how your ingredients are produced.

Flexibility is survival. Adaptation is good. Respect your present circumstances as much as you respect abstract ideas of tradition or the pronouncements of food experts.

Good home cooks—like good people in general—are curious. They don't just keep an open mind when new foods or techniques are presented to them, but seek them out. They ask questions and want to learn.

Authentic is a word that can be applied to whatever you're cooking or eating, and so it is essentially meaningless in the realm of food.

Anyone, of any age, can gain competence as a cook if they're allowed to make (age-appropriate, safe) mistakes. Be patient with yourself and the new cooks you're helping in the kitchen; most mistakes are edible or at least fixable, and all contribute to a cook's education.

When I consider what it means to be confident in the kitchen, to understand ingredients, to enjoy cooking and eating, and to be capable of sustaining yourself and your friends and family, the kinds of skills that come to mind now are considerably different from those that I might have considered important just a few years ago. Even before the stay-at-home orders went into effect in response to the coronavirus pandemic in 2020, I'd found myself more attuned to a general sense of extreme thrift. Living in Appalachia, learning about the region's long history of exploitation and struggle, reading old cookbooks of "make-do" recipes, helping fill boxes at the food pantry and realizing how many adults and children a single box was supposed to feed for a week (and then being told families are allowed only one box every *four or six* weeks): it's all revealed my own past efforts at efficiency in the kitchen to be frivolous and somewhat stupid. I'm sure moving to this part of the country changed how I cook, and then the coronavirus changed things further as I learned how to better use what we had on hand, repurpose, improvise more than I'd had to before. Full shutdown in West Virginia lasted only about a month and a half, but what I learned in that time (and throughout the summer and fall, as we continued to stay home as much as possible anyway) will stick with me forever, and it's partly why what began as a sweet kitchen handbook is now a manifesto.

How to achieve the perfect dice? Who cares. How to score the best bunch of carrots at the farmers' market? You have carrots? You're golden. How to be a member of a community, on the other hand, how to practice generosity with the sustenance we have, how to be curious about new foods while also appreciating what we already know and love? Those are the true essentials, the skills we should try to teach kids as early as possible—and learn ourselves if we haven't already. I'm still working on the community part myself, in all honesty. It's hard when the systems we live under and the built environments that surround us are designed in ways that discourage solidarity, from anti-labor laws and norms upholding long workdays that consume our leisure time, to elementary-school consolidation and zoning that favors giant houses and vast lawns to separate them, to highway projects that slice up neighborhoods. Food—talking about it, sharing it—has been a way for me to try to cut through all that and form relationships, some casual and fleeting (but still very necessary), some deep and permanent.

Just a couple of months ago, in the middle of writing this book—okay, not quite in the middle; in the *midst*, let's say, of *starting* this book—my family and I moved from Morgantown, West Virginia, a small college town in the hills, to a row house in the heart of Pittsburgh. People walk past our front windows almost every minute of the day, and I don't know any of them. My (over-?) reliance on food to spark early social engagement is all the more obvious when neighborly deliveries of baked goods to and from virtual strangers are made even more awkward by a pandemic, of all things. There are other ways to meet people, of course; I'm just not very good at them, and I suspect I'm not alone.

Americans move a lot, an average of about twelve moves in a lifetime—two or three times the rates in Europe. As part of a system in which GDP growth is valued above all, it's almost impossible to stay in place, though the number of people moving in the United States each year has been declining from its height during the postwar boom of the 1950s as the workforce ages; salaries flatten out, making the expense and hassle of moving a household less appealing; and jobs become more homogenous and less tied to specific places. Maybe, too, in times of uncertainty like these, when the possibility that growth won't or even shouldn't, in fact, continue its historical upward trend in this country begins to dawn on some of us, the idea of making a home in one place, preferably close to good friends and family, becomes more attractive. It certainly feels that way to me as I sense my own momentum slowing down on this move, my fourteenth, though I'll fully admit that it might just be that I'm getting old and tired of packing and unpacking kitchen supplies.

I have no idea whether my daughter will settle down somewhere as a young adult or continue to move around a lot, but I want her (and you, reader) to believe that one can make community wherever one is. Having the skills you need to cook and appreciate and share food with people you don't know well yet is a relatively straightforward way to do that. If you can cook well, you can help others, and if you can help others, they can help you. When I finish writing this, I'm going to unpack the mixer, make a big batch of ginger-molasses cookies, put on a mask, and drop off a container of them for our next-door neighbors, who moved in a couple of weeks after we did.

In an essay with nothing explicit to say about cooking that nevertheless clarified and deepened my own sense of how I want to be as a home cook, environmental historian William Cronon offers thoughts on the tricky question of what constitutes a liberal education. The liberally educated, he says, "nurture and empower the people around them." They "understand that they belong to a community whose prosperity and well-being are crucial to their own, and they help that community flourish by making the success of others possible." I like to think of a cook's education in a similar way, and I appreciate that Cronon talks of communities flourishing, not just surviving.

When I was a kid, I was fascinated by the literature of survival: Jack London and Laura Ingalls Wilder, Melville and *Mutiny on the Bounty*, the Foxfire series. I'd never call myself a survivalist, and I'm definitely not a prepper here in our dense new neighborhood in Pittsburgh, but I do read far too many articles about North American climate-change migration forecasts and run through imagined doomsday scenarios while studying maps with grim titles like "Geographic Range of Fire Ants Continues Northward March." In West Virginia I'd make mental notes of the locations of natural springs in the area (just in case), and where various edible plants would pop up each season—plants that really wouldn't be worth collecting unless it came to be absolutely necessary for whatever reason. A friend of mine has put together a file of survival resources that will fit on a flash drive, and out of curiosity and a little bit of panic I asked her to share it with me, while promising myself I would not open any

documents describing emergency at-home dental procedures until the shit had truly hit the fan. (At which point, of course, it'd all be academic anyway: the grid would be down, the flash drive useless to me, because owning a generator any larger than a crank-operated flashlight is kind of a personal Rubicon.)

My daughter shares my interest in this stuff. She knows how to start a fire with a couple of sticks and a length of self-fashioned dogbane cord—and she's good at it: when she was seven, she was the only kid at Survival and Awareness summer camp, at a prairie school in Nebraska, who got her fire lit. Her English class did a unit on "Survival," and the first assignment involved choosing four items you'd take with you as you escaped a sinking ship and swam to a desert island. I was inordinately proud and relieved to see that out of a couple dozen options she chose the tarp. She knows how to cast a fly rod (if not, yet, catch a fish with it) and build a rudimentary shelter. And, of course, now at fourteen, she can cook reasonably nutritious food by herself with random ingredients she finds in the fridge and pantry.

One afternoon not too long ago, though, I came into the kitchen to find her snacking on a pan of onions she'd sliced up and lightly sautéed. Just: onions. Cooked in olive oil. I knew there was much to be done. In Ling Ma's *Severance*, a novel about a young woman working in a lower-level position at the edges of book publishing in Manhattan when a plague hits (a story seemingly written just for me), the protagonist remembers when she was a child and her mother was considering going back to work. The mom asks if the daughter knows how to make rice.

"Yeah. You just put the rice and water in and hit the button!" The mom says, "No, you have to wash the rice first. So it doesn't taste dirty. You wash the rice in cold water for at least a minute. If you could learn how to do that, and also how to steam a fish with ginger and scallions, then I could work." What a beautifully concise depiction of our project here.

That's not to say that my daughter and I need to embark on a series of cooking lessons—or that you need to do anything like that either. Where there are lessons, there's a curriculum, and where there's a curriculum, there are judgments about what should be part of it. You'll find a selection of recipes in this book, of course, but I'll make no claim that they constitute anything like a program of study, much less a culinary canon. Cronon (the historian) lists examples of areas of interest that a person might pursue in the course of their life—meaningful engagement with art, the ability to identify wildlife, an appreciation for fine craftsmanship, facility with the "World Wide Web" (this was 1998), and so on. "None of us can possibly master all these forms of 'reading,' but educated people should be competent in many of them and curious about all of them." An educated cook, likewise, will be able to make many foods well, and will cultivate a lifelong interest in learning to cook and enjoy an ever-broader range of dishes. We've already moved in this direction, I think, but let's definitely bury the idea that an accomplished cook is one who's mastered this technique, or that classic sauce.

This isn't a new idea either, but to hell with the canon, along with outdated notions of authenticity. Are there certain techniques and foods you must be familiar with in order to be considered a sophisticated cook—tempering eggs and making a béchamel? Absolutely not. Who is allowed to cook certain dishes and ingredients, learn about them, write about them, have opinions about them, even sell them? You are. Anyone is. There are no limits other than your own curiosity, the trait I think adults should nurture most enthusiastically in the kids we care for. If you're cooking a dish the way your granddad taught you to, or the way you first learned to cook it from a recipe in a magazine you bought in the checkout line at the grocery store, or the way you've developed over years of tinkering with it yourself, it's a perfectly legitimate dish. It's part of your own tradition. Your repertoire is authentic.

The recipes here are part of one person's tradition (mine). They represent a chronicle of how I learned to cook but also of my ongoing efforts to help my daughter develop a level of competence with improvisatory home cooking I myself didn't have until years after I'd graduated from college and moved out on my own. The collection is meant to serve here not as a program of study, but as an example of how you might help a young person learn to cook, or how you might go about becoming more competent in the kitchen yourself if you feel you need refreshers. Think of the points of the manifesto as the frame of a somewhat shoddily built shed, the recipes as the siding that holds it together. Pry off the cabbage-and-noodles plank and replace it with something more appropriate to your taste—your grandma's homemade fettucine, maybe. Rice and steamed fish with ginger and scallions. The structure will stand just as well.

Cookbook authors write recipes in a state of fear. Either we assume too much knowledge and risk leading readers into catastrophe, or we include so much detail that our tone is condescending, as if we think our home-cook readers are incapable of basic judgment. The recipes here, especially in the early part of the book, will seem simple, erring on the side of condescension, but I've learned that just one innocent young child in the kitchen can make all hell break loose, and that it helps to have a written plan for even a grilled cheese sandwich if you're having *one of those days*. Much of cooking is intuitive and not tied to recipes on a page—Is this done yet? Does it taste right? Sometimes I do it this way, sometimes I do it that way—but when you're showing a young person how to make a dish for the first time, clarity is key, so I'm giving even the most basic dishes the full recipe treatment.

Because I wanted this book to be useful for cooks of all ages, at the top of each recipe I've included a list of skills that cooks (or their helpers) will need to draw on. If you're cooking with a five-year-old and you see that the dish involves "stovetop cooking over high heat," or "moving a full baking dish in and out of the oven," you know you'll need to stay close and help out a fair bit. I've tried to be fairly specific in describing each recipe's difficulty. Chopping an onion is a lot harder for inexperienced hands than slicing a tomato, but a careful young person might be able to handle it well enough.

Treating kids as only slightly less skillful equals while you cook with them is incredibly rewarding: You'll see them start to anticipate what needs to be done and attempt new tasks with confidence, even if they don't quite get the details. (Recall the self-assurance of the exclamation point: "You just put the rice and water in and hit the button!") Be generous with yourself and the kids you're cooking with, and try not to worry too much about perfection. With young kids, everything in the kitchen will take much longer than you think it should—start before anyone's cranky with hunger, and take your time. If the vegetables are chopped unevenly, let it go, and perhaps gently explain why the smaller bits will cook faster than the larger ones and will end up more tender in the finished dish. Whatever it is, it'll taste just fine, your co-chef will be proud, and maybe next time—or the time after that—the pieces will be more uniform. I know from fourteen years of experience how hard it is to refrain from continually issuing corrections or taking over a task when it's not going as well as you'd like it to, but if the dish will be okay and if the young person you're cooking with is happy and isn't asking for help, I'd suggest trying to let them work on their own as much as possible. Handle expensive ingredients yourself (no liquid flows more extravagantly from the bottle than pure vanilla extract!), or use less-dear substitutes. Expect mistakes, accept imperfections, and enjoy your time together in the kitchen and at the table.

Gaining kitchen skills that will see you through difficulty—learning to roast a whole chicken and use it for several days' worth of meals, to cook a pot of creamy beans and one of fluffy rice, to preserve foods when they're abundant—is not at all incompatible with living hopefully and with great pleasure.

Know how to start a fire in a clearing in the woods, and also how to make a simple but celebration-worthy layer cake. How to forage for wild greens when your body is telling you very clearly that it's lacking their nutrients, and how to make a mug of hot cocoa just because it's the first cold, gray day of fall.

The title of William Cronon's essay on liberal education is the famous epigraph from E. M. Forster's *Howards End*, "Only connect . . . ," words that appear, along with the more general idea of connection, several times in the novel. Cronon emphasizes Forster's use of the phrase to mean the connections we have with others. But in the most famous instance in the book, the exclamation "Only connect!" is clearly referring not to a connection with other people, but to a joining of seemingly opposing aspects of one's self, "the prose and the passion." At the risk of making an overwrought analogy, a liberally educated home cook will find comfort in a facility with the prose—the "survival" skills, the beans and rice, the bread—and the passion—the beauty and joy discovered through lifelong curiosity, the cakes, the special once-unfamiliar foods that become part of a new tradition, the roses. The project of reconciling those disparate parts, and cultivating them in ourselves and the young people we're helping through childhood, is at the heart of this manifesto and its cladding of recipes.

Following a Recipe

Read it all the way through before you start.

Add up all the cooking, baking, cooling, chilling, and freezing times and confirm that you'll have time to make the dish.

Note any ingredients that require advance preparation—a dough you need to make using another recipe, for example, or beans that need to be soaked overnight.

Gather all the ingredients—and figure out substitutions if you don't have everything.

Unless it says not to in the ingredients list, it's generally assumed that you'll peel onions and garlic, and wash all fruits and vegetables well before using them.

Most recipes are written so that the steps are listed in the most efficient order, so it's usually best not to skip around too much.

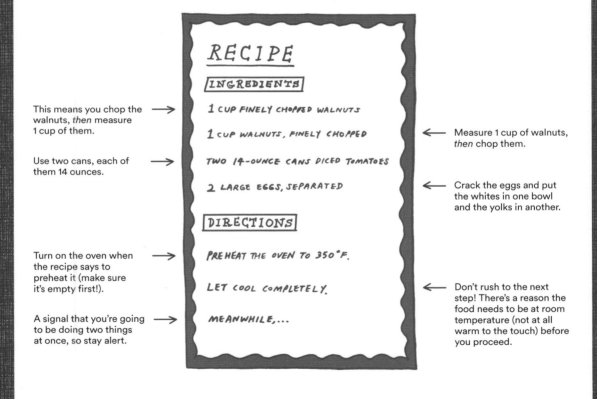

This means you chop the walnuts, *then* measure 1 cup of them. → **1 CUP FINELY CHOPPED WALNUTS**

1 CUP WALNUTS, FINELY CHOPPED ← Measure 1 cup of walnuts, *then* chop them.

Use two cans, each of them 14 ounces. → **TWO 14-OUNCE CANS DICED TOMATOES**

2 LARGE EGGS, SEPARATED ← Crack the eggs and put the whites in one bowl and the yolks in another.

Turn on the oven when the recipe says to preheat it (make sure it's empty first!). → **PREHEAT THE OVEN TO 350°F.**

LET COOL COMPLETELY. ← Don't rush to the next step! There's a reason the food needs to be at room temperature (not at all warm to the touch) before you proceed.

A signal that you're going to be doing two things at once, so stay alert. → **MEANWHILE,...**

(Recipe card contents:)

RECIPE

INGREDIENTS

1 CUP FINELY CHOPPED WALNUTS

1 CUP WALNUTS, FINELY CHOPPED

TWO 14-OUNCE CANS DICED TOMATOES

2 LARGE EGGS, SEPARATED

DIRECTIONS

PREHEAT THE OVEN TO 350°F.

LET COOL COMPLETELY.

MEANWHILE,...

A Few Friendly Tools for Small Hands (and Small Kitchens)

STOVETOP POTS AND PANS

Heavy is good, especially if your stovetop cooking involves kids, because sturdier pots will stay put better than lightweight ones—and will be less prone to hot spots. Young kids won't be lifting big pots and pans full of hot ingredients anyway, so stick with the good stuff, if you have a choice: cast iron and tri-ply stainless steel.

10-inch (25 cm) cast-iron skillet or not-nonstick stainless-steel skillet: An oven-proof handle is preferable. We also use a cheap 14-inch (35 cm) steel wok with a wok spatula (I pried the spatula's wooden end off because I found the extra length unwieldy), but just the skillet will do fine if space is an issue.

8-inch (20 cm) skillet, possibly nonstick ceramic-lined: Nonstick makes for the easiest egg cookery, but it doesn't last very long. If you choose nonstick, make sure you have a heat-safe plastic or silicone turner to use with it so it doesn't get scratched.

Small (1½- or 2-quart), heavy-bottom saucepan, preferably with a rolled lip for less-drippy pouring.

Medium (3-quart), heavy-bottom saucepan.

Something to cook pasta and stews in, like a Dutch oven.

COOKING UTENSILS

One of the smartest decisions I've made recently, kitchen-organization-wise, is to empty our utensil drawer, which had gotten to the hard-to-open-and-close stage, put everything in a big bag, and then add tools back only as we used them. I try to maintain control and return rarely used utensils to the overflow bag in deep storage so we don't have bulky potato mashers and specialty whisks tangling with the spatulas we need every day.

Lightweight 12-inch (30.5 cm) steel tongs: Not "heavy-duty," which can be hard for small hands to manage; the cheapest ones from a restaurant-supply store are best.

Metal spatula or turner: Thin but sturdy, for flipping burgers, breaking up ground meat as it browns, transferring hot cookies from baking sheet to cooling rack, and so on. Narrower ones are easier to maneuver in crowded pans than wide ones.

Spider strainer (aka wire skimmer): For scooping pasta or vegetables out of boiling water, which is easier for young kids than draining a whole pot in a colander.

Short, sharp paring knife with a wide blade: The kind of knife you'd use to slice, say, an apple, preferably serrated so you can also use it on soft fruits, like plums and tomatoes.

Sharp chef's knife and a honing steel: Yep.

A variety of potholders and oven mitts: Every cook and every set of hands has different needs, so find the potholders that work best for you. I like square fabric potholders (instructions for sewing them are on page 100) and bar mops that come in packs of two dozen, but some kids might be more comfortable with full-on mitts or silicone pot grabbers.

Long-handled wooden spoon and a couple of heatproof silicone spatulas.

Bench scraper: For unsticking pastry dough from the countertop, for transferring chopped ingredients from the cutting board to wherever you need them to be.

Classic American-style heavy rolling pin: Heavy is good for kids so they don't have to work too hard to apply pressure on their own.

Granite mortar and pestle.

Instant-read meat thermometer.

Graters: I honestly haven't yet found a decent one-size-fits-all grater that will handle hard cheese, ginger, citrus zest, and nutmeg in exactly the ways I prefer. I would like to suggest, though, a ceramic grater for ginger; it'll give you a fine, juicy pulp, free of long fibers. (It also works well for garlic.)

SMALL APPLIANCES

I have a respectable fleet of kitchen appliances now, and you can pry my electric pizzelle iron from my cold etc., but at various times in my home cooking life I have done without each of them. I won't claim that mincing a couple of bags' worth of fresh cranberries by hand in my first apartment kitchen was a *pleasant* way to pass the time, but the Thanksgiving relish got made, and it was years before I felt I needed a food processor of my own. That said, there are a few appliances that I'd keep above all others, and that happen to be easy enough for at least older kids to use safely.

Kitchen scale: Few of my favorite recipes, even those for baked goods, require pinpoint accuracy, but it's just so much easier to weigh certain ingredients than to measure them by volume, and requires fewer cups and bowls.

Slow cooker: Super safe, and it's really hard to mess up anything you cook in one. An Instant Pot or other electric pressure cooker with a slow-cooking function (and a yogurt setting!) is useful too, but not quite as young kid–friendly.

Stand mixer and/or an electric hand mixer: You can certainly get by without a mixer, but you'll need patience and forearm strength to do things like whip egg whites or cream butter and sugar together until fluffy. I have a fancy stand mixer and a $19 grocery-store hand mixer, and the latter will do fine.

Blender, either upright or immersion.

Electric tea kettle: I came to the electric kettle late in life, but I've seen how easy it is for my daughter to use to make tea, instant noodles, oatmeal—and of course I use it myself several times a day, to speed up boiling water for pasta or blanching vegetables or cooking potatoes. Well worth the counter space, as it turns out.

Electric pancake griddle: My parents gave us one a few years ago, and I thought it was ridiculous. I was wrong. It allows even young kids the *feeling* of active stovetop cooking without the open flames or exposed heating elements, and makes pancakes, eggs, sausage, scrapple—the whole Saturday-morning diner experience—much more doable.

BAKING SUPPLIES

As a professional recipe tester, I'm required to possess a whole lot of baking equipment I really don't want or need. I'll often have to buy an odd-sized cake pan or mini tart rings or whatever and then stash it in the giant "pan box" in the basement and never use it again. But you can do a lot with just a few basic pans and a slew of bowls.

Bowls, bowls, bowls: Small ones, medium-sized ones, large ones. I like stainless steel, but stoneware or tempered (heatproof) glass are fine too. Plastic isn't as versatile.

A handful of flexible rubber spatulas: The smallish white rubber spatulas from the restaurant-supply store have a good stiffness-to-flexibility ratio.

One (1) standard whisk: Sometimes in the middle of a cake recipe I think it's my fault that I don't have more than one whisk at hand, but you know what? It's a failure of the recipe, not me.

Pie dish: I like transparent glass ones, because you can check the bottom crust for browning.

9-inch (23 cm) round and 8- or 9-inch (20 or 23 cm) square baking pans: The kind with little handles on the sides are easy for small hands to grasp when hot.

9 by 13-inch (23 by 33 cm) baking pan: Metal or glass, doesn't matter too much.

Two 9¼ by 5¼ by 2¾-inch (23.5 by 13.3 by 7 cm) loaf pans: Quick breads and sandwich bread loaves should be made in pairs, if possible. One to keep (and taste-test) and one to take to a neighbor.

Baking sheets and rimmed sheet pans: Quarter sheet pans, measuring 9 by 13 inches (23 by 33 cm) and available pretty cheap at restaurant supply stores, are great for younger cooks—easier to slide two of them in and out of the oven or under the broiler than one large half sheet pan, and easier to wash in a small sink.

Parchment paper: Why make baking harder than it has to be?

Small offset spatula: If you're ever going to frost any sort of cake, spring for one of these and don't look back. It's also handy for PBJ spreading, applying cream cheese to bagels, and so on.

OUTDOOR COOKING SUPPLIES

Older kids can cook over live fire, with supervision and the right tools.

Charcoal grill.

Chimney starter (advanced) or firestarters (beginner) and long matches or one of those long lighters.

Long-handled turner and tongs.

Fireproof mitt.

Rural Experiment

When we moved to a farmhouse in rural Georgia, one of the first things I did was start planning to make it a comfortable home for chickens. I rented a big truck for a day and picked up a bunch of lumber in town, then spent the next month building a simple but clever chicken tractor, an A-frame coop with a set of kick-down wheels on the back end so the whole thing could be hauled around the yard and the chickens could scratch and fertilize fresh ground every couple of weeks.

My daughter was just a toddler, but when she wasn't digging for spent shotgun shells in the dirt or exploring the old double-seater outhouse (with its confounding *outward*-bound bullet holes in the metal door), she helped me "measure" and "drill pilot holes" and "hold boards in place." I'd never built anything so elaborate before, and I learned a few things: (1) wood is more flexible and forgiving than it looks, which is good if your measuring or math skills happen to be having an off day; (2) keeping *two* charged-up cordless drills on hand may seem like a luxury but speeds up construction by such a significant factor it's absolutely worth it; and (3) you should listen attentively to your lower back when it twinges in complaint. (I ended my summer of amateur carpentry with a nearly crushed spinal cord and a date with major surgery.)

For a couple of years we hosted an evolving complement of Ameraucana hens—the tractor was big enough to contain about four birds at a time. Every once in a while we'd let them roam outside the tractor for a while and then shuffle them back inside; occasionally a hen would disappear, probably due to hawks or roaming neighborhood dogs. On cold winter nights we covered the tractor with a blue tarp and ran a shop lamp on an extension cord through a kitchen window to the coop for warmth. There were no eggs in the winter other than the ones from the grocery store, but as the weather warmed we'd be back in deep golden frittatas and baked goods, and the shells in the compost pile would be pale blue and green.

Just before our experiment with rural life came to an end and we moved into town, my daughter and I cuddled the chickens in our laps one last time and left them and their coop with the house's new owner. To be honest, I don't miss the fresh eggs terribly much—they were aesthetically lovely but tasted and behaved about the same as store-bought—but I do miss the chickens once in a while. And in difficult times when we must limit public outings, I miss the feeling of being just slightly less reliant on grocery stores, as I've found eggs to be one of the few delimiting ingredients in my everyday cooking. An egg or two, cooked easily on the stovetop, is at least the start of a respectable meal. We also need plenty of egg yolks for comforting pudding and gelato, of course—and the whites for meringues and angel food cake. For my daughter, like many kids, eggs were the first foods cooked without help on the stovetop, and she still makes them almost every day. In the thick of the coronavirus stay-at-home order, we'd have three eighteen-packs of eggs in the fridge, and head out for groceries when we got down to the last one. If we run out of eggs, in other words, it's past time for a shopping trip.

Fried Egg Serves 1

Cracking an egg (crack into a small bowl, then transfer to the pan, if young kids find cracking it directly into a hot pan tricky)

Stovetop cooking over medium-low or medium heat

Spatula work—easier if you're using a nonstick pan

---

1 teaspoon butter, or a little less if using a nonstick pan

1 egg

Salt and freshly ground black pepper

One morning when my daughter was about three, she specifically requested an egg for breakfast. I'm not a short-order cook, so I didn't ask how she wanted them; I just cooked up an egg, flopped it onto a plate, and put it in front of her. She burst into tears, and I couldn't understand what was wrong. Eventually, after a few mornings of this, it emerged that she'd been expecting the eggs to look like the ones Max and Ruby eat for breakfast in the eponymous children's TV show: almost perfectly round, perfectly white whites, perfectly yellow-orange globes of yolk in the very center of each. In an early example of her interests nudging my own education in unexpected directions, I had to learn how to make a sunny-side-up egg even though I'd never in a million years want to eat one myself. (I'll take eggs over-medium, or whisked with fish sauce and lime juice and a bit of cornstarch, then fluffy-fried in a very hot wok, thank you.) Soon she was making them on her own, perched on a step stool at the stove.

For sunny-side-up: Put the butter in a small sauté pan (cast iron, steel, or nonstick) and place over medium-low heat. When the butter is melted, crack in the egg—it should not sizzle; if it does, turn down the heat. Sprinkle with a pinch each of salt and pepper and cook for about 5 minutes, until the white is solid at the edges and almost up to the yolk. Sprinkle a few drops of water around the edges of the egg and cover the pan. Cook for 30 seconds, or until the white is fully cooked, the yolk runny.

For over-medium: Put the butter in a small sauté pan (cast iron, steel, or nonstick) and place over medium heat. When the butter is melted, crack in the egg—it will sizzle and bubble. Sprinkle with salt and pepper and cook for about 6 minutes, until the white is curling up and crisp at the edges. Slide a spatula under the egg and lift it up; tilt the pan so the butter moves to the center, then flip the egg over and into the butter in the pan. Cook for 30 seconds.

Scrambled Eggs Serves 2

PRACTICE SKILLS

Cracking and whisking eggs

Stovetop cooking over medium-low heat

3 or 4 large eggs

Salt and freshly ground black pepper

1 teaspoon butter

I'm not sure I ever intentionally made scrambled eggs before my daughter started going to daycare a couple of days a week. The daycare would serve the kids breakfast—frozen French toast sticks with syrup for dipping, fresh fruit, and scrambled eggs with what looked like quite a lot of black pepper whisked in. The eggs looked so appealing—simple and fluffy and comforting (and peppery)—I found myself thinking about them after morning drop-off. But even in a well-seasoned cast-iron skillet, I'd almost always end up with a browned film of egg stuck to the pan, and I'd go months without making them again. When I finally broke down and bought a small ceramic-lined nonstick skillet, many years later, my family's scrambled egg consumption skyrocketed.

Crack the eggs into a small bowl and add a good pinch of salt and a grinding of pepper. Add a small splash of water (about 2 teaspoons). With a fork, whisk until well combined.

Put the butter in a small nonstick sauté pan over medium-low heat. When the butter is melted, pour in the eggs. Let cook for about 10 seconds, then slowly, gently stir with a heatproof spatula or wooden spoon, scraping the cooked egg at the outside of the pan into the center of the pan to form lumpy curds. Continue to cook and stir until there's almost no liquid egg remaining in the pan, about 4 minutes. Scrape onto plates and serve.

Variations: Add a couple of pinches of shredded cheese at the end of cooking, or sauté some sliced ramps or slivers of shallot in the butter before adding the eggs, or stir snipped fresh herbs (chives, basil, parsley, cilantro, or a little oregano or thyme) into the eggs in the bowl. Serve in a warmed tortilla with fresh tomatoes or salsa, or on top of buttered toast.

recipe continues

Tips: If you're using a cast-iron skillet or not-nonstick stainless-steel pan, melt at least 1 tablespoon butter over medium heat until almost all the foamy bubbles have disappeared and the butter just starts to brown, then turn down the heat to medium-low, add the eggs, and cook for just a minute.

To clean a cast-iron or steel pan with egg stuck to the bottom, pour water into the still-hot pan and scrape up the egg with a spatula or wooden spoon, then dump out and scrub with a cleaning brush to remove any stray bits. The main point is: don't leave the pan to cool before scrubbing (and don't leave it for the next person to clean).

Perfect Hard-Cooked Eggs

3 or 4 large eggs

Several times a week, especially during the school year, it occurs to me to be thankful that my child actually likes hard-cooked eggs. I don't care for them much myself, but they really are the perfect protein for chilled lunch boxes or a quick breakfast. We usually make three or four at a time—one for immediate needs, a couple to stick in the fridge for another day, and one for Piper, our dog, who goes bananas as soon as she hears the back of a spoon tapping an eggshell. The method below will yield a perfectly cooked egg with a creamy but not runny yolk and a tender white.

Put the eggs in a small saucepan and add cold water to just barely cover them. Place the pan over high heat and bring the water to a boil. As soon as the water is at a full boil—with bubbles vigorously breaking the surface in the center of the pan—remove from the heat, cover the pan with a lid, and let stand for 9 minutes (set a timer).

Fill a bowl with ice water. After 9 minutes, use a slotted spoon or spider skimmer to transfer the eggs to the ice water to cool. When they're cool enough to handle, hold an egg in your hand and gently tap the shell all over with the back of a spoon to crack it. Peel off the shell and rinse the egg in the ice water to remove any stray bits. (Use the cool water for watering plants.) Serve the eggs warm or cold, or put in an airtight container, cover with cold water, and store in the refrigerator for up to 5 days.

For a very simple egg salad sandwich: On the large holes of a grater, grate a hard-cooked egg or two into a small bowl. Stir in a couple spoonfuls of mayonnaise, a spoonful of sweet pickle relish if you have it, and a grinding of black pepper. Spoon onto rye bread.

Frittata Template

Cracking eggs

Shredding cheese

Moving a baking dish in and out of the oven

Here's an opportunity to improvise and for kids to make a dish the whole household can enjoy.

For the baking vessel: A glass baking dish like a pie plate is best so you can gauge doneness by peeking at the bottom of the frittata. Coat the inside generously with olive oil. If you'd like, sprinkle some breadcrumbs on the bottom and up the sides.

For the bulk: Find some leftover cooked vegetables in the fridge—braised kale (page 80) is great (drain the liquid off), spinach (you can just thaw some frozen spinach and squeeze it dry), baked potatoes (peel and slice them), steamed or sautéed zucchini or yellow squash (drain any accumulated liquid off). For a pie plate–sized frittata, you'll need about 2 cups' worth, or enough to fill the dish halfway. Distribute the vegetables in the oiled baking dish.

For the binding agents: Eggs, 5 or 6 of them. Crack them into a bowl and whisk well. Add a few handfuls of shredded semi-firm cheese—cheddar, Monterey Jack, Swiss, or Gruyère will do—and a few tablespoons of a grated hard cheese—Parmesan, pecorino Romano, or cotija, for depth and saltiness. Grind in some black pepper and maybe grate in a little nutmeg. Chopped fresh herbs are nice here too.

Pour the egg mixture over the vegetables in the baking dish, nudging the vegetables with a fork to let the egg run underneath.

Bake at 400°F (205°C) for about 25 minutes, until browned at the edges and set in the center. Let cool for at least 5 minutes before slicing into wedges and serving.

Bread + Cheese + Heat

One summer when my daughter was little—she'd just been fitted with her first round of braces—her grandma and aunt took her and a couple of cousins to the Jersey Shore for beach and board-game time. They stayed in an old-school motel the New York Krissoffs had been going to for years, had meals in beachy restaurants, and played in the water until they were sunburned. When she came home and told me about it, did she talk about building sandcastles, slumber parties, wave-jumping? A little, eventually, but the first thing she wanted me to know was that we'd been making her so-called grilled cheese sandwiches all wrong. In loving detail worthy of an ode on the back page of an issue of *Bon Appétit*, she described a Jersey diner sandwich oozing with this wonderfully gooey orange cheese (I'm guessing it was not the slivery extra-sharp cheddar of home) and—get this—it had been fried. In butter. She couldn't get over it. The gig was up.

I've been unable to determine if it's a regional distinction or not, but my mom says that what I'd been serving up to my poor daughter and teaching her to make for herself was a *toasted* cheese sandwich—bread and cheese browned and melted, respectively, in a dry skillet: basically a health food. For some reason the kind with lots of soft butter slathered on the bread (outside *and* inside, in some cases, god help us) before it hits the heat isn't called a fried cheese sandwich but is instead the true *grilled* cheese even though it has nothing to do with grilling or even broiling. (This is all not to be confused with *cheese toast*, of course, which is a piece of toast with cheese melted on top, preferably made in a countertop toaster oven. I remember my little brother doing the cheese toast thing between meals when he was a fast-growing kid.)

Plain cheese-filled sandwiches and variations thereon are easy for even young kids to make themselves, and they can experiment with add-ins and technique as they branch out. My daughter's innovation, which she came to surprisingly early in her cheese sandwich–cooking career: she purposely sprinkles a tiny bit of the shredded cheese off the edges of the bottom bread slice or tortilla so it melts and crisps in the pan, a halo of Fruilian frico.

When I lived in Astoria, Queens, in the nineties as a young adult in my first apartment, the cheapest bread-like product around was pitas, so I ate them often, usually just plain or dipped into yogurt. When I was flush with sweet, sweet editorial-assistant cash, I'd buy some halfway decent cheese, slit a pita partway, tuck slices of the cheese inside, sprinkle in some salt, pepper, and fennel seeds (how creative and urbane!), and toast it in a hot pan like a hearty quesadilla or a thin toasted cheese.

However you do it, the humble cheese-plus-bread formula is ideal food for kids to cook and eat—it's quick and satisfying, few won't gobble it up, and of course it's endlessly adaptable with different cheeses, some bits of protein or other add-ins, different kinds of bread, and so on.

Grilled Cheese Sandwich   Makes 1

Spreading butter on bread

Stovetop cooking over medium-low heat

Soft butter

2 slices bread

Jam, chutney, or mustard (optional)

1 handful of shredded or sliced melty cheese (or 2 slices American cheese)

If you want to make this more interesting, sprinkle the cheese with some spices (fennel seeds, caraway, cayenne, coarse black pepper, kalonji seeds . . .), or tear up a slice of ham or turkey or scoop up some kimchi or sauerkraut and scatter it over the cheese—just make sure you leave a little space between the pieces or clumps of filling so the cheese can ooze through to the top slice of bread and make it stick together. If you want to add slices of tomato or avocado, pry the cooked sandwich apart, put the slices inside, and close the sandwich back up again before cutting it in half.

Spread butter on one side of each slice of bread. If you'd like, spread a little jam, chutney, or mustard on the other sides of the bread slices.

Heat a skillet or flat griddle over medium-low heat, then add one slice of bread, butter side down. Spread the cheese over it, then top with the second slice of bread, butter side up. Cook slowly, lowering the heat if necessary, until nicely browned on the bottom. Press the sandwich down gently with a metal spatula so the melting cheese makes the sandwich stick together, then carefully flip the sandwich over and cook until the second side is browned and the cheese is completely melted, about 8 minutes total.

Remove to a cutting board and let it sit for a minute (this allows the cheese to settle and firm up a bit), then cut in half and serve.

Quesadilla or Sincronizada Makes 1

PRACTICE SKILLS

Stovetop cooking over
medium-low heat

Improvising fillings

1 or 2 flour tortillas

**1 handful of sliced or
shredded melting cheese
(Oaxaca, Monterey Jack,
Swiss, cheddar, Gouda,
fontina, etc.)**

**Kosher salt and freshly
ground black pepper**

Young kids might want to start with the single-tortilla folded model, which is easier to flip than the two-tortilla sincronizada because it's smaller and less leaky. When my daughter was first learning to cook quesadillas, we found that she was more comfortable filling a tortilla (slices of cheese are less prone to spilling out than shredded) and then placing it in the hot pan than putting the tortilla in the pan and then filling it.

When you get the hang of flipping and timing, try some add-ins, but keep them minimal so the quesadilla stays flat and the cheese melts properly before the tortilla burns: a bit of diced tomato, dollops of refried beans, slivers of roasted or pickled peppers and onion, shredded cooked meat or torn sliced ham, a few clumps of leftover cooked greens. For a crisper quesadilla, add a few drops of oil or a little ghee to the pan just before you add the tortilla. Eventually cooks who are deft with a spatula can move on to sincronizadas made with *corn* tortillas—they're sloppy, but delicious.

Heat a skillet or flat griddle over medium-low heat.

For a folded quesadilla (1 tortilla), put the cheese on one half of a tortilla, sprinkle with salt and pepper, and fold in half. Place the folded tortilla in the pan. For a sincronizada-style quesadilla (2 tortillas), put one tortilla in the hot skillet, top with cheese, sprinkle with salt and pepper, and top with the second tortilla.

Cook slowly, lowering the heat if necessary and pressing down on the quesadilla gently with a metal spatula, until nicely browned on the bottom, then flip it over and cook until the other side is browned and the cheese is completely melted, about 7 minutes total. Remove to a cutting board and let it sit for a minute (this allows the cheese to settle and firm up a bit), then cut into wedges and serve.

Packing a Lunch

CONDIMENTS + MISCELLANEOUS

Salt-and-pepper bottle for seasoning sliced tomatoes or a hard-cooked egg

Little bottle of simple soy sauce–vinegar mixture for sprinkling on dumplings (to fill, squeeze the sides of the bottle and dip the opening in a cup of sauce, then release to draw the sauce into the bottle via physics!)

Larger bottle of ketchup

Tiny containers with airtight lids for dips, yogurt with honey, shelled edamame, and snacks

Don't forget utensils and a napkin!

HOT LUNCH

Use a good Thermos-type container with a lid that seals tightly (fill with water, put the lid on, and tip it to check the seal).

Warm up the container by filling it with hot water from the kettle and setting the lid on top without sealing it. Don't screw the lid on tight, or the hot water could shoot out when you reopen it in a few minutes.

Heat soup or stew or pasta with sauce as evenly hot as possible. Empty the hot water from the Thermos, add the food, and close the lid completely. Carefully tip it to make sure there are no leaks.

Put the container in an insulated lunch bag that allows it to be toted upright.

Include accompaniments in the bag that don't need to be kept super-cold—a piece of whole fruit, crackers, a container of cut vegetables.

When you get home, wash the Thermos and its lid in hot soapy water in the sink.

COLD LUNCH

Use an insulated lunch bag.

Put a couple of frozen ice packs in the bag with your lunch.

Keep sloppier sandwich fixings separate from the bread—put tomato slices in their own container and add them to the sandwich at lunchtime. Keep lettuce crisp by wrapping it in a small piece of paper towel and putting the bundle in a baggie (which you can rinse out and reuse several times).

Make sure everything in the lunch is cold before you put it in the lunch bag, and put a few ice cubes in your water bottle if you carry it in the bag too, wrapping a napkin around it to absorb condensation.

As soon as you get home, rinse and dry the ice packs and return them to the freezer for tomorrow's lunch.

The Case for a Spoiled Appetite

There are periods of time—in my case it lasted for about a year and a half—when it feels almost impossible to get a decent meal on the table day after day while taking care of a young child. When they want to be a part of the action but aren't yet at the stage where they can be truly helpful—and they also tend to become suddenly, almost violently hungry. This isn't a new observation, but it's incredibly frustrating to be tugged in different directions by, on the one hand, an impatient human being who needs sustenance and, on the other, the sense that you should ("should") be offering her something better ("better") than convenience foods or a fistful of crackers.

Years ago, I attended a panel on child nutrition hosted by my daughter's school. One of the speakers, Janet Frick, a professor at the University of Georgia, delivered one simple, life-changing suggestion: set out a small plate of cut-up vegetables for snacking while you cook supper. That's it. A plate of vegetables, maybe some fruit. For those times when you want to cook a nice meal—and one that doesn't make you anxious in the preparation—consider starting with a vegetal offering to the gods of evening calm. You don't need a dip or anything to go with the vegetables, but I'd say go ahead, if it helps.

My mom almost always had a Tupperware container—the squared-off-oval one with the light blue lid—of carrot and celery sticks covered in ice-cold water in the fridge for snacking, and when I manage to engage in such forward-thinking behavior, everything else I do in the kitchen seems easier. When my mom made pizza, following a recipe clipped from a magazine in 1985, she'd stand a handful of crisp romaine leaves in a short drinking glass of water and set it on the table for a taste of something fresh between slices, or while my brother and I waited impatiently for the next small "Pizza Parlor Pizza" to come out of the oven.

She was and still is adamantly opposed to serving dips for those raw vegetables.

Why do *kids these days*, she says, have to *dip their vegetables in something* before they'll eat them?

I don't know, because it tastes good? Because it's fun? Because when I put a drinking glass of romaine leaves on the table my own family looks at me like I've gone mad? *We're just supposed to eat these, like this?*

Setting a bowl of dip on the table alongside those vegetables may well ruin a child's appetite for the main event, but it's a small price to pay for a little peace.

Yogurt-Herb Dip

Makes about 2 cups (410 g)

PRACTICE SKILLS

Chopping herbs and thawed frozen spinach

2 cups (480 ml) Greek yogurt

2 tablespoons finely chopped fresh parsley, chives, basil, or cilantro, or a combination

1 scallion, finely chopped

Handful of frozen spinach crumbles, thawed in a sieve under running water, squeezed dry, and finely chopped (about ¼ cup/55 g chopped)

½ teaspoon garlic powder

1 teaspoon kosher salt, or more to taste

Freshly ground black pepper

You may not want to eat much else after compulsively dipping sweet pepper slice after sweet pepper slice into this filling, green-flecked yogurt, but that's okay.

Line a fine-mesh sieve with 3 or 4 layers of rinsed and squeezed-out cheesecloth and set it over a bowl. Spoon in the yogurt and set aside in the refrigerator for at least 4 hours or overnight to drain and thicken.

Dump the thick yogurt into a medium bowl. Add the parsley, scallions, spinach, garlic powder, salt, and a few grinds of pepper and stir to combine. Cover and refrigerate for at least 1 hour and up to 2 days before serving. Taste and add more salt if needed just before serving.

Roasted Red Pepper Dip

Makes about 1½ cups (360 g)

PRACTICE SKILLS

Chopping roasted red peppers

Working with hot chiles (if you choose to)

Mashing ingredients in a bowl with a fork

½ cup (100 g) roasted and peeled red bell peppers (jarred is fine)

1 to 2 serrano chiles or jalapeños (optional)

8 ounces (225 g) feta cheese

2 tablespoons Greek yogurt

⅛ teaspoon ground cayenne

Kosher salt (if needed)

Olive oil for serving

This is similar to tirokafteri, the spicy Greek feta-based spread. I make things as easy on myself as possible, pop open a jar of store-bought roasted red peppers (or, for more heat, piquillo peppers), and just mash everything to a chunky orange paste with a fork. There's a more traditional version of tirokafteri, along with several other creative feta spreads, in a Greek cookbook I worked on a couple years ago, *Sea Salt and Honey*, by Nicholas, Olivia, and Chloe Tsakiris, if you're looking for further dip inspiration.

Feel free to leave out the spicy elements if you're serving this to antsy youngsters—or if they themselves are making it on their own.

Finely chop the roasted peppers, and seed and mince the serrano chiles (wear gloves when working with fresh chiles!). Put them in a bowl with the cheese, yogurt, and cayenne. Use a fork to mash all the ingredients together until all the feta is uniformly salmon-colored and the mixture has a dippable consistency. Season with salt if needed. Serve, drizzled with oil, or cover and keep in the refrigerator for up to 1 week.

Variations: To make a dollopy green feta sauce, use ½ cup (100 g) roasted and peeled green chiles (Hatch chiles, either fresh, frozen, or canned, work well) instead of the red bell peppers and serranos. Blend everything in a blender or food processor until smooth, adding yogurt or a little water if necessary until it's just pourable. This isn't a "real" Peruvian ají verde, of course, but it's terrific with chaufa (page 87) or roasted meats or vegetables.

Instead of the red bell peppers, use ½ cup (100 g) drained and finely chopped jarred artichoke hearts (in brine or marinated, they're both good). Replace the cayenne with a pinch of dried oregano.

Single Servings

It's all for you. Everything in this little container—this jam jar of chilled trifle, this paper muffin-cup liner filled with snacks, this mini bento box lunch of mostly vegetables—is yours to enjoy at your own pace, in your own way. It's special, a gift, and so are you.

I didn't truly appreciate the beauty of dishes prepared (or at least presented) as self-contained individual servings until I had a child to care for, largely by giving her food on a regular basis. In those early years, she certainly would have told me, if I'd asked her opinion, that it really didn't matter if I'd piled the handfuls of grapes and carrot sticks and crackers on a paper napkin or in three separate stainless-steel measuring cups of graduated sizes.

But it made a difference to me. The foods she was eating back then were simple. I lacked the energy and imagination, most days, to come up with anything very elaborate for lunches and snacks, and I wanted her to know, through this small gesture, that I cared more than it might seem—or, rather, I wanted to have some evidence to mentally point to when I started to doubt myself. It was silly, but most things about taking daily care of a young child are, in retrospect. I didn't think too much about it at the time.

We've both, for the most part, outgrown the cutesy snacks and have graduated to assembling layers of sweet things in jam jars, which have been an especially joyful treat during our year-and-counting pause in restaurant-going. We can imagine that the waiter has persuaded us to stay a while longer over dessert, and sets before each of us a tartlet, say—not a slice of pie, which is its own sort of pleasure, but a small pie, a whole thing-in-itself. Or a beautifully decorated petit-four of our own rather than a slice of a larger cake. That's what each of these jar sweets gives us: the delight of encountering the neatly contained single serving where it's not necessarily expected, in our refrigerator at home.

Jar Sweet Template

CREAMY LAYERS

yogurt

whipped cream cheese

quark

whipped cream

lemon curd folded into whipped cream*

custard or pudding*

ice cream or gelato*

SWEETENERS

honey

maple syrup or maple sugar

golden syrup

agave syrup

jam or preserves

marmalade

apple butter

powdered (confectioners') sugar

dry hot cocoa mix

FRUIT LAYERS

strawberries

kiwi

bananas

mangoes

berries

currants

peaches

cherries

butter-sautéed or steamed apples

quince preserves

CRUMBLY LAYERS

granola

graham crackers

cake scraps

gingersnaps

digestive biscuits

Maria cookies

biscotti

vanilla or chocolate wafer cookies

TOPPINGS AND EMBELLISHMENTS

toasted nuts and seeds

toasted coconut flakes

cacao nibs or cocoa powder

chia seeds

dried fruit soaked in juice or apple cider

These are easy to customize. Make the creamy layer and then mix and match it with different fruits and crumbly elements in each jar and trying out unusual combinations.

For six half-pint jars of dessert, you'll need about 3 cups (720 ml) of a creamy layer (either already sweet or sweetened to taste—honey-sweetened yogurt, for example), 2 cups (290 to 560 g) fruit (sliced or diced if necessary), 1 cup (about 100 g) of a crumbly layer (granola or crushed cookies, for example, or a couple cups of cake scraps), and, if you'd like, a handful of a topping or embellishment. If you use ice cream or gelato as layers, obviously put the jars in the freezer for storage.

* No need to add any sweeteners with these, of course.

Blueberry–Graham Parfait

Makes 6 half-pint (240 ml) jars

2 cups (290 g) blueberries
(fresh or frozen)

3 tablespoons granulated
sugar (optional)

**FOR THE WHIPPED
CREAM CHEESE LAYERS:**

8 ounces (225 g)
cream cheese, at room
temperature

1 cup (240 ml) heavy cream

½ cup (65 g) confectioners'
sugar

½ teaspoon vanilla extract

1 sleeve (135 g) graham
crackers

Yes, this is essentially a very lazy person's cheesecake.

If your blueberries need to be sweeter, toss them in a bowl with the granulated sugar.

Make the whipped cream cheese: In a deep bowl, using an electric mixer, beat the cream cheese until softened, adding a splash of the cream to help loosen it up. Add the confectioners' sugar and beat until smooth. Add the remaining cream and beat on high speed until thick and smooth, scraping the sides and bottom of the bowl with a rubber spatula a couple of times—if there are a few little lumps, that's okay; they won't be noticeable in the parfaits. Beat in the vanilla.

Put the crackers in a bowl—oops, we're up to three bowls here, but this one can be rinsed clean in a few seconds—and coarsely crush them with your fingers. Set aside.

Sprinkle a layer of cracker crumbs in the bottom of each of six half-pint jars. Top with a layer of whipped cream cheese, then a layer of blueberries. Continue layering to the tops of the jars, pressing down on the blueberry layers so everything's nice and compact. Reserve some of the fine cracker crumbs in the bottom of the bowl to sprinkle on top just before serving. Put the lids on and refrigerate for at least 2 hours and up to 2 days. Uncover, top with the reserved crackers, and serve.

Semi-Convenience Food

If I were asked by a major media outlet to name one cookbook that has influenced what and how I cook from week to week more than any other, I'd say, er, Julia Child and colleagues' *Mastering the Art of French Cooking*, both volumes. If I were being more honest, I'd say Yamuna Devi's *Lord Krishna's Cuisine: The Art of Indian Vegetarian Cooking* (the palak panir sak is the closest I've come to re-creating the world-changing dish I took the 7 train to Sunnyside, Queens, to eat three times in a week at Mina Foods & Restaurant). Or maybe *Betty Crocker's Cookbook* (it has the snickerdoodle recipe in it, along with several plain cake recipes that will never, ever fail).

If a close friend were asking and I wanted to be *completely* honest, though, I'd have to name *Make-a-Mix Cookery* (1978), or maybe *More Make-a-Mix Cookery* (1980). Whichever one has the taco spice mix recipe in it that my mom made in great quantities throughout the decades since those books were published and purchased. It was one of the few recipes I *needed* when I moved away from home to New York, and one of even fewer of those that I still use regularly. (The grasshopper brownies and whoopie pies and Hello Dolly bars I loved as a kid and thought I'd need as an adult are now far too cloying.) I haven't looked at a *Make-a-Mix* book since I left home, and haven't actually consulted the typed-out recipe my mom gave me in years, and I think my version has skewed from the original quite a bit, but in spirit it's the one I grew up with. I don't think my cupboard has been without a tall jar of taco mix, ready to scoop into a skilletful of browned meat for instant old-school seventies taco flavor, in at least twenty-five years.

I have eaten and cooked some of the best tacos al pastor, de lengua, and barbacoa ever made by human hands, and I know that taco-mix tacos are not even remotely in the same league. But I keep topping up the mix jar when it gets low and making that bastardized version anyway, and alongside the skillet of spiced meat I'll set out warmed tortillas (flour and/or corn), chopped tomatoes, shredded lettuce, sliced chiles, and shredded cheese—sometimes a mixture of Monterey Jack and extra-sharp orange cheddar because my husband, Derek, once proclaimed the bicolor confetti "festive." I don't even think of the things we assemble at the table on taco nights as *tacos*, really; they're just supper.

Why have I not moved on from the *Make-a-Mix* tacos? There are so many other, more interesting dishes that are reasonably easy to make on a weeknight after a busy day. So many other meals my family would appreciate just as much, festive cheese or not. Will I stop making it someday as another food takes its place? Various dishes have threatened its supremacy over the years—suya beef, yogurt-marinated chicken thighs, a curried tofu that until just now I'd completely forgotten I used to make constantly—but none has endured. None has been *as* effortless. If I had to pull out individual spices every time I made taco-mix taco meat, if I even had to chop an onion for it, I surely wouldn't make it

as often. The mix is key. It gets you almost all the way to supper, and that's no small thing.

From 1964 to 1974, women's share of the U.S. workforce grew by 43 percent. Not coincidentally, Old El Paso's taco dinner kit (crunchy tortilla shells, seasoning packet, taco sauce—just add meat and toppings!) was introduced to grocery store shelves in 1969, Hamburger Helper (dried pasta, seasoning packet—just add meat!) in 1970. I've never thought to buy either one, nor do I have a whole lot of experience with boxed cake mixes and instant puddings and the like, probably because I've been lucky enough in recent years as a parent to have a job with a flexible schedule that usually allows for futzing around in the kitchen at odd hours. I can't justify a meal delivery kit subscription. But on days when things are suddenly not so flexible I am a huge fan of convenience— and of thanking myself for my foresight in pre-preparing as much as possible.

As old-fashioned as they may seem, simple homemade mixes are ideal for people cooking for and with kids for at least two reasons: (1) The mixes themselves are of course easy to make, and are solid introductions to measuring carefully and combining thoroughly—and for some of them you get to use your largest bowls! (2) Having a well-thought-out mix on hand lowers the barrier to entry in the heat of the moment: dishes that might otherwise be a bit complicated are instead very much within reach. Brown some beef, add mix, and you're there. Empty a freezer bag of scone mix into a bowl, add buttermilk, cut, and bake. Scoop out cocoa or instant oatmeal mix, add water from the kettle, and you're done.

Seventies-Style Taco Meat Mix for the Cupboard

Makes enough for about 6 batches of ground meat

5 tablespoons ground cumin

4 tablespoons paprika

1 tablespoon onion powder

1 tablespoon garlic powder

½ tablespoon dried oregano

½ teaspoon freshly ground black pepper

3 tablespoons cornstarch

This makes a mild, foundational Old El Paso–style blend that will both flavor and thicken. The paprika gives good color and a comforting sweet pepper flavor, but you can add a little cayenne for heat, or replace some of the paprika with ancho chile powder or Kashmiri chile powder for more character. If you try this mix and like it, double the quantities next time and fill the whole jar.

Put all the ingredients in an airtight pint-sized container, cover, and shake to combine thoroughly. Store in a cool, dry, dark cupboard.

To use: In a skillet over medium-high heat, cook 1½ to 2 pounds (680 to 910 g) ground beef or turkey (or a combination), stirring with a wooden spoon, until no pink remains, about 5 minutes. If there's a lot of excess liquid fat in the skillet, drain it off: either hold a lid over the skillet and drain the liquid into a heatproof container, or set a colander or sieve in a bowl, dump in the meat, then return the meat to the skillet. (Let the fat cool, then discard it in the trash—don't pour it in the sink, or it could clog the drain.)

Return the skillet with the meat to medium heat and add 2 tablespoons of the mix (taste and add more at the end if needed) and 1 tablespoon tomato paste. Stir for 30 seconds to distribute the spices and tomato paste, then pour in 1 cup (240 ml) water, add kosher salt to taste, and lower the heat to medium-low. Cover, and cook for 20 minutes, stirring frequently and adding a little more water if it seems to be too dry. Season with more salt and spice mix if needed, cook for a few more minutes if you added more mix, and serve with warmed tortillas and bowls of fixings—chopped tomatoes or salsa, shredded cheese, shredded lettuce, sliced chiles, sprigs of cilantro, whatever you feel up for.

Scone and Biscuit Mix for the Freezer

Makes enough for four batches of 12 biscuits or 8 large scones

Mixing dry ingredients

Using a food processor (easier than a manual grater for frozen butter; you can also thinly slice cold butter and cut it into the dry ingredients with a pastry blender or your fingers, but it'll take a lot longer)

Moving a baking sheet out of a hot oven (to use mix)

10 cups (1.3 kg) all-purpose flour

1 cup (100 g) cornstarch

16 teaspoons (62 g) baking powder

4 teaspoons kosher salt

2 cups (4 sticks/1 pound/ 455 g) frozen unsalted butter, cut into pieces

Remembering I have a bag of scone mix in the back of the freezer is one of the great pleasures of my quiet, wannabe-English-thatched-cottage life. Feel free to play around with different types of flour and different add-ins—this mix is pretty resilient and has always rewarded my own experimentation.

In your largest bowl, whisk together the flour, cornstarch, baking powder, and salt until very well combined. Put a couple of cups of the mixture in the bowl of a food processor fitted with the blade attachment. With the motor running, drop the frozen butter through the feed tube and pulse until the bits of butter are no larger than peas, then dump it all into the large bowl with the rest of the flour mixture. (Break up any clumps with your fingers.) Use your hands to quickly but thoroughly toss the butter into the flour mixture so it's evenly distributed.

Divide the mixture among four quart-sized freezer bags: Put a glass measuring cup or similar container on a kitchen scale, fit a freezer bag in the cup, put a wide-mouth canning funnel in the opening, and zero out the scale. Scoop about 3½ cups (480 g) of the mixture into each bag. Seal the bags and store in the freezer.

To use for currant scones: Dump a bag of mix into a bowl, add ⅓ cup (65 g) sugar, ⅓ cup (50 g) dried currants, and 1¼ cups (300 ml) buttermilk, and fold gently to make a soft dough. Turn out onto a floured cutting board and pat out to a round 1 inch (2.5 cm) thick and about 8 inches (20 cm) in diameter. Use a knife to cut into eight wedges and place them 2 inches (5 cm) apart on a parchment paper–lined baking sheet. Brush with a little half-and-half and sprinkle with 1 teaspoon sugar. Bake at 475°F (245°C) for about 15 minutes, until nicely browned.

To use for fresh blueberry scones: Follow the instructions for currant scones above, omitting the currants and adding 1 cup (145 g) fresh blueberries tossed in a little flour just before the

dough is thoroughly combined—very gently pat and fold the dough until it just holds together, trying not to burst the berries.

To use for banana–chocolate chip scones: Dump a bag of mix into a bowl, add ¼ cup (50 g) sugar, ⅓ cup (60 g) chocolate chips, ¾ cup (180 ml) buttermilk, and ½ cup (120 ml) mashed ripe bananas (about 2 small), and fold gently to make a soft dough. Turn out onto a floured cutting board and pat out to a 4 by 12-inch (10 by 30 cm) rectangle. Use a knife or bench scraper to cut into twelve wedges and place them on a parchment paper–lined baking sheet as far apart as possible (they'll spread a bit but will all fit on one regular-sized pan). Brush with a little half-and-half and sprinkle with 1 teaspoon sugar.

Bake at 475°F (245°C) for about 15 minutes, until nicely browned.

To use for biscuits: Dump a bag of mix into a bowl, add 1 cup (240 ml) buttermilk, and fold it in gently to make a soft dough. Turn out onto a floured counter and pat out to ½ inch (12 mm) thick. Use a 2½- to 3-inch (6 to 7.5 cm) biscuit cutter to cut rounds and place them with their sides touching each other on a parchment paper–lined baking sheet. Bake at 475°F (245°C) for about 15 minutes, until nicely browned. Brush with melted butter.

Note: If you don't have buttermilk on hand, stir 1 teaspoon lemon juice into 1 cup (240 ml) regular milk and let it stand for 10 minutes to curdle a bit. Or use plain yogurt thinned with a little milk.

Hot Cocoa Mix for the Cupboard

Makes enough for about 70 mugs

PRACTICE SKILLS

Mixing dry ingredients in a food processor or blender

Boiling water in a kettle (to use mix)

3 cups (305 g) nonfat dry milk powder

1½ cups (145 g) cocoa powder

1½ cups (300 g) sugar

1 tablespoon cornstarch

½ teaspoon kosher salt

A little jar of cocoa mix makes a sweet gift for friends or neighbors. Mix a couple of drops of peppermint extract into the powder as it whirs in the food processor for a festive chocolate-mint cocoa.

Combine all the ingredients in a food processor or blender and process until completely combined and very powdery. Store in an airtight container in a cool, dry, dark cupboard.

To use: Put 3 tablespoons mix in a mug, add ¾ cup (6 fluid ounces/180 ml) boiling water, and stir well. Drink while it's hot, before the cocoa solids sink to the bottom.

Instant Oatmeal Mix for the Cupboard

Makes enough for 16 servings

PRACTICE SKILLS

Mixing dry ingredients

Using scissors or a knife to chop dried apple rings or slices

Boiling water in a kettle (to use mix)

---

7 cups (595 g) old-fashioned rolled oats

½ cup (110 g) packed brown sugar

½ teaspoon kosher salt

½ teaspoon ground cinnamon

1 cup (85 g) snipped dried apples, or raisins or any other dried fruit in small pieces

Oatmeal is so easy to make, why an instant mix? Somebody is buying those envelopes of weird-flavored, oversweetened instant oatmeal, so there must be some value in making porridge even easier. As with all of these mixes, please experiment: if you have it, use maple sugar instead of brown sugar, add different spices and dried fruits, use your fingers to pinch in some scraped vanilla bean seeds, even add a little dry milk powder to the mix for a creamier oatmeal.

Put the oats, brown sugar, salt, and cinnamon in a food processor and pulse until combined and the oats are partially pulverized—there should be some whole rolled oats, and some almost floury oats, but it should not be all flour. Transfer half of the mixture to an 8-cup airtight storage container and add half of the dried apples; toss to combine, then add the remaining oat mixture and apples and toss again. Cover and store in a cool, dry, dark cupboard.

To use: Put ½ cup (65 g) mix in a heatproof bowl and stir in ½ cup (120 ml) boiling water from the kettle (enough to just cover the oats—no need to measure too precisely). Let stand for 3 to 4 minutes, then serve with a little milk, a sprinkle of cinnamon on top, and chopped nuts if you like them.

The Cult of Homemade

"Preferably homemade." I read this sentiment in cookbooks and blogs and my first thought is: *Well, of course.* Homemade, all-natural, from-scratch cooking is the way and the light. My second thought is: *Wait. Is it really?*

Better for what? Long-simmered homemade stock is better than a carton of store-bought in several ways: you can add only as much salt as you want (or none at all), you can leave the fat in (or skim most of it off), you can use whatever flavorings suit your taste (lemongrass tops, ginger, galangal trimmings—these you won't find in most can or carton broths), and making stock yourself certainly can reduce food waste if you use scraps and trimmings. Is homemade more efficiently produced? It's possible that the gas or electric energy used to produce a quart of stock at home is less than that used by manufacturers to produce, package, and transport containers of it to grocery stores. But I don't think it's a given that economies of scale aren't massive in this case. Is homemade cheaper? If you're really using scraps and leftovers, it likely is cheaper (setting aside the value of time) than the $9-per-pint broth at Whole Foods. If you can make do with

lowbrow, store-bought is definitely cheaper. Is homemade more healthful? Again, maybe. Decent-quality commercial broths don't tend to contain a lot of weird ingredients. There may be added sugar listed on the label, but probably no more than if you used an extra carrot or two in your own pot of broth. If the hassle of making your own stock is keeping you from making your own soups, homemade is not better than store-bought at all.

What about more finished, ready-to-eat products, like bread? Are homemade versions always better? How good are you at making bread? My daughter and I have long made pretty good breads and soft rolls and focaccia and even sandwich loaves, but we can also get nice crusty sourdough and baguettes baked in a real steam oven (difficult to replicate at home) at our local grocery stores and at a bakery we can ride our bikes to. If I'm being honest, these, baked by skilled professionals, are almost always of better quality than our homemade breads. Over the course of the COVID-19 pandemic, many people discovered not only that homemade is better than no bread at all, but that it's not terribly hard to produce a very fine loaf from just flour, water, salt, and the natural yeasts in the air.

When the choice was to learn to bake bread or to become despondent, we fed sourdough starters, ordered large quantities of flour as the store shelves emptied, and baked.

My daughter and I made several loaves a week as we stayed home and stayed home and stayed home, alternating among a basic sourdough, a pain de mie in a Pullman bread pan (the kind with a neat slide-on lid to keep the loaf perfectly squared off), soft rolls, and challah. Some of those were legitimately better than store-bought; some were . . . well, survival bread, I guess. Better than nothing, and the bread-baking skills we and so many others acquired during the pandemic will stick with us even if we don't need to call on them out of necessity.

I sometimes think, ungenerously, that food writers who frequently implore us to make everything ourselves do so in order to maintain a sort of exclusivity, a separateness. This dish you're reading about, the one you're about to make with store-bought ketchup, they seem to be telling us, won't be as good as mine. If you don't have the time to make ricotta before layering that lasagna, or the fridge space to keep an extra gallon of milk on hand for making said ricotta, you're not like me. They're the evangelicals who show up at the front stoop the day after you move in and ask if you have a church yet, halfway hoping you'll rudely close the door so they will know with certainty that you're not living the kind of life you should be living, the kind they're living. I'm aware that my reaction to these recipes says more about my own feelings of inferiority than anything intentional on the part of the writers. I *want* to use nothing but homemade stock and fresh-from-the-cheesecloth ricotta, but it's just not possible.

Often, though, a recipe's ingredients list is written that way because the store-bought version simply won't work right in that context—it isn't fluffy enough, or doesn't contain enough fat to react with other ingredients in certain ways, or it's too salty—and in those cases I'm happy for the heads-up. Then there are the products that are truly better when they're homemade. Flour tortillas, for example. For a long time I thought flour tortillas in general were just sort of okay, and I didn't fully realize that everyday flour tortillas could be anything better than that. But then a friend—one who really knows food—mentioned missing the ones he'd buy from dedicated tortilla factories in the Southwest, and it spurred me to try making my own even though bags of perfectly serviceable grocery-store tortillas are readily available.

I'd been making corn tortillas for decades, but flour ones intimidated me, and it was only recently that I overcame my hesitancy and gave them a shot. As it turned out, it wasn't difficult at all to figure out the proportions and method that worked best. My daughter and I could easily make a good-sized batch in little more than half an hour and have plenty for tacos, plus some to stick in a freezer bag for later. And they really do taste better and behave more interestingly in the pan than the packaged ones, which now seem bland. I'll never write a recipe that specifies "flour tortillas, preferably home-made," but for the good tacos or the fancy quesadillas one might serve to a guest, that recommendation will be there in spirit.

Flour Tortillas

Makes about 12 (7-inch/18 cm) tortillas

PRACTICE SKILLS

Using a kitchen scale

Heating water in a kettle

Mixing and kneading dough by hand

Rolling out dough with a rolling pin

Stovetop cooking on a griddle or in a skillet over medium heat

Easy spatula work

---

3 cups (390 g) all-purpose flour, plus more as needed

1½ teaspoons kosher salt

⅓ cup (80 g) vegetable oil

¾ cup (175 g) hot water from a kettle

I've read that special soft-wheat flour from Texas or Mexico is the best for flour tortillas, but I've tried it side by side with plain old all-purpose flours and could not discern any difference among them. This recipe will give you a nice thin, stretchy tortilla that browns beautifully in the pan.

Put a medium bowl on a scale and zero out the scale. Add the 390 grams flour, then stir in the salt with your fingers. Make a well in the center of the flour. Zero out the scale and slowly add the oil to the well until it reads 80 grams. Zero out the scale and slowly add hot water to the well until it reads 175 grams.

Use a spatula or wooden spoon to mix everything together into a rough dough, then use your hands to gather it into a ball and transfer it to the countertop (no need to flour the work surface). Knead the warm dough for 5 minutes—it'll be uniform but dimply; if it's sticky, add a little flour as you knead. Put the dough back in the bowl on the scale and zero out the scale. Pinch off a walnut-sized piece of dough that's about 50 grams—the scale should read −50 grams. Roll it into a tight ball and cover loosely with plastic wrap or a damp kitchen towel on the counter. Zero out the scale and pinch off another piece of dough, adding or subtracting bits of dough until the scale reads −50 grams. Roll it into a ball, cover, and continue until you have used all the dough. Let the dough balls rest, covered, for 15 to 30 minutes.

Place a skillet or griddle, preferably cast-iron, over medium heat.

Take one dough ball from under the plastic wrap, sprinkle it with a little flour, then use a rolling pin to roll it out to 8 to 9 inches (20 to 23 cm) in diameter (it'll shrink in the hot pan): Start with the rolling pin in the center of the dough and roll outward away from you, almost but not quite over the edge, then return to the center and roll toward you; rotate the dough round and repeat until it's very thin, sprinkling with a little more flour if you start to create pleats in the dough.

Lift the dough round in your palm and lay it flat in the hot skillet. Cook on the first side for about 45 seconds, until speckled brown on the bottom, then use a large spoon or spatula to flip it. Cook on the second side for about 30 seconds, gently rubbing the top surface with the back of the spoon to help it puff up and bubble. Flip back to the first side and cook for 10 seconds longer, then transfer to a plate and cover with a paper towel or clean kitchen towel. Repeat to roll and cook all the tortillas, stacking them on the plate. Serve warm, or let cool and transfer to a zip-top bag to store for up to several days. Reheat briefly in the skillet or in a microwave oven before using.

Corn Tortillas

Makes about 10 (6-inch/15 cm) tortillas

2 cups (260 g) masa harina

About 1 cup (240 ml/g) warm water

Few things smell better than masa as you're mixing it into a soft, warm, Play-Doh-like mass in the bowl. One of those things is a masa tortilla just as it hits the hot cast-iron griddle and starts to cook.

In a medium bowl, combine the masa harina and enough warm water to make a soft dough.

Put a square of waxed paper on the bottom plate of a tortilla press. Pinch off a walnut-sized (55- to 60-gram) piece of dough and shape it into a ball. Set the ball on the waxed paper, cover with another square of waxed paper, then fold the top plate down, pressing on the handle to flatten the dough. Turn the paper-dough-paper sandwich 180 degrees, so the spine is opposite the hinge, and press again—gently this time—to make the tortilla evenly thin.

Place a skillet or griddle, preferably cast-iron, over medium heat. When it's hot enough that a drop of water sprinkled on the surface skitters and jumps, it's ready.

Unwrap the flattened tortilla and hold it in your palm, then flip it down onto the hot skillet. Cook on the first side for about 45 seconds, until speckled brown on the bottom, then use a large spoon or spatula to flip it. Cook on the second side for about 30 seconds, gently rubbing the top surface with the back of the spoon or spatula to help it puff up and bubble. Flip back to the first side and cook for 10 seconds longer, then transfer to a plate and cover with a paper towel or clean kitchen towel. Repeat to press and cook all the tortillas, stacking them on the plate. Serve warm. If you have leftovers, transfer them to a zip-top bag to store for up to several days and use for migas (page 118).

Make Two

I have two loaf pans of the same dimensions, and I almost always pull them both out when I'm making sandwich bread (or a quick bread like apple cake or zucchini bread or molasses bread). When my daughter sees them on the counter, buttered and ready to receive a sticky dough or sweet batter, she knows—or should know by now—that she'll be making a delivery to a neighbor after a few hours' cooling time, and after a taste-test of one loaf confirms we didn't inadvertently leave out an important ingredient. In most cases it isn't any more time-consuming to bake a little more than our family needs, and because we have the means I figure we might as well share the bounty. In our old neighborhood in West Virginia, we had friends who would readily accept the Second Loaf, and sometimes I even wrapped it nicely in parchment paper and bakery twine for transport.

I've always been exceedingly inept, socially, and have more than a few times been the person at the raucous party who quickly seeks out the quietest corner of the house or yard and a family dog willing to sit and chat. Genuinely happy to be there, among people I adore, and also a little overwhelmed by the human contact. I often find initiating conversation with those I don't know well to be excruciating, as rewarding as I know those conversations can be, and I've found that they're made much easier, on my end, if I'm handing over an apple cake at the same time.

My daughter is also shy, but she is braver by several orders of magnitude. On election night in 2020, a friend of Derek's invited us all to a socially distanced backyard party in our Pittsburgh neighborhood to watch the returns come in. Derek and I weren't up for *being outside the home* that night, but our fourteen-year-old wanted to go. So I mapped the address and dropped her off on the sidewalk in front of the house in the dark. I watched her walk with a confidence utterly foreign to me around the side of the house and through a gate, waited and listened for expressions of alarm (there were none), then went home and wondered what in the world I'd just done. She didn't know those people,

had never even met them (and neither had I), many of them were Belgian, and as far as we knew there would be no other teenagers or kids at the party. Derek picked her up at the curb an hour or so later, and she reported that indeed there were no other kids there, and that she'd wanted to try a (Belgian) beer or a whiskey but decided against it, and that she hadn't talked to many people but had enjoyed being there and felt welcome.

Her willingness—eagerness, even—to go to this rare in-person gathering, bearing no protective food offerings whatsoever, might well have been a function of the pandemic semi-lockdown she'd been living under for eight months by that time. But it might also have had something to do with the fact that I'd sent her out into the streets countless times over the past many years, baked goods in hand, to knock on neighbors' doors unannounced and offer our extra loaves of bread.

Kneading a Yeasted Bread Dough

Dough for yeasted bread like the sandwich loaf on page 60 is usually kneaded after everything's mixed together in the bowl so that the gluten in the wheat flour forms stretchy strands that help bread rise and give it a bready structure.

1 Clear off plenty of space on your countertop and sprinkle it with flour. Flour your palms, too, and keep a cup of flour handy in case things become sticky.

2 Scrape the dough onto the counter-top in front of you and gently fold it into a compact blob. Sprinkle the top with a little flour and you're ready to knead.

3 If you're right-handed, use the fingertips of your right hand to lift the edge of the blob that's farthest from you and pull it up and toward you, folding it over the top of the blob. In the same fluid motion, firmly press the heel of your right palm (not your fingers, just the heel!) into the edge of the dough you just folded over to kind of shove it down into the blob toward the counter and away from you.

4 With both hands, lift the whole blob slightly off the counter and turn it 90 degrees to the right (clockwise), then set it back down again.

5 Repeat the lifting of the far edge of the blob with the fingertips of your right hand, folding it over the top and pressing it down with the heel of your hand. Again turn the blob of dough 90 degrees to the right.

6 Keep lifting, pressing, and turning until the dough is smooth and elastic and no longer as sticky—add a little more flour to the counter, dough, and hands if you need to, but not too much. Knead vigorously for at least 5 minutes, or however long the recipe specifies.

7 Here's a fun extra step, something my mom taught me that I haven't seen many other bakers do. Use your left hand (if you're right-handed) to shove the ball of dough neatly into the palm of your right hand. Lift the dough high over the counter, then slam it down hard. (Stray utensils lying around on the countertop will rattle, and your neighbors may know you have bread in the works—best to bring them a half loaf when it's ready.) Repeat the shoving, lifting, and slamming as many as 50 times to get a nice smooth, compact ball of dough. Don't turn the dough ball over after you slam it or when you push it into your hand for the next slam: you want to slam the same side every time.

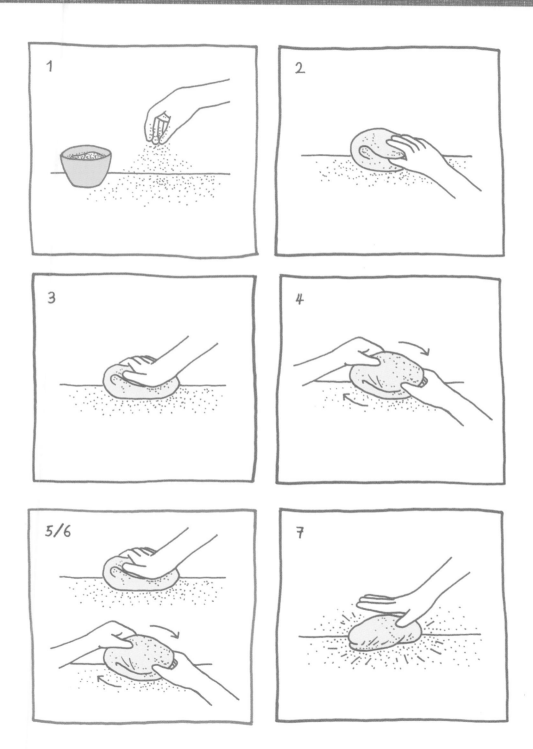

59

Seedy Sandwich Bread   Makes 2 loaves

A stand mixer is the easiest option for mixing this dough and kneading it in the bowl; the next best option is mixing with a spatula or spoon and kneading on the countertop by hand (a handheld electric mixer won't work so well here).

Put the oats and cornmeal in a heatproof bowl and pour in the boiling water. Stir with a rubber spatula to combine; set aside to cool to lukewarm.

In a stand mixer bowl (or any large bowl, if mixing by hand), stir together the warm water, honey, and yeast. Scoop in the bread flour and whole wheat flour and sprinkle the salt, sunflower seeds, and pepitas over the top. If using a mixer, attach the dough hook and mix on low speed to moisten all the flour. Stop the mixer, scrape down the sides of the bowl, then turn the speed to medium and mix for about 5 minutes to knead the dough; it will be quite sticky, but stretchy. (If mixing by hand, use the spatula or a wooden spoon to combine all the ingredients, then turn the dough out onto a well-floured countertop. With floured hands, knead the dough for at least 5 minutes. Use a wide metal spatula or a bench knife/dough scraper to lift the dough from the counter, and don't be shy with the flour—it's a sticky dough, but it's best when kneaded thoroughly. Return the dough to the bowl and pat and fold it into a ball.)

Cover the bowl with plastic wrap or a damp towel and set aside in a warm spot to rise for about 2 hours, until very puffy and almost doubled in volume.

Lightly oil two 9 by 5 by 3-inch (23 by 12 by 7 cm) loaf pans. Turn the dough out onto a floured countertop and cut it into two portions. With floured hands, pat one portion out into a rough rectangle, then fold the rectangle into thirds like a letter.

1 cup (90 g) old-fashioned rolled oats

¼ cup (45 g) cornmeal

1 cup (240 ml/g) boiling water

2 cups (480 ml/g) warm (not hot) water

2 tablespoons (42 g) honey

2 teaspoons instant yeast

3 cups (420 g) bread flour, plus more for kneading and shaping

2 cups (270 g) whole wheat flour

2½ teaspoons kosher salt

½ cup (70 g) unsalted hulled sunflower seeds

¼ cup (35 g) roasted unsalted pepitas

Pat the letter out flat, fold it into thirds in the opposite direction, then roll the folded dough so the seam side is down. Cradle the dough on the counter between your palms and swiftly rock it back and forth between your hands, using the outer edges of your hands to pull the dough's top surface taut and shape it into a loaf about the length of a bread pan. Lift it into a pan. Repeat with the second portion, cover both pans with plastic, and set in a warm spot for 1 to 2 hours, until the tops of the loaves are just about level with the rims of the pans.

Preheat the oven to 450°F (230°C). Position an oven shelf in the center of the oven.

Uncover the pans and use a sharp knife to make a slash ½ inch (12 mm) deep down the center of each loaf. Bake in the center of the oven for 25 to 30 minutes, until deeply browned. The interior temperature of the loaves should be about 200°F (93°C). Set the pans on a wire rack and loosen the edges of the loaves if necessary with a dull knife. Turn the loaves out onto the rack and set them upright to cool completely before slicing. The cooled bread will keep for several days in a plastic bag, though the crust will soften.

Great-Grandma Barron's Nut Bread

Makes 2 small loaves

PRACTICE SKILLS

Measuring dry ingredients

Cracking an egg

Chopping nuts

Moving hot loaf pans out of
the oven

Butter for the pan

1 cup (200 g) sugar

1 large egg

1½ cups (360 ml) milk

1 cup (120 g) coarsely
chopped nuts

4 cups (520 g) all-purpose
flour

4 teaspoons baking powder

1 teaspoon kosher salt

My mom gave my daughter a slender binder of old baking recipes, and the note with this one said that in her family it would often be the first bread a child could learn how to make on their own. It's as easy as a quick bread (leavened with baking powder, not yeast), but the resting time allows the gluten in the flour to develop so the finished loaf is more bread-like than cake-like. It's wonderful toasted, and freezes well. I like the narrow slices slathered with lots of salted butter or cream cheese, or topped with a shard of sharp cheddar to counterpunch the sweetness a little.

My grandma likely used black walnuts from her yard, but regular English walnuts or pecans are just fine.

Butter two 9 by 5 by 3-inch (23 by 12 by 7 cm) loaf pans.

In a large bowl, combine all the ingredients with a rubber spatula. Scrape into the prepared pans, spreading it evenly (it'll only be about ¾ inch/2 cm deep) and let rest for 20 minutes.

Preheat the oven to 350°F (175°C).

Bake for about 40 minutes, until pale golden on the top. Loosen the edges and turn out onto the rack to cool completely. Leftovers will keep for several days, well wrapped in plastic or in a plastic bread bag.

Apple Cake

Makes 1 or 2 loaves

PRACTICE SKILLS

Mixing dry ingredients

Cracking an egg

Peeling and dicing apples

Moving a loaf pan in and out of the oven

---

2 LOAVES	1 LOAF
4 cups (520 g)	2 cups (260 g) all-purpose flour
2 cups (400 g)	1 cup (200 g) sugar
3 teaspoons	1½ teaspoons baking powder
1 teaspoon	½ teaspoon baking soda
1 teaspoon	½ teaspoon kosher salt
2 teaspoons	1 teaspoon ground allspice
1 teaspoon	½ teaspoon ground cinnamon
½ cup (115 g)	¼ cup (55 g) unsalted butter
2 cups (600 g/ml)	1¼ cups (300 g/ml) plain yogurt
2 large	1 large egg
2 teaspoons	1 teaspoon vanilla extract
4 cups (640 g) (about 4)	2 cups (320 g) diced peeled apples (about 2)
2 cups (240 g)	1 cup (120 g) chopped walnuts

My mom seems to enjoy putting together notebooks and binders and folders for her granddaughter to page through. For a while, she was mailing a homemade magazine (called *Reach*) every month, with articles, puzzles, drawings, maps, projects, recipes, you name it. A couple years ago, she sent along a self-bound book containing the dozens and dozens of apple cake recipes she'd clipped and collected over the course of four or five decades— photocopies of recipe cards, crumbling newspaper columns, and so on. (Note that this recipe collection is separate from the one of old family recipes she'd sent earlier.)

Mom's current favorite apple cake is Rose Levy Berenbaum's Cinnamon Crumb Surprise cake, which is on page one, and a simplified version of the same cake is on page two. I've made both, and they are wonderful, but even the simplified one is a little fussy for me these days. So I've been baking my way through the rest of them in search of the very best apple cake, by which I mean one I can ask my daughter to make when she's looking for something to do on a crisp fall afternoon.

Each cake in the book has been *not quite right*. I want an apple cake with *loads* of apples. Subtle spices. A light and tender crumb with no hint of baking soda aftertaste. (Not sure why that's such a common feature of the many different apple cakes I've made.) One that's easy to double, natch, and that truly comes together quickly, preferably without the aid of a mixer.

Recently I remembered Mark Bittman's cranberry nut bread—*cake*, really; let's not fool ourselves. I used to make it every time I needed a portable treat to bring to a party when fresh cranberries were in the grocery stores. Doesn't everyone go through a two- or three-year cranberry nut bread phase in their early thirties? I decided to revisit that recipe and try to determine whether it could be the basis of my apple-studded holy grail. *How to Cook Everything* fell open to the cranberry nut bread page, and I saw that the technique was different from every other quick bread or cake recipe I'd used. Dry ingredients, including sugar, are whisked together, butter is cut or rubbed in, then the liquid ingredients are added. Here was a quick bread—cake—that was made using a biscuit method and not, as Alton Brown would call it, the muffin method, which is how most cake batters are made! The fact that this technique yields such an extraordinary apple cake (or muffins) is baffling, but it works.

———————————————

Preheat the oven to 350°F (175°C). Butter one (or two) 9 by 5 by 3-inch (23 by 12 by 7 cm) loaf pans.

In a large bowl, whisk together the flour, sugar, baking powder, baking soda, salt, allspice, and cinnamon. Cut the butter into thin slices, add them to the bowl, then use your fingertips to blend it into the flour mixture until the pieces are the size of coarse breadcrumbs.

In a large measuring cup or medium bowl, whisk together the yogurt, egg, and vanilla. Pour into the flour mixture and use a rubber spatula to fold stir until evenly combined—it will still be dry-ish, but don't overmix or the cake will be tough. Add the apples and walnuts and fold them into the batter. It'll be very thick, like chunks of apple held together by batter. Scrape the batter into the prepared pan (or divide it between two pans) and spread it evenly. Bake for about 1 hour, until a skewer inserted in the center of the cake comes out clean.

Let cool on a wire rack for 15 minutes, then loosen the edges with a thin knife and turn the cake out onto the rack, set it upright, and let cool completely. Slice and serve. Leftovers will keep, tightly wrapped in plastic wrap, for a few days.

Tip: This batter can also be baked as muffins (a single batch will yield about 12): Increase the oven temperature to 400°F. Generously butter a twelve-cup muffin tin or line it with paper liners and fill so the batter is mounded up a bit in each cup. Bake for 30 minutes.

The Daily Side

When I'm not writing cookbooks (and whatever this is), I have a day job as a freelance editor. I work on books about everything from the criminal justice system to climate change to French pâtisserie, with the occasional foray into heavy sci-fi, often the second or fourteenth novel in a series in which the preceding books are mysteries to me. In other words, like many people who work, even those of us who are lucky enough to be able to work from home, I'm tired and brain-fried and distracted a lot of the time. On those days it can be surprisingly hard to get a meal made—much less an interesting one.

Even when I'm in the throes of cookbook writing or a recipe-testing job, which involves nearly constant cooking (and grocery shopping and dishwashing and stovetop scrubbing and pantry reorganization that can feel like an unwinnable game of Blokus), it's often not the kind of food prep that ends with a particularly balanced meal. I'll find myself grilling lamb chops at 8 a.m. Or using every inch of the kitchen and, somehow, more bowls than I even own to make large quantities of several elements in a fancy dessert that has to be plated right as it's made—not exactly something one can cart leftovers of to neighbors at the spur of the moment, and not a nutritious meal. I'll have to make an electric-blue cocktail that *smokes* at noon on a Tuesday. And sometimes, of course, the recipe is a failure altogether. I've cooked all day and have nothing for my family to eat for supper.

It's a glamorous life.

I ogle food magazines and page through gorgeous cookbooks in my free moments, mentally filling imaginary dinner plates with several different but perfectly complementary vegetable- and spice-heavy dishes, each more complex and deeply flavorful than the next:

- Steamed asparagus with segmented blood oranges, fresh oregano, minced shallot, and white wine vinegar
- Toasted almond and garlic couscous flecked with more minced fresh herbs
- Roasted carrots with honey and caraway, alongside a dollop of homemade ajvar–swirled labneh
- A paprika butter–fried egg

Or perhaps:

- Berbere-spiced roasted winter squash drizzled with cilantro cream
- Dried apricot brown basmati pilaf with caramelized onion
- A cucumber-tomato-mint-lime-chile-cumin salad topped with toasted sesame seeds that hiss and sizzle when they hit the cool salad
- Ginger-garlic pan-seared lacinato kale

Or, if you will:

- Gouda mac and cheese baked with garlic breadcrumbs
- Succotash of lima beans, okra, fresh sweet corn, tomatoes, and basil
- A mess of collards with smoked ham hock and vinegar
- A hot skillet of crisp-bottomed roasted Hatch chile cornbread

Alas, a confession: Instead of chopping vegetables for a succotash, at the last minute I'll pat some ground beef into burgers, sprinkle on some Goya Adobo, and cook them while reheating some frozen peas in a saucepan with a splash of water and toasting buns. You want condiments? They're in the fridge. Butter on those peas? The butter's on the table. I was going to sauté them in a touch of olive oil with asparagus tips and minced sweet peppers and onion and I was going to tear in some mint from the yard, but, among other things, all of that would necessitate the use of a cutting board, which today was a hurdle too high to even contemplate.

If I'm thinking ahead a little bit, I'll put a chuck roast in the slow cooker. *Maybe* drop some root vegetables in there too. Or, of course, I'll say yes when someone suggests picking up pizza or Lenten fish-fry takeout.

The meals I cook in a given week are fine, solid even, and—sometimes—relatively nutritious. They can be enjoyed by everyone in my family despite dietary constraints and idiosyncratic preferences; almost all of the fancier dishes I dreamt up and listed above would be verboten for one or more of the three of us. And they're almost entirely stress-free, especially when I can ask my daughter to take a break from homework to cook a vegetable, preferably one that requires only an oven (if the main part of the meal is cooked on the stovetop) or one burner (vice versa); I know that she is capable of taking on that responsibility easily and we'll have a supper that includes an actual vegetable side dish.

Baked Potatoes

PRACTICE SKILLS

Moving a small baking sheet in and out of a hot oven

Testing doneness with a small knife

When my daughter observed my mom rubbing bacon fat on potatoes before baking them she was verklempt. Why hadn't we been doing this all along? Why had I been keeping this from her all these years? In truth, I'd just never paid that much attention to what my mom was doing when she was making potatoes.

For russets or sweet potatoes, poke a few holes in the outside with a fork; rub the skins all over with saved bacon fat, soft butter, or oil; and sprinkle with kosher salt. Put on a small rimmed baking sheet and bake for about 1 hour (for 12-ounce/340 g russet or sweet potatoes at 400°F/205°C), until you can easily slip a small sharp knife all the way to the center (carefully open the foil partway), lift the potato a bit, and the potato slides right back off the knife.

Roasted Potato Wedges   Serves 4

PRACTICE SKILLS

Cutting potatoes into wedges

Moving a baking sheet into and out of a hot oven

Using a spatula to flip hot potato wedges on the baking sheet

4 russet potatoes, scrubbed

2 tablespoons olive oil

1 teaspoon kosher salt

Super basic, but wide open for experimentation with spices tossed with the potatoes, either before or after roasting. You can also use these as the start of a warm potato salad: just toss with one of the dressings on page 144, and add as many other crunchy vegetables as you have time to chop (celery, onion, sweet pepper, and so on).

Preheat the oven to 400°F (205°C).

Cut the potatoes lengthwise into wedges ½ inch (12 mm) wide (into sixths or eighths), and pile them on a baking sheet. Drizzle with the oil and sprinkle with the salt and toss to coat well. Spread out in a single layer, cut sides down. Roast for 30 minutes, then move the baking sheet to the stovetop and use a metal spatula to flip them onto their other cut sides. Return to the oven and roast for another 5 to 10 minutes, until golden and tender. Serve.

Roasted Winter Squash Slices   Serves 4

1 delicata squash, or ½ kabocha or similar squash

1 tablespoon olive oil

½ teaspoon kosher salt

Winter squashes that have thinner, edible peels are a godsend: delicata, kabocha, and red kuri are favorites. If they've been coated in wax (to preserve their shelf life), just scrub with a vegetable brush, cold water, and a little baking soda.

Preheat the oven to 400°F (205°C).

Cut the delicata squash in half lengthwise. Scrape out the seeds and stringy bits and cut off the ends and stems of the squash. Cut into half circles or wedges ¼ to ½ inch (6 to 12 mm) thick. Pile on a rimmed baking sheet, drizzle with the oil and sprinkle with the salt, and toss to coat the slices. Arrange the slices in a single layer, cut sides down, then roast for about 35 minutes, until tender and browned on the bottom (no need to flip them). Serve hot or at room temperature.

Make it fancier: Roast some sliced onion along with the squash. Transfer everything to a platter and drizzle with a hot sweet-and-sour dressing: heat cider vinegar or a wine vinegar with honey, salt, and hot pepper flakes while the squash roasts. Sprinkle with lots of fresh parsley and maybe some mint.

Roasted Florets   Serves 4

PRACTICE SKILLS

Cutting cauliflower and/or broccoli into florets

Moving a baking sheet into and out of a hot oven

1½ pounds (680 g) cauliflower and/or broccoli florets

3 tablespoons olive oil

1 teaspoon kosher salt

Be sure to roast until the bottoms are very well browned. If you have a spare wedge of onion, slice it and add to the baking sheet to crisp up as well.

Preheat the oven to 400°F (205°C).

Pile the florets on a rimmed baking sheet, drizzle with the oil and sprinkle with the salt, and toss to coat. Arrange the florets in a single layer, then roast for 35 to 40 minutes, until tender and browned on the bottom (no need to flip them). Serve hot or at room temperature.

Steamed Vegetables

PRACTICE SKILLS

Chopping vegetables (perhaps)

Stovetop cooking over high heat

You can absolutely steam an assortment of vegetables together, as long as they're ones that cook at a similar rate, or add delicate, quick-cooking ones partway through. Quick-cooking vegetables: shelled peas, snow peas, corn kernels, asparagus, pea-sized cubes of carrot and other root vegetables, thin or fussily "frenched" (sliced lengthwise) green beans. Longer-cooking vegetables: whole regular green beans, broccoli and cauliflower florets, chunks of carrot and other root vegetables.

Put a little water in a saucepan with a good pinch of salt and add vegetables—peas, green beans, chopped asparagus (cook whole asparagus in a wide skillet with a lid), chopped carrots, or cauliflower florets, for example. The water won't cover the vegetables completely, and that's okay. Put the lid on and place over high heat. Bring to a boil and cook, lifting the lid carefully and stirring the vegetables around with a slotted spoon or tongs occasionally, until as tender as you'd like them. Drain and serve. (For broccoli, I put thick slices of the stalk in the bottom of the pot, then the florets on top, and cook without stirring.)

Soft Mashed Potatoes   Serves 4

PRACTICE SKILLS

Chopping potatoes; peeling is optional

Stovetop cooking over high heat

Draining a large saucepan of hot water and potatoes in a colander

Mashing

Pouring hot milk slowly from a saucepan (one with a rolled lip is best for a drip-free pour)

2 pounds (910 g) potatoes (russet or Yukon Gold–style varieties are best here)

1½ cups (360 ml) milk

¼ cup (55 g) unsalted butter, cut into four pieces

1½ teaspoons kosher salt

Freshly ground black pepper

Mashed potatoes or other root vegetables is a little more involved than I like to get on the average weekday, but if I have a helper, and one who loves mashed potatoes enough to tear herself away from old *M*A*S*H* episodes, it's doable.

Peel the potatoes, or leave them unpeeled—up to you. In any case, cut them into 2-inch (5 cm) chunks (or just cut small unpeeled ones in half) and put them in a large saucepan. Add cold water to cover them well. Bring to a boil, uncovered, over high heat, then lower the heat and simmer briskly for about 15 minutes, until the potatoes are very tender and easily broken apart with a spoon. Drain in a colander and return the potatoes to the hot saucepan.

Meanwhile, in a small saucepan, heat the milk, butter, and salt over medium heat just until the butter is melted.

With a potato masher or some other makeshift implement, mash the potatoes coarsely, then add the milk mixture a little at a time and mash and fold it in until the potatoes are as smooth as you'd like. Season with a few grindings of pepper and serve hot.

Variations: Cook a few peeled garlic cloves with the potatoes and mash them along with the potatoes. Or, if you have oven-roasted garlic, squeeze a half head's worth of cloves into the potatoes as you mash.

Fold in snipped fresh chives or other herbs at the end.

Reduce the milk quantity a bit and fold a big dollop of cold crème fraîche into the mashed potatoes.

Replace some of the potatoes with peeled and chopped celery root or parsnips.

I, for One, Welcomed Our New Cruciferous Overlords

Almost from the beginning of its reign of terror, in around 2009 if internet search trends are any indicator, kale has been the object of undeserved derision, the fibrous vegetal symbol of healthful excess and virtuous consumption. It's an easy punchline for the lazy commentariat who'd mocked arugula and eventually moved on to foods like toast with the flesh of a certain mashable avocado-green fruit spread across it. I actually wasn't very familiar with kale before it became wildly popular, but I jumped on the bandwagon with no hesitation. I made kale chips and kale smoothies and kale salads and pushed handfuls of kale down into countless simmering soups—and I still do (make kale salads and soups, that is; the smoothies have faded into memory). It's an incredibly versatile green, easy to grow nearly year round in abundance, that I'll never apologize for sincerely enjoying. The substantial toothsomeness of a full-meal-of-its-own kale salad, the slight bittersweetness kale brings to a soup of creamy white beans in broth . . . I take these pleasures for granted now, but I shouldn't. Wan tender lettuces and slippery cooked spinach are sad substitutes.

I'll acknowledge that there are disincentives to bringing home a week's worth of kale from the farmers' market. Long bunches of crisp greens peeking out of a reusable shopping tote look charming, but they can certainly fill a fridge in a hurry. And I've found that the mere thought that cooking supper will begin with a session of washing kale in our kitchen's small, shallow sink is a strong indicator that we'll end up ordering pizza. So, while I'm not the most forward-thinking home cook in most respects, I make an exception for kale: it's one of the few ingredients I break down and get ready to use as soon as I get home, when I'm still basking in the full flush of kale appreciation. I strip the leaves off the tough lower stems with a satisfying *zip* from bottom to mid-stem (an excellent task for young prep cooks in the house), swish them in a big bowl of water, lift and drain, and stuff into a sealable plastic bag, compressing it and pushing as much air out as possible before sealing it—the squishing-down of the bag has no negative effects on the leaves themselves, and saves space. Wedging the bag into a free spot in the fridge, I congratulate myself for setting up ready-to-use kale that will be available for any meal I decide to make in the next five or six days. (And when the kale is gone I rinse the bag, drip-dry it, and use it again and again.)

I would love to apply my foresight with kale to other ingredients, extending it even into that hallowed territory that is weekly meal-planning and Sunday precooking of multiple meals and parts of meals. And every once in a while I try to make a plan, usually after a friend mentions doing a "weekly shop" and filling in their family's meal chart on a whiteboard. It sounds so appealing—not to have to come up with a new idea every single day. I am a food professional (in a way) and I'm pretty good at planning, for example, cookbook photo shoots, mapping out which dish will be prepared on which day and at what time, making pages-long multiday shopping lists that take fridge space and relative perishability of ingredients into account, prepping individual parts of each dish as far in advance as possible while preserving the finished dish's aesthetic appeal. (For one shoot, I drove from northern West Virginia to Georgia with all my equipment and most of my ingredients, including bagged and Tupperware'd premixes for foods like biscuits, cornbread, and pancakes so I could just add the liquids on the day of, straight to the container.)

But knowing on Saturday what my family and I will want to eat as far in the future as Tuesday evening, and having the various components ready to cook those foods? It seems an impossible stretch! Every time I've written out a "meal plan" and gotten as far as buying the ingredients, we've ended up with far too much food, meat that didn't even make it to the use-by date on the package, and too many just plain unappealing meals. I consistently fail to take leftovers into account (both having more than anticipated and having less desire for them than anticipated) and what's known around here as fend-for-yourself days, those blank breathing spaces in the week when my daughter will make a pot of oatmeal for her own dinner, Derek will scramble a couple eggs and pile them on a roll, and I'll have an orange meal of Cheez-Its and dried apricots because I somehow neglected to wash and stash the kale when I brought it home and a nice salad or a quick soup feels *just* out of reach.

Washing Dishes

As my daughter and I are baking or cooking, we'll stack bowls and pots in the sink as we're done with them, filling them with hot soapy water to soak, then wash them as we cook with a soapy dish rag, if there's spare time. We're lucky enough to have a dishwasher, so dinner plates and glasses go in there (dirty sides facing the sprayers, and like items with like). But it's good to know how to use a sink when the dishwasher inevitably goes on the fritz, or in kitchens without dishwashers, or the morning after a party when there are more dishes than usual.

Because life is complicated and some kitchens are more awkward than others, this isn't always how dishwashing shakes out in our family and I wouldn't necessarily expect it to do so in yours. But when circumstances allow, here's how I do it.

When clearing a table, scrape scraps into the trash, stack plates next to—not in— the sink, utensils gathered on top, and pour undrunk drinks down the drain.

IN A DOUBLE-BASIN SINK

1 Make sure the sink itself is clean, and plug both basins. Fill one basin with hot soapy water for washing, the other with clean hot water for rinsing. Put on some rubber gloves so you can work comfortably in hot water.

2 Start with drinking glasses. Gently submerge them in the soapy water and wipe clean with a dish rag. Transfer them to the rinsing water as you go, then remove them and drain in a dish drainer or dry them off with a clean kitchen towel.

3 Move on to any delicate plates or bowls, then utensils (and, one at a time, knives), working from less to more messy. Drain and replace the rinse water if it gets too soapy.

4 Finally, wash dirty pots and pans, letting the especially crusty ones soak for a bit if necessary, switching from dish rag to scrub brush, and adding a little more dish soap if needed. (Hold back on any cast-iron pans—wash them in plain water separately.) Remember to scrub the outsides and handles. Dry off the pots and pans and put them back where they belong.

5 Drain and rinse out the sink basins. Squeeze the rag and hang it some-where to dry.

IN A SINGLE-BASIN SINK (EUROPEAN STYLE)

1 Set a plastic washing-up basin in the sink and fill it with hot soapy water. This way you can wash in the basin, then rinse under running water in the sink alongside it.

2 In the soapy water, a few at a time, wash drinking glasses, then delicate plates, then utensils and knives (one at a time). Rinse them quickly in hot running water as you work, and put them in a dish drainer.

3 If you can fit pots and pans in the washing-up basin, wash them there; if not, dump out the basin and wash and rinse them under running water with a soapy dish rag. (Remember to wash cast-iron pans in plain hot water unless they really need a little mild soap.) Rinse and dry them off and put them away.

Kale, Clementine, and Cranberry Salad

Serves 2 to 4

PRACTICE SKILLS

Slicing kale (or tearing it into small pieces)

Juicing and slicing clementines

Toasting almonds over medium heat

---

1 bunch kale (about 9 ounces/250 g)

½ teaspoon kosher salt

⅓ cup (30 g) sliced almonds

5 clementines

¼ cup dried sweetened cranberries (or currants, raisins, or chopped dates or dried apricots)

⅛ red onion, very thinly sliced

1 tablespoon olive oil

Bocconcini or torn fresh mozzarella (optional)

This alliterative salad is designed to be appealing to young kids with sensitive taste buds, though your success rate may vary. The sweetness of the dried fruit and the juicy clementines—if you live within a hundred feet of a child, I suspect you have a bag of them in the fridge throughout the winter—alleviates some of kale's bitterness.

Strip the kale leaves off the thick stems, leaving only the parts of the stems thinner than a pencil attached. Put the leaves in a large bowl, cover with water, and swish around. Lift them into a colander and repeat with fresh water until the water is no longer sandy. Drain very well, and shake out or spin out all the excess water. Stack a bunch of leaves and thinly slice them crosswise with a chef's knife. Put in a clean large bowl and sprinkle with ½ teaspoon salt. Use your clean hand to massage the salt into the kale until it's wilted. Set aside.

In a small skillet with sloping sides (the easier to flip with), toast the almonds over medium heat, tossing them every 5 to 10 seconds, for 4 to 5 minutes, until most of them are evenly golden. Immediately scrape onto a piece of paper and set aside to cool.

Juice 3 of the clementines (to yield about ¼ cup/60 ml) and pour the juice over the kale. Peel the remaining 2 clementines, separate the sections, and cut each in half. Toss them into the kale, along with the cranberries, red onion, and half of the almonds.

Drizzle the salad with the oil and toss well. Serve topped with the remaining almonds and the bocconcini, if you'd like.

Garlic Kale Serves 2 or 3

1 large bunch curly kale

6 cloves garlic

2 tablespoons olive oil

1 cup vegetable stock or
water

Kosher salt

This is one of my most-cooked foods simply because it goes with just about any kind of main dish, from curries to roasted meats to soupy beans. Still—al dente curly kale catches and holds on to sauces as well as pasta does, and makes a fine plate-filling substitute for rice and other grains. Drop leftovers into a frittata, hash, fried rice, stewed lentils, or a bowl of instant ramen, or layer a handful into a roast pork and provolone sandwich and heat it, open-faced, under the broiler or in a toaster oven.

Starting at the bottom of each stem, use your fingers to strip the leaf off the stem, breaking the stem off at the point where it's about the thickness of a pencil. Tear the leaves into bite-sized pieces, put them in a large bowl of water, and swish them around to wash them well. Lift them from the water into a colander and set aside to drain.

Put the garlic cloves on a cutting board, set the side of a chef's knife over them, and pound the side of the knife with your fist to smash the garlic. Hold each clove by the "tail" of its peel and tap the garlic gently with the back of the knife to release the clove; discard the skins.

In a deep skillet or Dutch oven, heat the oil over medium heat. Add the smashed but still mostly intact garlic cloves and cook, stirring frequently with tongs, until nicely browned all over, about 4 minutes. Carefully (it'll splatter a bit) pile in the kale and pour in the stock. Sprinkle with a pinch of salt, cover the pan, and cook for 1 minute. Uncover and use the tongs to turn the kale so it's evenly wilted. Cover the pan again and cook for another 8 to 10 minutes, turning once or twice with the tongs, until tender. Season with more salt if needed, and serve.

Soy-Braised Bok Choy

Serves 3 or 4

PRACTICE SKILLS

Chopping heads of bok choy

Peeling and chopping garlic and ginger

Stovetop cooking over high heat

---

3 heads baby bok choy (about 1 pound/455 g total)

3 cloves garlic

3 coins peeled fresh or frozen ginger

1 tablespoon vegetable oil

1 tablespoon soy sauce

A super-simple go-to side dish that pairs well with just about any kind of main dish. But the best reason to make this is that it's incredibly useful as leftovers: Fry some rice or chopped leftover potatoes, spoon in the greens and some of the flavorful braising liquid, and a healthful breakfast practically makes itself.

Trim the bottoms off the bok choy heads, then slice the white and light green parts crosswise into pieces ½ inch (12 mm) wide, leaving the dark green leafy tops whole. Submerge the slices and leaves in a bowl of water and swish them around to wash them well. Let stand for a minute, then lift them out of the water and drain in a colander. (This lifting ensures that any sand that's been rinsed off sinks to the bottom of the bowl and doesn't cling to the greens.)

Chop the garlic and ginger and set aside.

In a dry skillet or wok, heat the oil over medium-high heat. Add the garlic and ginger and stir with tongs for 30 seconds. Add the greens, turn them with the tongs for a minute, then add the soy sauce and ½ cup (120 ml) water and lower the heat to medium. Simmer until the bok choy is nice and tender and the liquid has reduced a little, 8 to 10 minutes. Serve hot.

She's Gone Already; She's Still Here

As I write this, my daughter is making a cup of tea and a pan of basic fried rice with egg for her lunch. (Remote schooling during a pandemic has its positives, hot lunches at home being one of them.) The scent of ginger and garlic sizzling in hot oil, the rising then falling whoosh of the electric kettle, my daughter's murmurings to our dog, who waits at her feet for tiny offerings of food and attention as she cooks—it's familiar and comforting, and I almost don't even notice it's all happening without me.

She's using cold leftover rice she'd cooked last night to go with a pot of red beans she'd tended throughout the day. It was the first time she'd made rice using the "advanced" method of boiling it in a large saucepan and then draining and gently steaming the grains. When I came into the kitchen to help her drain it from the heavy pot into the sieve, she'd already done it. It was perfect rice, and it made two meals she needed no help from me to prepare. I was quietly proud, but also felt that an ending was imminent. I've been experiencing this premonition of an ending for years.

When my daughter was very small, she'd sometimes look at me silently with an expression of deep seriousness that conveyed nothing less than the fact that soon she would know much more than me, would be better at many things than I could ever

82

be, would be a more compassionate and thoughtful person than I ever was. That look was unnerving, almost accusatory: *One day I won't need you. And it's possible I won't even like you.* It's my responsibility to keep this child safe and happy, while also making sure that she will be so even without my help. As an adult those responsibilities are frequently in conflict, and the trick is to understand that the real goal is to raise a highly capable, independent adult who loves me as an individual whether she actually needs me or not.

My no-nonsense friend with three daughters in high school and middle school speaks of her role with more clarity: kids have to learn to be functioning humans in every way, and it's our job to get them there. "You can't change the world," she tells her daughters, "if you're still learning how to make scrambled eggs." When her husband was commuting to a job several large western states away, the kids learned to take care of themselves and each other, one making meals for a younger sibling while their mom was taking the other to an extracurricular activity. The concept of self-efficacy—the degree to which a person feels in control of aspects of their own life because they've developed competence in related skills—has been pinging around a lot throughout the coronavirus pandemic, as kids and adults alike reckon with a bizarre loss of agency and an overall uncertainty. But letting kids take on a little more than they might feel ready to handle, not only so those tasks get done but so kids continue to *learn that they can learn*, is really just common sense, and it applies neatly to cooking whether we're stuck at home under a pandemic lockdown or not. It's not the same as learning to be self-sufficient, which is almost never an option in the modern world, despite my preteen fantasies, inspired by the wilderness novels I devoured, about living completely on my own, maybe with a wolf companion—very few people manage to live in a state of self-sufficiency, and I probably wouldn't care to know them anyway.

When I was about twenty and newly in possession of a thick book of persnickety but comfortingly exacting Italian recipes by Giuliani Bugialli, my uncle Roy, in my parents' backyard in Virginia, taught me how to slaughter and skin a rabbit. I took the carcass inside, opened up the book, and carefully followed the several pages of instructions and a series of grainy black-and-white photographs to debone it in one piece. I had little call to slaughter live rabbits after I moved to New York City to take a job in book publishing. But the more important thing I'd learned, and I'm sure I was internalizing this long before the rabbit, was that I could learn how to do anything, and I could keep figuring out what I'd need to know, not just about food but about living and being with other people in the world. I could learn how to get lost in the city and find my way home without a map or a phone, how to be disappointed (my friend had a party and didn't invite me; I didn't get the job; plans are canceled), how to cook a vegetable I'd never seen before but couldn't pass up when I encountered it for sale at a sidewalk stand in Chinatown, how to make a wokful of basic fried rice (something I didn't learn until I was about thirty). I could become competent in just about anything.

Here is a thought that occurs to me with each of my daughter's cooking successes: After this, whatever else I teach her will be gravy, just for fun. She doesn't need to know how to smoke a pork shoulder or how to hold and squeeze a pastry bag in just the right way so that frosting comes out in even strands and rosettes—skills that, honestly, I'm still working on myself and which I've managed just fine without mastering. *My work here is done*, and so on. I forget, though, that there will forever be more milestones, some she'll pass through with me and some she'll overtake on her own. She'll figure out how to top a baked potato with plain yogurt and eat it slowly with a handful of generic corn chips from a 99-cent 1-pound bag, my early-twenties-in-an-expensive-city staple meal. And that when you live by yourself it might make more sense, from a home-ec standpoint, to stir up a little milk from powder in a cereal bowl for oatmeal in the morning than to buy a full jug of fresh. She'll work out how to make toast without a toaster, a pie without a pie plate, gnocchi without a potato ricer, a healthful supper with less-than-ideal ingredients if she has to or wants to. If the teachers in her life—her family as well as the formal educators she encounters—have done the work of showing her how to learn, she'll come up with her own, better iterations of those skills and develop others we might not even know she'll need.

"You work too hard," my daughter says as she sets a plate of rice next to my laptop on the dining room table—she's made enough for both of us. Her lunch period is absurdly early, so it'll be my breakfast.

"Sweetie, I barely work at all," I tell her.

Fried Rice   Serves 2

2 tablespoons vegetable oil

2 large eggs, cracked into a small bowl

Pinch of kosher salt

½ cup (100 g) chopped or shredded cooked meat (optional)

2 coins fresh ginger, chopped

2 cloves garlic, chopped

2 scallions, chopped, white and green parts kept separate

1 cup (140 g) frozen peas and carrots, or ½ cup (65 g) frozen peas alone

3 cups (475 g) cold leftover cooked rice

1 to 2 tablespoons soy sauce

Fried rice is one of the best ways to use random quantities of leftover meat or vegetables—that last half pork chop from the night before, or just about any vegetable: a couple forkfuls of leftover braised greens, some chopped roasted or steamed broccoli or cauliflower or asparagus, raw or cooked zucchini, raw or cooked sweet corn sliced off the cobs, sugar snap peas cut into thirds, and so on.

Have all your ingredients chopped and ready near the stovetop, because this will go quickly—you'll be done cooking in about 6 minutes.

Heat a wok or cast-iron skillet over medium-high heat. Add 1 tablespoon of the oil and pour in the eggs. Sprinkle the eggs with the salt and let them cook for a few seconds, then use a metal spatula to break them up and scramble them in the pan. When they're almost completely cooked (after about 1 minute), scoop them back into the bowl, scraping the pan as clean of egg as you can.

Still over medium-high heat, add the remaining 1 tablespoon oil to the pan, along with the meat (if using), ginger, garlic, and the white parts of the scallions, and stir for 15 to 30 seconds, until fragrant. Add the rice and frozen vegetables and use the back of the spatula to spread them out evenly in the pan and gently break up any clumps of rice. Let cook for a few seconds, then turn with the spatula and stir everything together, cooking and turning for about 2 minutes, until the rice and vegetables are heated through and some of the rice grains are starting to crisp up just a bit. Sprinkle in the soy sauce, stir to distribute it, then stir in the green parts of the scallions and the cooked eggs. Serve immediately.

Chaufa de Pollo   Serves 2

Serve this with the green feta sauce (the variation of the roasted red pepper dip on page 36) for an approximation of a Peruvian restaurant version.

PRACTICE SKILLS

Chopping cooked chicken, ginger, garlic, and scallions

Stovetop cooking over medium-high heat

Cracking eggs

---

2 tablespoons vegetable oil

2 large eggs, cracked into a small bowl

Pinch of kosher salt

1 cooked boneless, skinless chicken breast (see Note), cut into ½-inch (12 mm) cubes (about 1 heaping cup/160 g)

2 coins fresh ginger, chopped

2 cloves garlic, chopped

4 scallions, chopped, white and green parts kept separate

Pinch of toasted red chile powder or chile flakes (optional)

3 cups (475 g) cold leftover cooked rice

¼ teaspoon Ajinomoto (MSG powder; optional)

1 to 2 tablespoons soy sauce

Have all of your ingredients chopped and ready near the stovetop, because this will go quickly—you'll be done cooking in about 6 minutes.

Heat a wok or cast-iron skillet over medium-high heat. Add 1 tablespoon of the oil and pour in the eggs. Sprinkle the eggs with the salt and let them cook for a few seconds, then use a metal spatula to break them up and scramble them in the pan. When they're almost completely cooked (after about 1 minute), scoop them back into the bowl, scraping the pan as clean of egg as you can.

Still over medium-high heat, add the remaining 1 tablespoon oil to the pan, along with the chicken, ginger, garlic, the white parts of the scallions, and the chile powder (if using) and stir for 15 to 30 seconds, until fragrant. Add the rice, sprinkle with the Ajinomoto (if using) and the soy sauce, and use the back of the spatula to spread them out evenly in the pan and gently break up any clumps of rice. Let cook for a few seconds, then turn with the spatula and stir everything together, cooking and turning for about 2 minutes, until the rice is heated through and some of the rice grains are starting to crisp up just a bit. Stir in the green parts of the scallions and the cooked eggs. Serve immediately.

Note: To poach 1 boneless, skinless chicken breast, put it in a small saucepan and cover with cold water; add a couple of big pinches of salt. Bring to a boil over medium heat, then lower the heat to a bare simmer and cook until the chicken is opaque throughout: remove the chicken to a cutting board with tongs or a slotted spoon and cut into it to check after about 8 minutes, or stick an instant-read meat thermometer into the thickest part—it should read 165°F (74°C) when it's done.

The Holy Grail

I once found myself (long story) in the rural Louisiana kitchen of a Cajun businessman I didn't know at all who was making breakfast for houseguests, including me. He'd been drinking black coffee for hours and had started a beef roast and a big Magnalite pot of red beans and andouille before dawn. I offered to help by making rice.

He looked at me with a subtle but unmistakable expression of deep skepticism.

"You know how to make rice?"

"Um, sure." I realized suddenly that I did not know how to make rice. I was in my mid-twenties. I'd cooked rice at home in New York countless times, of course, but each pot was a crapshoot. Sometimes whatever I did worked fine, sometimes I did the exact same thing and ended up with mush or with crunchy grains.

"You measure the water with your knuckle?"

"Uh . . . yeah. Sometimes?" I was panicking.

His suspicions about New Yorkers had been confirmed. "I'll make the rice," he said.

I observed him as closely as I could while appearing casual, nonchalant.

I'd tried his technique once or twice before. Put rinsed rice in a saucepan and smooth it out. Put your fingertip right on the surface of the rice and add water to come up to the crease of your first knuckle. It was bunk, I'd decided.

His rice, of course, was perfectly cooked—as was the spoonable pot roast and the creamy red beans and smoky sausage.

When I got home to my own kitchen, I cooked pot after pot of rice. I read about different techniques for measuring with your hand (resting your palm flat on the rice and adding water to just cover your knuckles, and so on), and I tried those, too. When I made a successful pot, I tried replicating the results, and you can guess how that went.

I pored through Asian and Indian and Persian cookbooks looking for hints, but the main one in those books seemed to be "Use a rice cooker." Buy a bulky appliance to cook a simple grain in water? *Je refuse!* For many years, I remained stubbornly opposed to such a thing.

Here's where you might expect me to tell you that I bought a rice cooker and discovered the error of my ways. I have been tempted, it's true, and certainly would have given in to the siren song of a chirruping machine ruled by fuzzy logic had my struggle not ended, at long last, with a perfect pot of basmati rice. But not just one. *Multiple* pots of basmati, jasmine, regular long-grain rice, every one of them perfectly cooked and fluffy. I'd held out just long enough to finally discover, in a wonderful book I'd used many times before while somehow missing the rice technique, the single most foolproof method that doesn't involve an appliance. It's Method 2 (page 91).

I'm going to give you two methods here, though, because the foolproof one is not young child–proof. If you can safely lift a large saucepan of rice and simmering water, carry it to the sink, and drain it in a colander, skip straight to Method 2 and never look back.

White Rice on the Stovetop: Method 1

Makes 5 to 6 cups (800 to 960 g)

1½ cups (275 g) long-grain
white rice (regular, jasmine,
or basmati)

The standard steaming method here is a little more finicky than the one that follows (different kinds of rice require slightly more or less water and cooking time), but it doesn't involve lifting a large saucepan of water to drain the rice so it's easier for shorter or younger or more hesitant cooks.

Put the rice in a medium (2-quart/2 L) saucepan and rinse in cold water, swishing it around with your hand. Slowly pour off the water, then rinse a few more times in fresh water, until the water you're pouring off is mostly clear.

Add 2½ cups (600 ml) water to the rice. Place over high heat, bring to a boil, stir once to separate the rice grains, then cover and turn the heat to the lowest possible setting. Cook for 15 minutes without lifting the lid. Remove from the heat and let stand, still covered, for 5 minutes, then fluff with a fork and serve.

White Rice on the Stovetop: Method 2

Makes 5 to 6 cups (800 to 960 g)

PRACTICE SKILLS

Rinsing rice and pouring off the water

Stovetop cooking

Lifting a large saucepan of hot water and rice and draining in a sieve

---

About 1½ cups (about 275 g) long-grain white rice (regular, jasmine, or basmati)

This is the best way to cook rice in a pan on the stovetop, and I'm kicking myself for not trying it until 2018, when I was in my forties. The technique is based on the one in Neelam Batra's *1,000 Indian Recipes*. After you've followed this recipe once, you'll never have to measure the rice or water again. It works with smaller quantities and larger ones, and results in fluffy, perfectly cooked rice every time.

Put the rice in a large (3-quart/2.8 L) saucepan and rinse in cold water, swishing it around with your hand. Slowly pour off the water, then rinse a few more times in fresh water, until the water you're pouring off is mostly clear.

Add 5 to 6 cups (1.2 to 1.4 L) water—or just fill the pot to about 1½ inches (4 cm) from the top of the pan. Place over high heat and bring to a boil, stirring occasionally to unstick rice grains from the bottom. Lower the heat and simmer, uncovered and stirring occasionally, for 6 to 7 minutes, until the rice is swollen and almost cooked through: taste a grain; it should not be crunchy, just a little firmer than fully cooked rice. Drain the rice in a sieve and shake the sieve to remove as much excess water as you can.

Dump the rice back into the pan, cover the pan (for best results, put a clean kitchen towel or paper towels underneath the lid and fold the corners up over the top of the lid), and place over the lowest possible heat for 10 minutes. Remove from the heat, let stand, still covered, for 5 minutes, then fluff with a fork and serve.

Use this method for brown rice, too: I'd be tempted to tell you to just use an Instant Pot, because it works so well for brown rice (not so for white rice, in my experience). But the simmer-drain-steam method is just as good. Simmer for 18 to 20 minutes, until the grains are just tender, then drain, return to the pot, cover with a towel and lid, and steam over the lowest heat for 10 minutes. No need to let it stand before fluffing and serving.

Age
Appropriate

Some of the dishes my friends' kids, ages six to seventeen, make for themselves without help from an adult:

- arepas
- banana "ice cream"
- black beans
- blueberry muffins
- boxed mac and cheese
- bread
- brownies
- buttered noodles
- cakes
- canned beans
- cereal and milk
- cheesecakes
- chili
- chocolate chip cookies
- cinnamon pastries with leftover piecrust dough
- clafoutis
- cupcakes
- cuppa (tea)
- curries with jarred sauce
- Dutch baby
- eggs
- English muffin or pita pizza in the toaster oven

- "everything" (this particular wunderkind is all of nine years old)
- four-quarter tortilla (the TikTok phenomenon)
- French toast
- fresh pasta
- frozen chocolate-covered banana slices
- frozen pizza
- frozen waffles
- gazpacho of cut-up tomato, lemon juice, salt, and herbs
- grilled cheese sandwiches
- guacamole
- homemade pasta
- instant ramen with leftover meat and frozen peas
- ketchup sandwiches
- lemon tarts
- oatmeal in the microwave
- pasta carbonara
- pasta with tomato sauce
- pesto in a molcajete
- poached salmon
- quiches
- reheated delivery pizza
- rice
- salsa in a molcajete
- scrambled eggs
- seared tuna
- sincronizadas and quesadillas
- snacks
- soups with beans and vegetables
- stir-fries
- sunbutter sandwiches
- tacos
- Thai curry noodle soup
- toad in the hole
- toast with peanut butter
- toasties
- tofu stir-fries
- vegetarian breakfast sausage
- vegetarian shepherd's pie

I don't know about you, but to me this seems like a darn good selection. If even half of these are in your home-cooking rotation, whether you're a kid or an adult, you'll be eating pretty well indeed. And I'll bet you couldn't guess which foods the seventeen-year-olds cook and which the six-year-olds.

At some point in the last few years as I was starting to think more closely about how kids learn to cook and how adults teach them, I bought a used book with the awkward title (I should talk, right?) *Fun to Cook Book*. It's full of recipes and kitchen tips for kids. Well, girls, anyway. It's a thin stapled paperback with cute fifties-style illustrations that were retro even when it was published, in 1978—when I was just a little younger than the target audience. I didn't realize until I got it home and flipped through it more intentionally that it was put out by the Carnation company, and all the recipes include evaporated milk or dry milk powder. (Worth hanging on to, if only as a reference for reliable shelf-stable dairy recipes in the event of another hard lockdown.) The book is narrated by a girl of indeterminate age, maybe ten or eleven: "My first day in the kitchen, I *watched*! Mother knows all about cooking, but I had to learn about knives, bowls, and kitchen things." She goes on to learn about different kitchen things, aka utensils ("EGG BEATER: Used for beating eggs or Carnation Evaporated Milk"), and eventually cooks supper for herself and her older sister and Sis's boyfriend while stylishly dressed-up Father and Mother are out for the evening. She writes out a menu in cursive—canned soup, sandwiches, (regular) milk to drink, fudge sundaes for dessert—and sets the table with five (5) pieces of silverware per plate.

With notable exceptions, like Claudine Pépin's delightful *Kids Cook French*, this is how even most newer, not-sexist cookbooks for kids are organized, as a linear progression from learning about tools and micro-techniques to cooking full meals. While the tips and techniques are helpful, overall this doesn't seem like a particularly useful way to help kids in the kitchen. Learning to cook is less like learning algebra, with its basic ideas built out and expanded to encompass more difficult concepts, than like learning a language as it's spoken at home: cooking (or, at least, eating) is all around us nearly every day, in the ether of the home of every family lucky enough to have the time and resources to do it often. There's no "first day in the kitchen." Imagine an adult pulling out all the bowls and pots and utensils in the house and explaining the uses of each one to a kid who lives there too. This is an *egg beater*. This is how we *peel an apple*. Once you've learned to do that, we'll move on to coring and slicing. How dreary. How like your least-favorite class in school.

The best cookbooks for kids—or for adults cooking with kids—are the ones that mirror the somewhat haphazard, often fanciful way real-world learning occurs. Pépin, for example, just dives right in to gougères. My daughter used *Kids Cook French*, a gift from her aunt Elizabeth, for the first time when she was nine to make us all a supper of sautéed chicken breast with persillade (garlic and parsley butter), and mashed potatoes and parsnips (marginalia on that page says, "Buttery! —Mom"). Simple dishes, but ones any adult would be happy to cook and serve to family and friends. She couldn't do everything by herself at that point, and I stayed with her to wash up and clear space as she worked, and to step in when she seemed uncertain. She learned to gather ingredients and plan ahead, to read recipes closely, to ask for help when she needed it. Most important, though, is that even though she'd yet to master peeling an apple or brunoise-ing a carrot, she learned she could cook a real meal.

I'm not sure how much I cooked with it by myself, without my parents' help, but my favorite cookbook when I was very young was *Peter Rabbit's Natural Foods Cookbook*, by Arnold Dobrin. The recipes are simple, of course, plenty of salads and carrot-centric dishes, but there's no hemming and hawing about knives and dicing and stovetop cooking safety. It's almost ridiculously charming, and I can see now why I loved it so much. It's written in a kind, encouraging voice, and assumes a keen intelligence and a strong sense of agency in its readers. I wish I could write recipes like these! I've been so conditioned as a writer and editor of cookbooks to anticipate every mistake and write like hell to avoid them, to make sure every dish ends up looking like the stunning photograph of it on the opposite page. At the end of the Peter Rabbit book, there's a small section of helpful hints. One of them is "How to Stir-Fry Vegetables," and it's shorter than the paragraph you're reading now.

A surprising number of my friends' younger kids have been inspired to prepare dishes they might otherwise not have felt confident enough to try by watching short cooking videos online—on TikTok or YouTube. A couple of years ago my daughter, without telling me what she was doing before she was quite far along in the process, made piroshki using a recipe from a YouTube video. The recipe posted with the video was a little vague and confusing to this professional recipe-evaluator, but I'll be damned if she didn't end up with excellent piroshki. I'll admit I jumped into the assembly line and stuck around for the deep-frying when I saw that was about to happen. And we baked some of them for comparison's sake—the recipe yielded *a lot* of beef-stuffed breads. For Christmas that year, I gave her Bonnie Morales's brilliant *Kachka: A Return to Russian Cooking*—the first cookbook I'd bought specifically for her. I think the main appeal of these snappy cooking videos, some of them made by kids or teenagers themselves, is not only that they make cooking look easy and fun, but that they guide viewers without any judgment about what they might be doing wrong or whether they're even old enough to be preparing that dish or whether they've diced the vegetables just right—because, of course, the YouTubers aren't there in the kitchen with the kids who are watching.

I'd like to be able to teach my daughter in a way that mimics the straightforward attitude of Claudine Pépin's book, the simplicity and intelligence of the Peter Rabbit stir-fry how-to, and the fun and nonjudgmental obliviousness of a YouTuber in a tracksuit.

Pork and Pepper Stir-Fry Serves 2 or 3

PRACTICE SKILLS

Slicing and chopping
vegetables

Thinly slicing raw pork

Stovetop cooking over
medium-high heat

1½ cups (185 g) sliced red
bell pepper (about 1 small)

1½ cups (115 g) snow peas

4 scallions, cut into pieces

2 cloves garlic, chopped

4 coins ginger, chopped

1 cup (240 ml) chicken
stock, preferably unsalted

1 tablespoon cornstarch

2 to 3 tablespoons Chinese
light (not "lite") or regular
soy sauce

1 tablespoon sweet soy
sauce (optional; a good
pinch of brown sugar works
if you don't have sweet soy
sauce)

Several grinds of black
pepper

2 tablespoons vegetable oil

8 ounces (225 g) pork loin
or lean steak, cut into very
thin slivers

Pinch of kosher salt

Cooked rice for serving

Several of my friends mentioned that their kids like to cook stir-fries, and I realized it was a blind spot in my daughter's education, probably because I just tend to make stir-fries up as I go.

When I buy a large-ish pork loin or tenderloin, I'll lop off one end and slice it thinly to freeze for a future stir-fry so all I have to do is thaw it and dump the slices straight into the wok. If you're having trouble thinly slicing the meat—⅛-inch (3 mm) matchsticks are ideal here, but anything close will do fine—put the meat in the freezer for half an hour to firm it up so it's easier to shave off slivers with your chef's knife.

Cooking a stir-fry goes quickly, so set out all the ingredients before you turn on the burner: Put the bell pepper, snow peas, and scallions in a bowl. Put the garlic and ginger in a little pile on the cutting board or in a small cup. In a glass measuring cup, stir together the stock, cornstarch, 2 tablespoons of the light soy sauce, the sweet soy sauce, and black pepper and leave the spoon in the cup.

In a large skillet or a wok, heat 1 tablespoon of the oil over medium-high heat. When it's hot, add the pork, spreading it out evenly in the pan. Cook, undisturbed, for 3 minutes so the pork browns nicely on the bottom, then use a thin metal spatula (or wok spatula) to turn and stir the slices. Cook for another 1 to 2 minutes or so, until no pink remains on the surface of the slices.

Scoot the pork to one side of the pan and add the remaining 1 tablespoon oil to the empty side of the pan. Add the garlic and ginger and stir for 30 seconds, then mix it in with the pork. Pile the bell pepper, snow peas, and scallions into the pan and cook, stirring frequently, for about 3 minutes, until the snow peas are a brighter shade of green. Give the stock mixture a stir and pour it into the pan. Stir and turn the vegetables and pork in the pan for about 2 minutes, until the bell pepper is just tender and the sauce is thickened and glossy. Taste and add more soy sauce if necessary. Spoon over hot rice in individual plates and serve.

Beef with Lime, Sweet Peppers, and Basil Serves 4

PRACTICE SKILLS

Working with raw meat

Peeling and chopping garlic

Slicing sweet peppers

Stovetop cooking over medium-high heat

1 tablespoon vegetable oil

2 pounds (910 g) ground beef

6 cloves garlic, smashed and coarsely chopped

1 cup (240 ml) beef or vegetable broth or water

3 tablespoons soy sauce, or more to taste

1 tablespoon brown sugar or grated palm sugar, or more to taste

1 cup (90 g) julienned (thinly sliced) sweet peppers

1 cup (40 g) packed fresh basil leaves, torn if large

3 tablespoons fresh lime juice, plus lime wedges for serving

Cooked jasmine or regular long-grain rice for serving

This is a crowd-pleaser adapted from a recipe I saw online years ago that I can't find now. It's easy to love even though it's not spicy at all (hence: crowd-pleaser). I personally keep at all times a tiny container of sliced chiles covered in fish sauce in the fridge, and one of toasted chile powder in an accessible spot in the cupboard, for adding to dishes like this at the table.

In a skillet, heat the oil over medium-high heat. Add the beef and cook, stirring with a wooden spoon to break it up into pieces, for about 5 minutes, until no pink remains. Pour off the excess liquid fat: either hold a lid over the skillet and drain the liquid into a heatproof container, or set a colander or sieve in a bowl, dump in the meat, then return the meat to the skillet. (Let the fat cool, then discard it in the trash—don't pour it in the sink, or it could clog the drain.) Return the skillet with the beef to the heat. Scoot the beef over to one side of the pan. In the empty space, add the garlic. Cook, stirring with a wooden spoon, for about 5 minutes, until the garlic is tender, then stir the garlic into the beef. Add the broth, soy sauce, and brown sugar and stir well. Bring to a simmer, then lower the heat, cover, and cook for 10 minutes.

Stir in the peppers, basil, and lime juice and cook for 2 minutes. Taste and add more soy sauce or sugar if needed—it should be quite salty and just a little sweet. Serve with rice and lime wedges.

Social Media— Unfriendly

The baked apple always sounds like a great idea. Wholesome and not too sweet, stolid and New England–y, the humblest of the apple dessert genre. I sometimes fantasize about slipping on a pair of pretty, colorful oven mitts and pulling a little baking dish of perfectly tender whole apples from the oven while leaves fall autumnally outside steamed-up kitchen windows. But then the background music in my fantasy sequence darkens and speeds up into an ominous montage: I take a few photos, run them through a saturation filter or two, post them to the internet with a bunch of search-engine-optimized hashtags, and wait anxiously for the likes to roll in and the dopamine to flood my system.

What if phone cameras weren't that great, food photos not so easy to upload, and the internet weren't the essential site of community and commerce it is now? What if we could make a simple, seasonally appropriate, reasonably healthful dessert without feeling compelled to show it to *everyone*? What if we could bake something, enjoy it, and use our short- and then long-term memory to keep it close? Don't tell my publisher's hardworking publicity department, but I've been thinking more about what it would mean to just *not* spend so much time in the ether.

Among other things, I would never be tempted by anything I see on social media to bake another whole apple in my life. Because they are an unholy pain! Even if you have exactly the right sharp-edged, narrow-bowled spoon for scooping out the cores, it's an incredibly awkward process. Pinching little bits of brown sugar and cinnamon into the narrow cavities—this level of fussiness is worth it if you're making a fancy cake or piping meringues, but feels way out of proportion when what you end up with is a slightly sweetened and spiced . . . apple. And then serving and eating the wobbly, hot-syrup-filled orbs, which are always either still a little crunchy or already turned to mush, is even more awkward. But god forbid you let them cool down before you cut into one, because in a cold, drafty Instagrammable farmhouse the butter that melted so nicely into the syrup will solidify into unappetizing flecks in record time. Why would we do this to ourselves, unless we were more concerned about how the food looks than the experience of making and consuming it?

There are much, much better (and simpler) ways to bake apples. They won't make you a star of the various photo-sharing sites on the internet, but they'll check all the other, more important boxes.

Baked Apples

Serves 4

PRACTICE SKILLS

Coring and chopping apples; older kids can quarter and core them, young kids coarsely chop the quarters with a small knife. No peeling needed!

Transferring a small baking dish to and from the oven

4 or 5 sweet, crisp apples (like Gala)

¼ cup (55 g) packed brown sugar

½ teaspoon ground cinnamon

Pinch of ground cloves or cardamom

Simply spooned from the baking dish with some of the syrup into small bowls, these baked apple chunks make an easy cold-weather dessert—you can put them in the oven just before supper. For something a little fancier, serve with a scoop of vanilla ice cream, a dollop of lightly sweetened whipped cream, or just a drizzle of cold heavy cream. Save a few pieces of apple to stir into a bowl of oatmeal in the morning.

If you have a couple of cups' worth of leftovers, you can blend them with some of their liquid in a blender or food processor and use the resulting puree in place of the oil in the batter for the spice cake on page 111.

Preheat the oven to 350°F (175°C).

Cut the apples into quarters, cut out the cores, then coarsely chop them (no need to peel). Put them in an 8-inch (20 cm) square baking dish and sprinkle the brown sugar, cinnamon, and cloves over them. Pour in ½ cup (120 ml) water and cover the dish with aluminum foil. Bake until the apples are tender, about 45 minutes. Serve warm.

Sewing a Potholder

This is the easiest way to make a quick potholder. If your sewing is not perfect, don't sweat it: it's just a potholder, it'll get stained and raggedy pretty quickly anyway.

1 Cut 2 squares of 100-percent cotton quilting fabric or linen (the same or different fabrics):

8 inches (20 cm)

2 Cut 2 squares from an old cotton bath towel, *or* 1 square of towel and 1 of Insul-Bright insulating fabric:

8 inches (20 cm)

3 Stack the squares like this (top to bottom) and pin them together:

quilting fabric *wrong* side up

quilting fabric *right* side up

towel

towel or Insul-Bright

4 Sew about ⅝ inch (1.5 cm) in from the edges almost all the way around, leaving a 4-inch (10 cm) opening on one end. Trim the fabric corners off, being careful not to cut the stitching.

5 Turn the stack inside out through the opening so that the quilting fabrics are on the outsides, with their right sides out. Nudge the corners out with a knitting needle or a dull pencil. Iron the stack so it's nice and flat and square, tucking in the raw edges at the opening.

6 Sew about ⅜ inch (1 cm) from the edges all the way around, making sure to catch the raw edges at the opening. If you'd like, sew around the edges again, close to the first line of stitching, to make a flatter edge, then sew lines across the whole potholder in a pattern or randomly to quilt it. Trim the threads and go bake something!

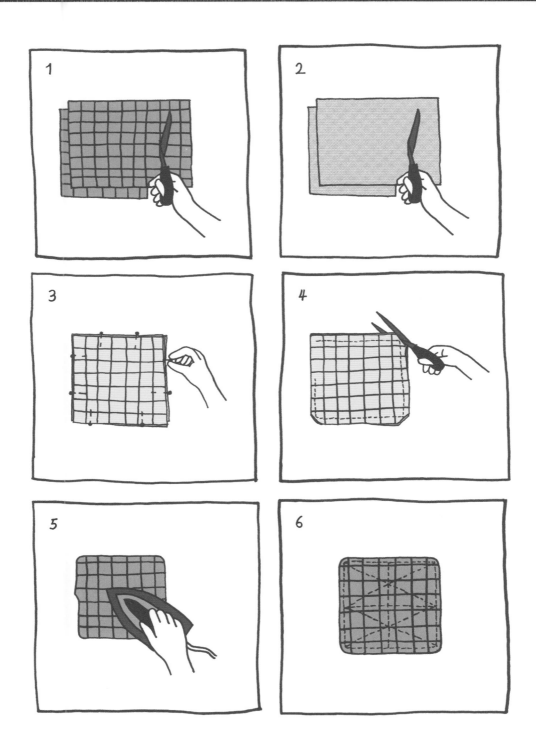

Apple-Nut Crisp Serves 4

PRACTICE SKILLS

Coring and slicing apples; peeling is optional (yay!)

Measuring ingredients, but it doesn't have to be exact

Mixing soft butter and dry ingredients with a fork

Transferring a small baking dish to and from the oven

4 or 5 sweet, crisp apples (like Gala), peeled or not

1 teaspoon fresh lemon juice (from 1 wedge)

6 tablespoons (80 g) brown sugar

6 tablespoons (80 g) unsalted butter, at room temperature

½ cup (45 g) rolled oats

½ cup (60 g) chopped walnuts or pecans

2 tablespoons flour

½ teaspoon ground cinnamon

Pinch of salt

The crisp is a truly beautiful thing, offering most of the pleasures associated with a fruit pie—tender, lightly sweetened and spiced fruit with a crisp-crunchy element—but without any of the hassle of making a crust. (We'll get to pies with crusts later.) I like to toss the apples with just a little brown sugar; if you prefer that the apple juices thicken a bit feel free to add a couple teaspoons of flour to the apple–lemon juice–brown sugar mixture.

Preheat the oven to 350°F (175°C).

Cut the apples into quarters, cut out the cores, then thinly slice them or cut into ½-inch (12 mm) chunks. (Or run them through a peeler-corer-slicer and then cut the spiral of slices into quarters.) Put in an 8-inch (20 cm) square baking dish and toss with the lemon juice and 2 tablespoons of the brown sugar.

In a small bowl, use a fork to mash together the remaining 4 tablespoons (55 g) brown sugar, the butter, oats, walnuts, flour, cinnamon, and salt until evenly combined. Distribute wads of the mixture over the apples in the baking dish. Bake until the apples are tender and bubbling and the topping is browned and crisp, about 50 minutes. Serve warm.

Variations: Use pears or peaches instead of apples, or toss some berries in with the harder fruit to melt into the expressed juices.

Use solid coconut oil instead of butter in the crisp topping.

Add small amounts of different spices to the topping instead of or in addition to the cinnamon—cardamom, cloves, and allspice are classic additions.

That Certain Spatula

Do you have an odd attachment to an otherwise unre-markable cooking implement? A vivid memory of a specific baking dish your grandma used for soaking fruitcake? Is there one dinner fork you never use for dinner and always—always—use for beating an egg wash to brush on a puffy risen braid of enriched dough? Can you picture the electric skillet your aunt pulled from the cupboard seemingly *only* when it was time for strawberry dumplings? Do you have one dented cake pan that's too small for anything but oven-toasting nuts, and you hold on to it across interstate moves because it's *just the thing* for oven-toasting nuts? Surely there's a thin, dull old knife you've designated the Cake-Loosener, naming it like a sword in *The Lord of the Rings*? Even if it's been used by some unthinking person to schmear a bagel and dropped, streaked with cream cheese, into the dishwasher utensil basket, if you've just removed a cake from the oven, you will extract and wash and dry and wield that knife on the edges of that cake knowing you're employing exactly the right tool for the job. It can't be just me.

Tradition has never been terribly important to me when it comes to food. There are too many new dishes to try and too few days. I can go several Thanksgivings without the fresh cran-berry relish my mom made "every year"—or, rather, on proba-bly only five or six occasions in all the years I lived at home; it made an impression in a childhood that for the most part lacked the sturdy ties of food ritual. If I miss pizzelle season, or if a spring goes by without a single bowl of asparagus soup, it's not the end of the world, and it doesn't mean I've forgotten about them. It just means I was busy making fatig cookies or rhubarb-and-parsley khoresh instead. Of course there are long-loved foods I'll revisit again and again, and many that evoke powerful memories when I taste them after an extended period of abandonment. Some of those will filter through to my daughter, and some we'll let fade. Aside from the handful of recipes in the collection my mom put together for my daughter, and the ones I asked for, like the kardemummakaka here, what's filtered most reliably to me aren't specific dishes and storied annual traditions but something more ephemeral: a Pennsylvania farm family's sense of thrift, an aversion to waste (which, as a food writer who at times produces a lot more in the kitchen than my family of three can easily handle, can be quite a challenge to overcome), and the idea that some tasks in the kitchen can be best carried out with the right tool—whether the tool was intended for that use or not.

In my mom's recipe collection, she describes how her grandma would have her mix stiff cookie dough in a crockery bowl with a metal spoon (I cringe just thinking about the sound that would make). She remembers the enormous high-sided blackened steel or tin baking pans her grandma would use in the coal stove's Hansel and Gretel oven. Grandma Bovard, born in 1884, would grease the pans with bacon fat and on them bake ginger cookies, which she called "black cookies" on the days she also made "white cookies" (plain sugar cookies), and apparently they were truly black, possibly because of the unpredictable heat of her oven, possibly because of the smoke it produced, possibly because her molasses was strong and her spices were old and kept in a plain dark-colored tin that held individual small tins inside (a Germanic masala dabba!). The black and the white cookies were kept in two glass dishes with heavy lids that made sneaking them difficult. What's striking to me about this recipe as my mom has related it is that the tools seem more memorable than the cookies themselves. I've yet to bake Great-Grandma Bovard's black cookies.

At some point in my young adulthood, my mom gave me the snack-cake spatula, a stamped-stainless-steel server with an ever-so-slightly rounded, barely sharpened end. It was the only tool she used for cutting squares of the small cakes she'd sometimes bake to welcome my brother and me home from school and levering them out of that one square pan she made them in. What kinds of cakes? I don't remember exactly. Spices, maybe apples, maybe bran, or maybe it was always gingerbread. What I can definitively claim to remember is the spatula, and it affords me a tangible, tactile connection to those mis-recalled cakes. Sometimes—in moments when I clearly have too much time on my hands—I wonder what pans and utensils and serving dishes my daughter will notice we use for highly specialized purposes, and whether she'll want to use any of them herself when she's living on her own as a way of remembering, a little more clearly, her time with her parents.

Whole-Wheat Applesauce Cake

Makes one 9-inch (23 cm) square cake

PRACTICE SKILLS

Mixing ingredients all in one bowl

Grating nutmeg

Moving a cake pan into and out of a hot oven

½ cup (120 g) vegetable oil, plus more for the pan

¾ cup (110 g) raisins

2½ cups (325 g) whole-wheat flour, or 2 cups (260 g) whole-wheat flour plus 1 cup (55 g) wheat bran

1 cup (220 g) packed light brown sugar

1½ teaspoons ground cinnamon

½ teaspoon freshly grated nutmeg (about ¼ nutmeg)

¼ teaspoon ground cloves

1½ teaspoons baking soda

½ teaspoon kosher salt

1½ cups (360 g) applesauce

One bowl, no egg, no dairy, and all whole grain. This is a tender and flavorful cake that seems more luxurious than it is. It's plenty sweet on its own, but you could dust the top with confectioners' sugar for looks, or serve it in little bowls with a vanilla custard sauce (simply make the pudding on page 206 with no cornstarch—and yes, I know this because I was in the midst of pudding experiments and one of them was too thin because I'd forgotten the cornstarch, so I then had to make this cake to go with it).

If you have wheat bran on hand, definitely try using it here in place of some of the flour—it gives the cake a satisfying bran-muffin-like toothiness. And, of course, if all you have on hand is all-purpose flour, that works well too.

Preheat the oven to 350°F. Oil a 9-inch (23 cm) square baking pan.

Put the raisins in a small bowl and cover them with water to plump a bit. Set aside.

In a deep bowl, use your fingers to combine the flour, brown sugar, cinnamon, nutmeg, cloves, baking soda, and salt. Make a well (an indentation) in the center and pour in the applesauce and oil. Drain the raisins and add them, too. Use a rubber spatula to stir the wet ingredients into the dry until all the dry ingredients are just moistened. Scrape into the prepared pan and smooth the top. Bake for about 40 minutes, until a toothpick or skewer inserted in the center comes out clean. Let cool for a bit, then cut into squares and serve warm or at room temperature. It'll keep, covered with plastic wrap, for several days.

Measuring Ingredients

For baking, it's easier and more accurate to weigh most ingredients than to measure them by volume—a cup of flour, for example, if it's too packed down in the measuring cup, might be more than you need.

DRY THINGS (USE INDIVIDUAL MEASURING CUPS)

Flour: Set a measuring cup on a piece of paper. Stir the flour in its container to lighten it. Use a large spoon to pile flour into the cup above the rim. Use a straight edge (an offset spatula works well) to level off the top. Use the paper to return excess flour to the container.

Brown sugar: If the recipe says "1 cup packed," for example, scoop a bunch of sugar into a measuring cup and press it down with your hand to pack it in, then level the top with a straight edge. If it just says "1 cup," just scoop in the sugar and level the top without packing it down.

Confectioners' sugar: Confectioners' (or "powdered") sugar can be pretty lumpy in the bag or box. Measure it as you would flour. If you can, push it through a sieve when you add it to your bowl to remove lumps.

Kosher salt, baking powder and soda, spices: Use a set of teaspoon and tablespoon measures and level off the powder after spooning it. If your baking soda is lumpy, break up the lumps before spooning it into your teaspoon. The size of a "pinch" of kosher salt is up to you! Pick up salt between your thumb and two fingers (if you've adult-sized hands) or three fingers (if your hands are smaller). 1 tablespoon = 3 teaspoons

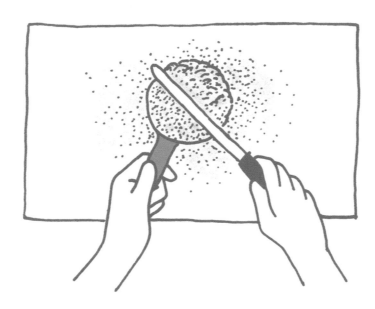

LIQUID THINGS (USE 2- OR 4-CUP GLASS MEASURING CUPS)

Water, milk, juice: Put a glass measuring cup on a level surface and add liquid. Hunch down so the cup is at eye level for the most accurate reading.

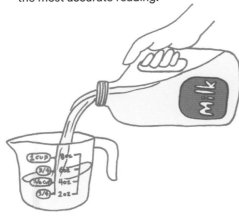

THICKER LIQUIDY INGREDIENTS

Yogurt, mayonnaise, sour cream: For quantities of a cup or more of these in-between ingredients, consider using a scale and spooning them straight from their containers a little at a time. You can use either a glass measuring cup or individual measuring cups instead if you'd like. Be sure to scrape the cup well with a rubber spatula to get it all out.

FATS

Butter: Sticks of butter have the measurements marked on the paper wrapping each stick so you can just lop off what you need. Thoughtful packaging!

Lard, shortening: These are dastardly substances to measure by volume (unless you want to spend extra for shortening packaged in stick form like butter), so it's best to use a scale if you can. The old trick of dropping spoonfuls of the fat into a measuring cup of cold water is great for demonstrating the displacement effect, but I've found it to be less than exact—and kind of a mess.

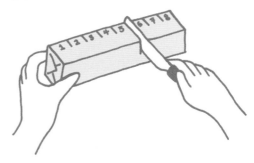

Spicy Gingerbread

Makes one 9-inch (23 cm) square cake

PRACTICE SKILLS

Mixing dry ingredients

Grating nutmeg

Grating fresh ginger

Heating water in a kettle

Moving a cake pan into and
out of a hot oven

2½ cups (325 g) all-purpose
flour, plus more for the pan

1 teaspoon baking soda

1½ teaspoons ground
ginger

1 teaspoon ground
cinnamon

½ teaspoon freshly grated
nutmeg (about ¼ nutmeg)

¼ teaspoon ground cloves

1 teaspoon kosher salt

½ cup (1 stick/115 g)
unsalted butter, at room
temperature, plus more for
the pan

½ cup (100 g) sugar

1 cup (335 g) molasses

1 large egg

1 teaspoon grated fresh
ginger

¾ cup (180 g) very hot
water from a kettle

This is a hot-water cake based on a classic Betty Crocker recipe I'm sure my mom has made scores of times. The water makes a smooth, thin batter that bakes up into an especially moist and tender cake. The chocolate cake on page 231 is another example that uses a hot-water batter, if you like how this one works and want to try another.

Note that I've given a weight for the molasses, even though it's usually measured by volume (cups or milliliters). I just find it easier to pour molasses directly from the bottle—slowly, watching the numbers on the scale inch up—until the scale says I've added 335 grams, or 1 cup. Saves scraping out and washing a measuring cup. Do the same with the hot water, adding 180 grams of it straight from the kettle, again, slowly, because extra water is hard to remove from a bowl of batter.

In fact, many messy-to-measure ingredients whose quantities are often listed by volume in recipes—peanut butter, yogurt, ricotta, shortening, and so on—can be converted to weights: check the top of the nutritional information box on the label, where it might specify a serving size that will tell you how many grams are in a certain volume, and then do some light math to figure out how many grams you need to add. For example, this jar of peanut butter I'm looking at right now says, "Serving size 2 Tbsp (32 g)." If I want to add ½ cup of it without futzing with a measuring cup, I'll multiply 32 by 4, because there are 8 tablespoons in ½ cup, and then scoop 128 grams of the peanut butter directly into the bowl on the zeroed-out scale.

Preheat the oven to 325°F (165°C). Butter and flour a 9-inch (23 cm) square baking pan. Put a kettle of water on to heat up.

In a large bowl, whisk together the flour, baking soda, ground ginger, cinnamon, nutmeg, cloves, and salt.

recipe continues

In a separate, deep bowl, use an electric mixer to beat together the butter and sugar until combined, then beat in the molasses, egg, and fresh ginger. With the mixer at low speed, mix in about one-third of the flour mixture until just combined. Add half of the hot water and mix to incorporate it. Add another third of the flour mixture, then the remaining hot water, then the remaining flour mixture. Turn the mixer to high and beat until the batter is smooth. Scrape it into the prepared pan. Bake for 45 to 50 minutes, until a toothpick or skewer inserted in the center comes out clean. Let cool for a bit, then cut into squares and serve warm or at room temperature. It'll keep, covered with plastic wrap, for several days.

Cardamom Butter Cake

Makes one 9-inch (23 cm) square cake

PRACTICE SKILLS

Mixing dry ingredients

Cracking an egg

Whisking egg and sugar

Warming milk and melting butter

Moving a cake pan into and out of a hot oven

2½ cups (325 g) all-purpose flour, plus more for the pan

2½ teaspoons baking powder

½ teaspoon kosher salt

1 large egg

1¼ cups (250 g) plus 1 table-spoon sugar

1½ teaspoons ground cardamom seeds (freshly ground, if possible)

¾ cup (180 ml) milk

1 cup (2 sticks/225 g) unsalted butter, plus more for the pan

1 teaspoon ground cinnamon

2 tablespoons chopped walnuts or pecans

When I left home for my first job in New York, my mom photo-copied a few recipes for me, and a version of this perfect, fun-to-say Swedish coffee cake (kardemummakaka) was one of them. It's extremely tender and buttery, with a bit of crunch from freshly ground cardamom and a sugar-and-nut topping. I'm not sure where the recipe came from (note to publishers of books and magazines: please use running feet and heads on every page), but the photocopy itself is well worn, wrinkly and stained with what appears to have been a nearly full cup of coffee. You can tell it's an older recipe, because it calls for just "nuts."

Preheat the oven to 350°F (175°C). Butter and flour a 9-inch (23 cm) square cake pan.

In a medium bowl, whisk together the flour, baking powder, and salt.

In a large bowl, whisk the egg until fluffy, then whisk in the 1¼ cups (250 g) sugar and the cardamom.

In a small saucepan over low heat, warm the milk to lukewarm. To the egg mixture, add a little of the flour mixture, stirring with a rubber spatula to combine, then a little of the milk, then flour, and so on until all the milk and flour have been added. In the same saucepan, melt the butter, then fold it into the batter— slowly at first so it doesn't slop out of the bowl, then beating until smooth. Scrape into the prepared pan. Mix together the remaining 1 tablespoon sugar, the nuts, and cinnamon and sprin-kle the mixture evenly over the batter. Bake for 35 minutes, or until a toothpick inserted in the center comes out clean. Let cool on a rack, then cut into squares and serve.

As *You* Like It

I f you find me cooking something in a skillet on the stovetop, it's more likely to be migas than anything else. Or, rather, *what I think of* as migas, as what I cook would be almost unrecognizable as such to anyone familiar with the classic fried-tortillas-and-eggs dish. I remember making the more traditional Tex-Mex version, years ago, but everything about my migas now has morphed so much that I feel a little uncomfortable even calling it that. I'd also be uncomfortable calling it anything else, because it draws so heavily on a long tradition that I'm decidedly not a part of.

Who am I to write about migas—or, really, any dish that isn't one my parents taught me to make or introduced me to? By writing about migas and even publishing a recipe with that word at the top of the page as the noun describing the finished product, am I taking unearned space from food writers who have much more claim to the dish than I do, writers with Mexican, Spanish, or Portuguese backgrounds, for example? Should I just keep my weird version of migas to myself?

These questions have niggled at me to varying degrees throughout my career as a food writer. My work (not to mention my work *life*) would be dull indeed if I limited myself to, say, the western Pennsylvania farmhouse cooking I'm probably most "qualified" to write about because that's mostly what I learned from my mom, even though I've never lived on a western Pennsylvania farm, and my mom made not only meatloaf and raisin-filled cookies but also on-point b'stilla and sopaipillas and a lot more when I was growing up. Those foods are just as much a part of my base of knowledge and experience, aren't they? If I don't have what some people would claim is the necessary cultural background to write authoritatively—or at least convincingly—about foods I don't find bland, should I be writing about food at all?

I'm often nearly paralyzed by this question. My job is developing and writing recipes that work, and I'd like to think I'm helping people make more delicious meals more easily, but am I not the right person to be doing this work? Should I learn to code or go to law school or just write about something else? Should I open up a restaurant—or would I be even more uncomfortable serving these foods than I am writing about them? I think often about my friend who offers a ramen special at his barbecue restaurant. He insists that his ramen, which features pulled smoked pork, collard greens, and other fully appropriate add-ins, is "inauthentic," and has said that if a good Japanese noodle shop opened up in his small town he'd never serve another bowl of it himself (which in my opinion would be a great loss to that community even as it gained a dedicated ramen restaurant). And I think of the woman who had the audacity to open a food truck featuring egg rolls with nontraditional fillings like mac and cheese and buffalo chicken. Whatever you think about the wisdom of a mac

and cheese egg roll, the public criticism of her business as appropriating Chinese food culture and unfairly making money from it is nonsensical. Treading the line between cooking and sharing food you love while knowing you're being seen by some as an interloper sounds exhausting, frankly, and I couldn't do it.

As a freelance cookbook editor and occasional ghostwriter, I'm in a position to help shape food writing by people who are much more knowledgeable than I am about a wide variety of foods, but even in that back-end role I sometimes feel as if I'm there to make "interesting" food "accessible" (meaning: recipes that work, for as many home cooks as possible), which can be just as problematic as sharing my own recipes in print. Do we need to include substitution suggestions for ingredients like dried shrimp or fermented crab, piment d'Espelette or amchur, papalo or holy basil? Is it condescending to ask authors of color to explain an ingredient or technique that might be unfamiliar to white readers? In a thoughtful, frustrating conversation on *Bon Appétit*'s website, Priya Krishna and Yewande Komolafe commiserate about dealing with editors who insist that they explain ingredients or offer substitutions. Komolafe, whose article featuring "essential" Nigerian recipes in the *New York Times* was no less than a revelation to me as a cook, says, "I want to see people who make my recipes commit to the full dish." I committed fully when I made several of the recipes in her story as soon as it dropped, and was deeply rewarded, but I've cooked those same dishes since with slight changes—in ingredients, in process—and they have been just as good, possibly even better because I've been able to fit them into my own system of kitchen management, haphazard as it may be at times. I cook those foods often, and with less effort (because sometimes I'd just rather eat than cook), and I've decided what staples I need and don't need to keep on hand. Am I still making "jollof rice"?

I don't think there will ever be a clear-cut way to apply universal standards across different cookbooks and media, and that's a difficult thing for me, as someone whose day job is essentially to apply standards with reasonable consistency, to accept. Should recipes that don't translate perfectly to the kitchen of a reasonably adventurous and resourceful cook be translated at all? I'd answer with a qualified yes.

There's something to be said for offering suggestions for substitutions even if they aren't exactly right, in the hopes that the finished product will be close enough to the spirit of the dish that people might be inspired to seek out the "real" thing next time. I don't know many people whose ingredient-storage situations are accommodating enough to keep all the supposedly correct foods in stock, and does that mean they shouldn't try to make even a facsimile of a dish they hunger for? For many years after leaving New York, I experienced nearly debilitating cravings for a sour long bean dish I'd ordered at least every couple of weeks from a Chinese restaurant near my apartment in Hell's Kitchen. I couldn't find sour long beans, didn't quite know what they were, couldn't find a recipe or reference to them in any book. And of course none of the restaurants near me offered anything similar (though I did later find the dish on the alternative Chinese menu at one place in Georgia). So I pickled some fresh long beans in vinegar, which wasn't quite right, and then I fermented beans in a salt brine, which was closer. But all the iterations I came up with—before I learned that in fact sour long beans were a ready-made product one could find in Asian grocery stores—were delicious and satisfying, and I was happy enough with those long beans that I wrote about them, hoping others would derive similar pleasures from cooking the dish (for which, incidentally, I've yet to find another published recipe). Recently I had a version of the same dish from a restaurant in my new neighborhood in Pittsburgh that was *wildly* different from the Hunan one I'd become used to: It featured a copious quantity of Szechuan peppercorns where the New York version had none, and you can imagine how jarring (and delightful!) that was. I'll bet nobody at the Pittsburgh restaurant is losing sleep over whether their pork with sour long beans is "legitimate" or "authentic" or not, and maybe I should worry less about that sort of thing myself.

I'll never stop trying to make all the foods my family and I want to eat, of course, and I'll always be intensely curious about foods I'm unfamiliar with. I probably won't stop writing about them and doing the work to bring them to other people's kitchens, either. The esteemed and award-festooned Madhur Jaffrey obviously feels comfortable cooking and writing about a wide range of foods, and she does it very well—her *World Vegetarian* is a classic for a reason and has broadened the vision of likely hundreds of thousands of home cooks in its life span. Anyone else who wants to take a stab at covering food from a culture other than their own should feel as free to do so as Jaffrey does. I say this with confidence, but I'll always be conflicted about it. I know I won't strike the right balance every time—there are more than a few recipes I've published in the past that make me cringe now, and I suspect this very book contains some I'll want to shove down the memory hole at some point. But I've heard from readers that some of my recipes have introduced them to foods they'd not had contact with before, and it's not a stretch to imagine that an encounter with a decidedly personalized, too-much-lime-juice version of, say, an Isaan-style laap led them to seek out better ones.

Of course there's more I could have done and can be doing now to open up the food-writing world to people who deserve to be a part of it more than I do. If he were less averse to punching down (way down),

Tunde Wey, the Nigerian American restaurateur-provocateur who in a tense webinar asked longtime Southern Foodways Alliance head John T. Edge, a white man who's held the position for decades, to resign from his post, would tell me to quit right now and make way. And then what? Would home cooks suddenly be willing to keep bottles of six kinds of cooking oil in their pantries, for foods from different traditions? Probably not, and as of right now I think that's okay. Each time I start a new editing or writing project I wrestle with all of these questions anew.

My daughter has expressed zero interest in becoming a food professional of any kind, but I hope that the way we cook and eat as a family now will make her comfortable in her own kitchen someday to experiment with dishes like migas, which is quite simply one of the best foods in the world, no matter who you are, where you come from, or how you make it. She's grown up with it, after all.

Migas, of a Sort   Serves 1

1 tablespoon unsalted butter or vegetable oil

½ cup (100 g) chopped vegetables

3 stale corn tortillas, torn into pieces

1 large egg

Salt and freshly ground black pepper

Sprinkle of shredded or grated cheese of any kind, or cotija

A few halved cherry or grape tomatoes; or 1 small tomato, diced

Vinegary hot sauce

Chopped fresh cilantro (optional)

You don't need to add any vegetables to this, but it's such a good way to use up stray leftovers that I almost always do. I like sweet peppers and onion, but you can use almost any quick-cooking or already cooked vegetables—raw asparagus or zucchini, finely chopped broccoli, leftover roasted vegetables like sweet potatoes or cauliflower, or braised kale. A bit of shredded roast beef, or taco meat, or a diced half of a pork chop from last night's supper are also fine additions.

In a small skillet, heat the butter over medium heat. Add the vegetables and tortillas. Cook, turning occasionally with a thin metal spatula, until the vegetables are just tender and most of the tortilla pieces are crisped and browned, 3 to 5 minutes. Spread everything out in the pan, then crack in the egg and sprinkle with a good pinch of salt and grinding of pepper. Use the spatula to break up the yolk and stir it into the white. When it starts to set on the bottom, after 30 seconds or so, turn and stir the egg into the other ingredients; cook until the egg is mostly solidified, about 2 minutes. Distribute the cheese over the so-called migas and let it melt a bit, then scrape the whole mess onto a plate. Top with tomatoes, hot sauce, and cilantro if you'd like, and serve.

The Sap Is Running

A week ago I was sure the winter was here in western Pennsylvania for good. The ice would never melt from our gutters or our sidewalks and paths through the parks; the sky would be gray forever. But today the spring thaw has arrived, if temporarily—I know that the sky in Pittsburgh is gray in all seasons. I'm driving out of city with my daughter, car windows open and my jacket thrown in the back seat with our dog, Piper, the ice scraper, the emergency mini snow shovel with telescoping handle, random bungee cords and coils of rope, flame-orange safety vests for hiking during deer season, and detritus from the Christmas tree I hauled from the local tree place and then to the recycling center. (My car is, in practice, more of a truck.)

Deep, lumpy snow still covers the ground in the woods behind my parents' house, spots of dark leaf litter peeking up from underneath like the irregular swooshes of chocolate my mom brushed on the fluffy white meringue frosting on the first birthday cake I remember. In a day or two the snow will have disappeared.

When the leaves were out and the hills beyond my parents' woods were obscured by them, my dad had marked a half dozen maple trees with string. Now he hands my daughter a cordless drill, and my mom and I take handfuls of tubing with black plastic taps attached and a stack of clean twenty-liter Cambro containers with them to the first tree. It's the largest in diameter, big enough to accept two taps. On the sunny side of the trunk, my dad shows my daughter where to drill, about four feet from the ground and angled up a bit. He's marked the drill bit with tape at the right depth. When the edge of the tape meets the bark, my daughter pulls the drill out, and it's damp with sap. My dad has another tool ready for her, a sort of dental pick she uses to clean wet wood shavings from the hole she's made. She selects a tube from my bouquet and pushes the tap in. Beads of thin maple sap start flowing at once, and she quickly inserts the free end of the tube through a hole in a Cambro lid, and we move on to the next tree, then the next tree and the next. There's a string-marked tree way down the steep hill behind the house, but the snow is too slippery for us to get to that one today. When it melts, my mom or dad will tap it, too.

After some snow play with Piper and one of my mom's smorgasbord-y lunches—baked chicken wings, sourdough rye spread with horseradish cream cheese and topped with thick slices of corned beef and tangy slaw, sweet pickles, potato chips, and the usual big bowls of fresh fruit—we check the trees. One sap container has blown over in the warm wind, and my daughter finds heavy rocks to stabilize it. The sap at the other trees is pooling generously in the bottom of each container. Over the course of the next month or so, each tap will yield gallons and gallons of sap—my dad says forty; my mom says half that. When there's a good amount of liquid in the containers but before they're too heavy to carry from the woods, in a few days maybe, depending on whether it stays warm enough during the daytime for the sap to keep flowing fast, my parents will start to cook it down to syrup. In the gazebo, my dad's already set up a big two-burner propane stove

with a large, shallow rectangular steel pan on top. Last spring, he and my mom boiled each batch down as they collected it, but this year my dad thinks they'll just keep adding fresh sap and letting it all boil down in bigger, more efficient batches. They'll finish the boiling on the stovetop in the kitchen for about an hour, so they can watch it more carefully as the water evaporates further and the syrup's temperature rises to exactly 219°F (104°C).

"Too much and it burns, too little and it's thin," my dad says. Forty gallons of maple sap will yield no more than one of syrup.

It's precious stuff, and I rarely had it as a kid, probably because my family had syrup-appropriate breakfast foods fairly often, and so store-bought "pancake syrup" or honey from my mom's extremely productive bees or runny fruit preserves was more economical—and we didn't have maple trees to tap.

I seem to remember that for a short time in the early to mid-aughts it was fashionable for parents (at least those who were being written about in newspaper style sections) to effect exasperation when telling a story about how their foodie offspring went to a friend's house for dinner and complained that the pesto wasn't homemade or about how much their toddler loves sushi—and just as fashionable to mock those people. My daughter is no snob, but once, when she was five or six and visiting her grandparents, my mom asked her what she'd like on her pancakes.

"Maplesyrup," she said as one word because at that point she'd neither eaten nor known any other kind. Now she spoons the syrup even more judiciously from the half-pint jars of home-gathered her grandparents give her.

Pancakes   Makes about six 5-inch (12 cm) pancakes

PRACTICE SKILLS

Cracking an egg

Mixing a batter

Using an electric griddle, or stovetop cooking in a skillet over medium heat

Spatula work

1 cup (130 g) all-purpose or whole-wheat flour

2 tablespoons sugar

2 teaspoons baking powder

¼ teaspoon kosher salt

1 cup (240 ml/g) milk

1 large egg

2 tablespoons unsalted butter, melted, plus more for cooking

This recipe, one of the first I tape to the inside of a cupboard door when we move to a new house, is based on—well, just about every basic pancake recipe you'll see in cookbooks and online. It's a small batch, but easy to double, and easy to personalize with different flours and additions.

In a medium bowl, whisk together the flour, sugar, baking powder, and salt.

In a glass measuring cup, whisk the milk, egg, and melted butter until the egg is completely broken up. Pour into the flour mixture and stir with a spatula until just combined. The batter will be thin and a little lumpy.

Heat an electric griddle to 350°F (175°C), or heat a skillet over medium heat. Melt some butter on the griddle or in the skillet. Working in batches, scoop in ⅓-cup (75 ml) portions of batter. Cook for about 2 minutes, until the edges look dry, bubbles are popping in the center of the pancakes, and the bottom is golden brown, then flip with a spatula and cook until the other side is golden. Serve them as they're ready, or put them on a plate in a warm oven until they're all cooked.

Variations: Add a handful of broken pecans or walnuts to the batter. This is especially good if using whole-wheat flour.

Just after ladling portions onto the griddle, drop some fresh or frozen blueberries (or chocolate chips, or a few thin slices of banana) into the batter.

Use all or part buckwheat flour—but be sure it's a nice light buckwheat flour from a mill somewhere in central Appalachia, not the harsh, bitter, coarser flour that's more common in supermarkets.

Add ¼ teaspoon baking soda to the dry ingredients and use buttermilk in place of regular milk.

French Toast   Serves 4

PRACTICE SKILLS

Cracking eggs

Stovetop cooking in a skillet over medium-low heat

Spatula work

---

3 large eggs

2 tablespoons sugar

½ cup (120 ml) milk

1 teaspoon vanilla extract

3 teaspoons unsalted butter

8 slices of bread

The only trick here is making sure you cook the soaked bread slices slowly so the custardy inside is cooked through by the time the outside is crusty.

In a shallow bowl or pie plate, whisk together the eggs and sugar until smooth, then whisk in the milk and vanilla.

In a skillet, melt a little of the butter over medium-low heat. Put a slice of bread in the egg mixture and soak it for about 10 seconds, then turn and soak the other side for 10 seconds. Lift it up, letting any excess egg drip off, and place it in the skillet. Repeat with another slice. Cook until deeply browned on the bottom, then use a thin metal spatula to turn each slice over and cook on the other side until browned and just cooked in the center—this should take about 4 minutes total; turn down the heat if the bread is browning too quickly. Remove to a plate and serve right away. Repeat with the remaining bread and egg mixture, adding butter to the pan as needed.

Sweeter variation: Spread jam (or, my favorite, apple butter) very thinly on two slices of bread and top one slice with thin slivers of almond paste. Sandwich the bread slices together, then dip the sandwich into the egg mixture on each side. Cook over low heat, as in the recipe above, pressing down on the sandwich gently so the two halves adhere. No need for syrup with this French toast, but you might dust the tops with a bit of confectioners' sugar tapped through a small sieve, and serve fresh fruit on the side.

Kids Using Knives

Risk assessment—determining the probability of an adverse event, and the severity of the effects should the event occur—lurks in the background of every happy session in the kitchen with a young child. NIOSH inspectors have nothing on the eagle-eyed adult watching a young person pick up a knife and settle its edge on the curve of an onion. We are constantly calculating: likelihood the knife will cut flesh = toughness/slipperiness of onion (pull off all of the papery peel first for better traction!) × cutlery ergonomics[looseness of long shirtsleeves as measured in excess cm] ÷ sharpness of knife × experience and skill of the individual; severity of potential injury = sharpness of knife (or is it dullness—would you prefer a clean, deep cut with a sharper knife or a messy, shallow cut with a duller one?) × softness of skin ÷ pain tolerance. Similar formulae apply to stovetop cooking, moving full baking sheets in and out of a hot oven, lighting a charcoal fire, draining pasta or rice, operating multi-bladed small appliances or ones with fast-moving parts.

I began to help my daughter use real knives—progressing from table knife to chef's knife—at what I considered to be a young age. She always seemed *just a little too young* to be wielding this kind of knife or that kind of knife, which is probably how it will always be. She was just a little too young to walk home from the library by herself, I thought, the first time she did it. A little too young to be unsupervised on the internet. Still just a little too young to fry her own egg over a burner or light a charcoal fire or spatchcock a chicken. Sometimes it really was too soon for a certain kind of knife work, and we'd take a step back: I'd gently re-assume prep-cook duties while she assembled a dish or stirred batter or rinsed produce. We'd return to that knife later.

It's a rare dish that absolutely requires mastery of a specific knife skill. Once when I worked in the restaurant kitchen, I was instructed to brunoise a bunch of vegetables—cut them into very tiny cubes—for a gazpacho (of sorts). I'd gotten partway through the vegetables when the chef came over to my cutting board and swept them all into the garbage bin. He explained, with more patience than I would've expected, that my cubes were too large and too non-cube-like for his gazpacho, and that the smallness and regularity were "*what make it nice.*" He was trying hard not to raise his voice for that last part. Until then, I hadn't thought much about texture as a component of the experience of eating, but after the gazpacho incident I noticed it everywhere, and tried to appreciate it as much as flavor. As I've learned to cook alongside a child, of course, I've become lazier—or, let's say, more flexible—in my approach. The onions might get neatly diced with a chef's knife, they might just get chopped into weird rhombuses with a paring knife, and that's—almost always—just fine.

If a child isn't ready for the knife that's most appropriate to the task but is ready for the task, think of ways one can achieve similar results. For a long time, my daughter wasn't able to smash a garlic clove under the side of a chef's knife tapped with the heel of her hand; the force required felt awkward to her. So we improvised: she'd drop the garlic into the heavy granite mortar we use for Thai curry pastes and bring the pestle down on it a couple times, pull off the peels and smash some more, and she'd have sort-of-not-exactly-minced garlic. Grate ginger on a ceramic ginger grater that can't really cut or shred anything sensitive but is an excellent tool for that job (works on peeled garlic cloves, too, but your fingers will smell like garlic for at least seventy-two hours afterward). Tear lettuces, herbs, even tomatoes into pieces with your hands, break up asparagus and green beans manually. Divvy up the task, with the adult halving the onion so it sits steady on the cutting board, the kid using a small knife to break it down further.

Or, where you can, substitute produce that doesn't need peeling or chopping—fresh or frozen peas, canned tomatoes, hearty greens, bite-sized new potatoes. A pot of vegetable soup is not just an essential dish to know how to cook but also a fine project for figuring out what a new cook is capable of doing with a knife, and adjusting technique and ingredients to match skill levels.

Using Knives Safely and Well

Never try to catch a knife you've dropped or knocked off the counter, and never put a sharp knife in the sink—it's too easy to accidentally grab the blade.

Make sure your hands and the knife handle are *clean and completely dry* before you pick up the knife.

Use a sturdy cutting board: wood and resin boards are my favorites. Very important: dampen a kitchen towel or a piece of paper towel and spread it underneath the board to keep it from slipping while you work.

Keep fingers of your non-knife hand clear of the blade by tucking your fingertips in toward your palm when holding the food you're cutting: Make your non-knife hand into an attacking-tiger claw. Your knuckles can help guide the knife as you slice.

Practice with small (but still sharp) knives and easy-to-cut foods: bananas, celery, cucumbers.

Use a *serrated* knife to cut tomatoes.

Use a long serrated bread knife for crusty bread—and be especially careful as you start cutting through a loaf of bread, using short back-and-forth sawing motions and light pressure, as the knife might slip on the crusty surface.

A sharp chef's knife is ideal for almost everything else. Hone it frequently if you use it a lot.

Carefully wash your good knives by hand with a dish rag or soft, clean sponge and hot soapy water. Wipe them dry and put them away when you're done with them.

Vegetable Soup Template   Serves 4

1 tablespoon olive oil

1 onion, chopped

Kosher salt and freshly ground black pepper

4 to 5 cups (960 ml to 1.2 L) vegetable broth or water, or a combination

One 14½-ounce (411 g) can diced or whole tomatoes; or 2 cups (335 g) diced fresh tomatoes, with their juices

¼ head green cabbage, cored and chopped

2 russet potatoes, chopped

2 carrots, peeled if you'd like, chopped

2 cups (290 g) sweet corn kernels (fresh or frozen)

1. Sauté aromatics—onion, garlic, ginger, leeks, shallots, whole or ground spices or spice blends.

2. Add liquids—water, broth, canned or ripe fresh tomatoes with juices, tomato juice.

3. Add hearty greens—cabbage, kale, collards, dandelion, escarole.

4. Add long-cooking vegetables—potatoes, carrots, sweet potatoes, winter squash, beets, turnips, parsnips, rutabagas.

5. Add quick-cooking vegetables—sweet corn, peas (shelled, sugar-snap, or snow peas), mung bean sprouts, small pieces of summer squash and zucchini, asparagus, green beans, spinach, bok choy, precooked beans, precooked whole grains.

In a Dutch oven, heat the oil over medium-high heat. Add the onion, a pinch of salt, and a few grindings of pepper and cook, stirring frequently, for 5 to 7 minutes, until the onion is tender and lightly browned. Add the broth, tomatoes, cabbage, potatoes, and carrots. Stir in 1 teaspoon salt. Bring to a boil, then lower the heat and simmer, uncovered, for 30 minutes, or until the vegetables are tender. Add the corn and simmer for 10 to 15 minutes, until tender. Season with more salt and pepper if needed, then serve.

A Pot,
a Pot of Beans,
and Thee!

I n *Bean by Bean*, Crescent Dragonwagon, one of my favorite cookbook writers, says of the bean: "In its life as an ingredient, it is humble, an object of potential, not actuality." She adds, "Nothing wrong with that," then goes on to reference Shakespeare. But I would invoke a more recent English poet, Samuel Taylor Coleridge.

YA Coleridge was the OG of the cottagecore aesthetic (and yes, I know the term "cottagecore" only because my daughter explained the concept to me in between Moomin embroidery projects), dreaming of a utopian community he planned to establish in Pennsylvania with his fellow poet Robert Southey and a pair of sisters—along with some wealthy potential utopians the poets hoped would bankroll the endeavor. The idea was to learn carpentry and farming over the course of an English winter, then hop on a boat to the New World, where they would enjoy a country life in which private property didn't exist, all decision making was conducted democratically, and each person would need work no more than three hours per day to maintain the commune and educate the kids. (Nothing wrong with that.) Coleridge and Southey were certain that such an arrangement would allow for long periods of metaphysical inquiry, that they would "write sonnets whilst following the plough," as Southey put it. They never made it to Pennsylvania, as you might have guessed, but apparently Coleridge had a hard time giving up on the idea of a bucolic life in nature surrounded by conversational friends. By many accounts he managed to construct something like it for a while in a thatched cottage outside Nether Stowey, in South West England. (He eventually moved to London to give lectures on Shakespeare; his later, opium-addicted years were more in line with the *dark academia* aesthetic, as it's been explained to me, than cottagecore.)

For possibly age-related or neurological reasons I don't want to think too much about, whenever I start to cook *a pot of beans*, I hear the phrase in my head in the same cadence as a line from Coleridge's "Constancy to an Ideal Object," which I must've studied when my mind was more sponge, less colander, because I'd forgotten it until recently: ". . . a home, an English home, and thee!" "Constancy" is a complex Romantic work of despair and longing, an attempt to reconcile the ideal, the potential or thought of an object, with the thing itself. The poem is . . . definitely not about beans, but it's possible my *pot of beans, and thee!* brainworm has been trying to tell me something all these years.

> *"Ah! loveliest friend!*
> *That this the meed of all my toils*
>   *might be,*
> *To have a home, an English home,*
>   *and thee!"*
> *Vain repetition! Home and Thou are one.*

There's not much else a person needs, right? A pot of beans, a lovely friend—and often they're one and the same. Creamy and substantial, protein- and fiber-rich, easy to store dried or canned, and as easy to cook, a warm pot of beans is a friendly thing. It's exceedingly cozy.

If there's any food besides, say, berry cobbler or apple dumplings—a favorite of Coleridge's, according to Charles Lamb—that could be considered pure late eighteenth- and early nineteenth-century cottagecore, it's a homey pot of beans. Several of the famous Romantic poets were vegetarians, and Lord Byron once described himself, while on a sadly restrictive diet, as a "leguminous-eating Ascetic." Clearly he was eating the sort of beans Dragonwagon would call objects of unrealized potential. I personally have little interest in restrictive diets or asceticism: while I appreciate plain-ish beans as much as the next person—though maybe not as much as my daughter, who has been known to serve herself up platefuls of the ones I cook solely to put in the freezer and use in other, more interesting dishes later—I'm more inclined to enjoy them in an advanced state, after they've "had greatness thrust upon them." Greatness in our kitchen often taking the form of chiles, some dried herbs (epazote especially—it not only tastes good, but is said to reduce beans' effects on digestion), and maybe even a piece of smoked pork for good measure.

Smoky, Savory Pinto Beans Serves 4 to 6

PRACTICE SKILLS

Using an Instant Pot or slow cooker, or stovetop cooking

Using an immersion or standing blender (or just smooshing some beans with a wooden spoon in the pot)

1 pound (455 g) dried pinto beans

1 piece of smoked pork jowl, or 1 smoked ham hock

½ onion, chopped

2 teaspoons garlic powder

1 teaspoon ground cumin

1 teaspoon ancho chile powder

½ teaspoon chipotle chile powder

1½ teaspoons crushed dried epazote

1 teaspoon dried thyme

1 bay leaf

Freshly ground black pepper

Kosher salt

I'll often rinse a pound of dried beans and dump them into a slow cooker with lots of water and nothing else and just let them cook all day, whether I have immediate plans for them or not. I'll use some in a soup or chili, funneling the rest into freezer bags and squirreling them away for a busier day.

Most people will tell you to soak dried beans overnight before draining and cooking them in fresh water, but I don't usually bother, if only because I don't usually remember in time. Soaking doesn't reduce the cooking time *that* much, and I haven't noticed a huge difference in either the evenness of cooking or the ease of digestion one way or the other.

Serve these with a grain (to soak up the flavorful cooking liquid), and maybe some braised hearty collard greens or kale.

Put the beans in a sieve and rinse them under running water. Dump them into an Instant Pot, slow cooker, or Dutch oven and add the smoked pork, onion, garlic powder, cumin, ancho powder, chipotle powder, epazote, thyme, bay leaf, and several grindings of black pepper. Pour in water to cover by at least a couple inches—about 7 cups (1.7 L).

If *pressure cooking* in an Instant Pot, put on the lid and lock it closed, set the valve to "sealing," and cook on the manual high or "more" pressure-cooking setting for 25 minutes. Turn off the Instant Pot, let pressure release naturally for 10 minutes or so, then carefully (using tongs if necessary) turn the valve to "venting" to release the remaining pressure.

If *slow cooking* in an Instant Pot, put on the lid and lock it closed, set the valve to "venting," and slow-cook on the high or "more" setting for about 6 hours, until the beans are tender and creamy on the inside.

If using a slow cooker, put on the lid and cook on the high setting for about 6 hours.

If using a Dutch oven on the stovetop, bring to a boil over high heat, then lower the heat and cook, uncovered, at a brisk simmer, adding more water if needed to keep everything submerged, until the beans are tender and creamy on the insides—the cooking time will vary considerably, from 1½ to 2½ hours, depending on how old the beans are. Add salt to the beans toward the end of the cooking time—start with 1½ teaspoons, then taste them again just before serving.

Use tongs or a slotted spoon to fish out the smoked pork and put it in a bowl. If you'd like, use an immersion blender to blend a bit of the beans to thicken the liquid; scoop some of them into a regular blender and puree, then return them to the pot; or just smash some of the beans against the side of the pot with a wooden spoon to thicken the cooking liquid a bit. When the pork is cool enough to handle, pick off the meat and discard any skin, fat, and—in the case of a ham hock—bones. Stir the meat back into the pot. Serve warm.

Sharing Food

AT A DISTANCE

Have a supply of food containers of various sizes that you wouldn't mind not getting back right away (or ever), and flat-bottomed totes or paper grocery bags with handles. My parents will often make a slew of wood-fired pizzas at a time, so many that they have a stash of small pizza boxes and one of those horizontal-carry insulated pizza-delivery bags from Restaurant Depot for taking them fresh off the grill to homebound neighbors. But they have a tendency to do things big. All you really need are some generic plastic food-storage containers.

Tote hot and cold foods in separate bags, if possible, or put hot containers in the bottom of a bag, then a neutral item like a sturdy loaf of bread or a container of cookies, then cool and lightweight foods like salads or a few cookies.

Remember toppings! Put a little grated cheese or chopped herbs or toasted nuts or extra chile flakes in a little baggie or wrap it in a piece of plastic or waxed paper. If it's feasible (for example, if the cheese won't melt from the heat of the container), tape the packet to the appropriate food container; if not, you can instead tape it to the inside of the paper bag so it doesn't get lost in the bottom.

If the recipient is incapacitated or very busy—and these are the friends we often want to bring food to if they're open to receiving it—let them know when you're coming by, drop off the food at the doorstep (or hand it off quickly if there's no doorstep), and take your leave. Make it clear that you don't need the containers returned.

HOSTING

I'm a fan of the old-fashioned non-potluck dinner party, at least as an occasional indulgence. You know: the kind where the host makes a meal, a simple and untaxing one, and nobody else is expected to bring anything to complete it. Guests might be inspired to add something to the table as an extra treat, a bottle of wine or nice sparkling water or a loaf of bakery bread, but they don't feel obligated to concoct an important part of the meal and figure out food-transportation logistics themselves. Time constraints, budgets, dietary requirements . . . there are plenty of reasons to forgo this kind of gathering in favor of a potluck scenario, but I think it's nice if it can happen every once in a while.

Offer plenty of food—more than enough, if you can, even if you suspect you'll have lots of leftovers. These can be packaged in saved plastic takeout containers for friends to take home with them, or enjoyed yourself. Few things are more pleasant than a lazy day-after-a-party when you don't have to scrounge for sustenance.

Consider candlelight. Except in the kitchen while you're actually preparing food, there's no need for harsh overhead lights.

For a potluck, ask people to bring a certain kind of food ("a salad," "a vegetable side dish," "a dessert"), leaving the details open to interpretation—and remaining, yourself, open to surprises. Unless they have a specific theme, potlucks rarely feature foods that all go perfectly together, and that's part of their charm.

It's been said better by many other writers, but I too would urge you not to worry if your house or apartment isn't perfectly suited to hosting a get-together, or perfectly rid up and sparkling clean, or if you don't have the energy to prepare an elaborate, multi-course spread (who ever will?). I go through periods of hermitage during which these are easy excuses for putting off cooking a simple meal for friends in my own home. I know few people who wouldn't be more than happy to sit on a stoop or around a kitchen table with a plate of cheese and crackers and crisp cold raw fruit and vegetables between them to share.

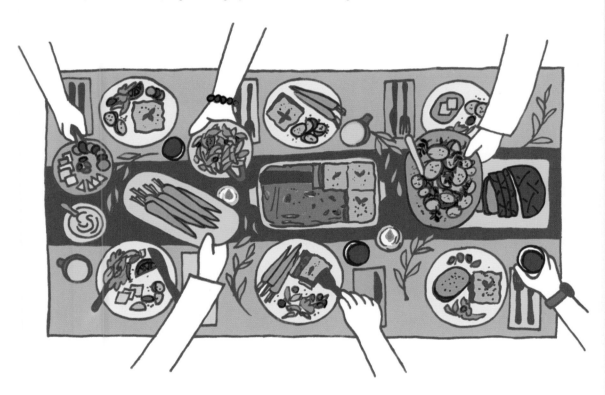

Tastes Acquired and Lost

As a kid I despised cilantro, just could not tolerate it. Chewing the leaves, I'd think I might as well be licking a stainless-steel bowl. Then, sometime in my early twenties, it quite suddenly became—and remains—the herb I use more than any other. In 2011 and 2012, researchers published studies in which they identified genetic variants that appeared to be related to whether a person loves cilantro or believes it smells and tastes strongly of soap (and thus dislikes it). I read countless articles about the possibility that cilantro preferences are heritable in an attempt to discover why my own taste for it had shifted so dramatically.

My mom posited that the cilantro she grew at home, the stuff I was trying to eat throughout my childhood, had a stronger flavor because she used little fertilizer in her herb garden—just a touch of compost—and didn't water it regularly. Commercially grown cilantro, those lush bunches skillfully lopped off and twist-tied by farmworkers along the west coast and in Mexico (the world's largest producer), are grown in more heavily amended soil, often with more generous irrigation. Maybe the milder cilantro I was buying in New York City was more palatable to me. It was a plausible theory, but I've grown cilantro myself since then, with not-ideal fertilizing and watering, and love it as much as the store-bought stuff. My daughter currently tolerates but doesn't adore it, and I wonder if she too will experience it differently as an adult. Some studies have suggested that repeated exposure to cilantro can overcome one's genetics, so it's theoretically possible that having one or more of those genetic variants that encode a sensitivity to aldehyde chemicals (present in cilantro, soap, and, weirdly, the scent released by stinkbugs, which indeed smell like cilantro to me and not *entirely* off-putting) can be powered through if that seems preferable to trying to avoid it altogether.

Genes also (probably) play a role in how people perceive sour flavors, but the science of it is complicated and still not entirely understood. When you think of an extremely sour food and your mouth waters, that's a biological response: the saliva produced is (likely) intended to dilute the acid you're presumably about to eat in order to help protect the enamel of your teeth. The amount of saliva produced is dependent on genetics, and if your saliva glands tend to produce less you will experience more intense sourness and will *seem* to be more sensitive to it than people who tend to produce more saliva and thus experience the same food as less intensely tart. In addition, there may also be a sour taste receptor gene, like the soapy-cilantro gene, that makes some people more sensitive to sourness.

Taste perceptions change with age, and there are biological and physiological reasons for this. Humans, it's believed, are born with a strong preference for sweetness (which characterizes "safe" foods, and those with the calories necessary for a growing body) and a heightened sensitivity to bitterness

(poisonous substances; danger) that persists through adolescence. With age and experience, it's less essential to our survival that we distinguish foods by taste alone, and so we're free to explore more-bitter and less-sweet foods—and whether we enjoy them or not could depend on specific gene variants. It could also depend on our literal taste buds: how many we have, and how sensitive they are. Taste cells die off and are replaced every couple of weeks, but as we get older some of them just . . . aren't replaced, which means older people aren't as sensitive to strong flavors as younger people, who generally have far more active taste receptors. Still, there's disagreement about whether the density of fungiform papillae, the tiny bumps on the tongue, is what primarily determines sensitivity to bitterness. A large study conducted at the Denver Museum of Nature & Science by trained citizen scientists found that intense reaction to bitterness correlates more closely to the presence of a variation in a certain taste receptor gene than it does to the density of papillae on the tongue. So-called supertasters, the authors of the study argue, don't necessarily have more taste buds, but they might be more likely to carry that genetic variation.

Culture plays a role in children's experiences of different foods too, of course. Persian kids snack on sour unripe plums and unsweetened sour cherry fruit leather that would probably make the average American kid's eyes tear up. Children in India tend to be eased into spicy foods much earlier than are American children. Key word: *eased*. The capsaicin in chiles activates not only taste receptors but pain receptors, and kids are more sensitive to stimulus received through both. There's some evidence that children who were exposed to spicy foods in utero might be more open to trying those foods at a relatively young age.

Anecdotal evidence, however, points to the fact that kids—like adults—are wildly different and have individual preferences that it's foolish and often counterproductive to try *too* hard to control. I didn't exercise a lot of intentionality when my daughter was very young and just learning to eat solid foods, but I think we hewed fairly close to the "division of responsibility" ethos. As Bettina Elias Siegel describes it in her book *Kid Food*, the division is this: Adults are responsible for providing a variety of nutritious foods, while the decisions about whether and how much of it to eat are up to kids themselves. It helps to remember that when a child—or an adult, for that matter—expresses a food preference it probably has very little to do with being "picky."

My daughter won't eat a green salad, but she could easily polish off a quarter sheet pan of roasted broccoli before it gets to the table, and that's fine with me. I still offer salad, even if it means I'm likely to be eating all of it myself. She doesn't care for as much heat in her curry or her chili as I do, but she's an adventurous taster in other ways, snacking on packets of dried anchovies, sipping fermented-pickle juice from the jar (her sour tolerance is at a level similar to my own), sneaking small bowls of whole raw garlic cloves into her bedroom to munch on while she reads, ordering the most unusual-sounding seafood dish on any given menu. She loves the darkest chocolate and the strongest Russian tea. Eventually she may come to love cayenne and habaneros and cilantro as much as I do, and perhaps she won't be as enamored of tart brine as she is now. Tastes come and go. In the meantime I'll slice chiles to add to my own plates, and keep bird's eyes soaking in fish sauce to spoon onto my fried rice. (I've seen her try a few drops from the fish sauce and chile container when I forget to put the bottle of plain fish sauce on the table.)

She'll have all the dried anchovies to herself for now; I'll work up to them.

Fresh Tarragon Salsa

Makes about 3 cups (600 g)

Finely chopping tomatoes and onion

Working with a hot chile (wear gloves)

1 pound (455 g) tomatoes (about 4 large plum tomatoes)

½ small sweet onion

1 to 2 jalapeño peppers

1 bunch (14 g) fresh tarragon, tough stems removed

1 teaspoon kosher salt

½ teaspoon garlic powder

3 tablespoons vinegar (cider, white or red wine, white balsamic, sherry)

When I was a teenager in Virginia, I made salsa from the vegetables and herbs in my mom and dad's garden several times a week throughout the growing season. I remember very carefully removing from a single chile every seed and fiber of white membrane, which is where the heat is, and mincing the jalapeño or serrano into the tiniest possible cubes so that in any one bite I'd be less likely to encounter more than a hint of heat. Now I broil a dozen whole chiles at a time so I can snack on them while my family eats normally spiced food. I also remember that my favorite salsa during that time featured not cilantro but tarragon, and not lime juice but tarragon vinegar. I recently tried to re-create it, just to see whether I still liked it. I'm not sure it was "salsa," but it was delicious.

Finely chop the tomatoes, onion, and jalapeños (remove the seeds and membrane first, if you'd like, and be sure to protect your hands with gloves), mince the tarragon, and combine in a bowl. Stir in the salt, garlic powder, and vinegar and let stand for at least 30 minutes before serving.

Simple Roasted Tomato Salsa

Makes about
3 cups (720 ml)

PRACTICE SKILLS

Moving a large baking sheet
(or two smaller ones) in and
out of a hot oven

Working with hot chiles (wear
gloves)

Using a blender or food
processor

2 pounds (910 g) plum
tomatoes (about 8 plum
tomatoes), cut in half

1 small onion, peeled and
cut into quarters

1 or more serrano or other
hot chiles

6 cloves garlic, unpeeled

Olive oil

Pinch of ground cumin

1½ to 2 teaspoons kosher
salt

Fresh lime juice

The thought of finely dicing a colander's worth of vegetables for
a fresh salsa after a long workday is often enough to make me
give up on fresh produce forever. The true beauty of this charac-
terful, customizable blender salsa, if I'm being honest, is that it
requires only about two minutes of easy knife work.

Position an oven rack in the top third of the oven (about
8 inches/20 cm from the heating element) and preheat the
broiler to high.

On a rimmed baking sheet (a half sheet pan or two quarter sheet
pans), arrange the tomatoes, onion, chiles, and garlic in a single
layer. Drizzle with a little oil and sprinkle with cumin. Broil
until all the vegetables are softened and nicely blackened in
spots, about 15 minutes; the tomatoes will have collapsed a bit,
while the onion will be softened but will keep its shape.

Set the pan aside until the vegetables are cool enough to handle.
Pick the peels off the tomato halves and put the tomatoes in a
blender or food processor; pinch the blackened bits off the peels
and add them as well. Pull the stems off the chiles (wearing
gloves or holding the chiles with tongs as you pull the stems)
and peel the garlic, and put them in a blender or food processor,
along with the onion, 1½ teaspoons salt, and a squeeze of lime
juice. Pulse until pretty smooth and uniform, with some chunks
remaining. Add more salt and lime juice if needed. Transfer to
a container, cover, and refrigerate until ready to serve. The salsa
will keep for about 1 week in the refrigerator.

Variation: To make a salsa verde, use tomatillos instead of tomatoes (remove the papery husks and rinse well), blend in plenty
of chopped fresh cilantro (finely chopping or blending it helps
enzymes break down the aldehyde chemicals in the herb that
some people find unpleasant), and go easy on the lime juice.

Make Do

One morning, about a month into our 2020 stay-at-home adventure in West Virginia, I found myself desperate for greens. I was like an infant in the ethically challenged experiment in Cleveland in the 1920s and '30s, in which babies were allowed to have whatever foods they indicated they wanted from a selection of (reasonably healthful) foods, the hypothesis being that human bodies know what nutrients they might be lacking and will naturally gravitate toward foods that contain them. I needed fresh greens, preferably dark, preferably bitter, preferably immediately. It was a powerful want, unlike anything I'd experienced with more conventionally crave-able foods, like pie or potato chips or chocolate. We'd done our grocery shopping maybe a week before, and I couldn't justify another trip into the potential maw of disease, swirling with COVID particles (or whatever viruses are), just to satisfy a craving.

I went out into the backyard that evening. I plucked from the edges of the overgrown lawn every dandelion leaf I could find. The plants hadn't yet bloomed, but I knew where *Taraxacum officinale* would be and what the leaves looked like—not rounded-off or fuzzy like cat's ear (*Hypochaeris radicata*), which is also edible but not what I was after. I filled my colander to the brim. I heated my cast-iron skillet as hot as it would go, poured in some olive oil, then dropped in handfuls of the washed and spun-dry leaves and several good pinches of salt. I let them crisp a bit, tossed with tongs, put them—much reduced—in a small bowl, and offered them to my family with the rest of our meal. Luckily there were no takers, and I was able to eat the entire bowl, ignoring whatever else was on the table. I'll never forget how delicious those greens were.

My husband surely thought I'd finally cracked, but it's how I grew up.

If you're in the country and driving a car behind one driven by my mom, leave braking space and be alert: she will not hesitate to swerve suddenly onto the shoulder of a dirt road whenever she sees something growing nearby that may be edible, medicinal, rare, or just interesting. She is an inveterate forager of edible greens and flowers and fruits, and would take my brother and me, and often the neighbor kids in Georgia, to pick black raspberries in a disused patch of land down the road and to the right and down a ways again, always on the hottest, sunniest, most ant-infested days of summer. I silently seethed every time, thinking she'd intentionally waited for that miserable weather to pull me from the cool, muddy creekside in the woods between our house and the neighbors' or from my stack of beloved Trixie Belden books in the breezy treehouse my dad had built high in a sweetgum tree. I can still picture my parents' ancient beige-jacketed copy of Euell Gibbons's classic *Stalking the Wild Asparagus* sitting out next to the *Field Guide to North American [Birds/Trees/Wildflowers]* on one of the wide windowsills in our kitchen in Virginia. She'd learned a lot from her family, growing up on a farm in western Pennsylvania, but I think just as much of her knowledge of wild things has come from books, from extension service classes, from various "enrichment programs." She knows how to learn.

The mushroom hunter in the family is my dad, who knows where morels and chanterelles are likely to pop up from year to year, and fries a mean puffball cutlet. My younger brother and I loved to stomp on the grayed-out old puffballs to spread their dark, powdery spores so we'd have more of them after another soaking rain or two.

Throughout a year and change of limited grocery trips, I never worried that my parents wouldn't manage. Once, after hearing about other older folks having trouble keeping food and supplies stocked and remembering that they left their chest freezer in Washington State when they moved back to Pennsylvania, I asked if they needed anything. My mom started rattling off all the foods she could collect from the woods that sloped steeply down from the wisteria trellis behind their house. (She also reported that a neighbor had been sending their kid over every few days with a plate of cookies.) If my mom felt she needed more vitamin A or C or K or any of the multitude of nutrients offered by wild greens but not cookies, she'd just go outside and stalk them.

My daughter knows more than I did at her age about wild edibles. She collected mulberries and cooked lamb's quarters (*Chenopodium album*—from the same genus as quinoa) at a summer camp in Nebraska, and learned about dock and ramps, along with the medicinal uses of countless plants like wild carrot, in a nature school in West Virginia. She has her own small collection of books about wild edibles. She's taught me as much about foraging as I've taught her, and we both still have a lot to learn.

Green Salad

Mixing and matching

Developing an affection for
fresh greens

Find or carefully forage greens—a mixture of them is nice, or you can just use a head of lettuce of any sort. Wash them very well, swishing them in a deep bowl of cold water. Lift them out into a colander, and wash in another change of water. Drain well. If you have a salad spinner, use that to get as much of the water clinging to the leaves off them as possible—you don't want it to water down your dressing and make everything soggy. If you don't have a spinner (I don't have one myself—I've decided they're just too unwieldy in cupboards already full of awkward items), put the washed and drained greens on a clean dish towel, gather up the corners and edges to enclose them, then swing the purse of greens around vigorously to extract the water. Do this outdoors, or in a shower stall so you don't drench the walls of your kitchen.

All a green salad really needs are the greens, salt, a sprinkle of something acidic (lemon juice, vinegar), and a drizzle of good oil (olive oil is best). I tend to keep things quite simple, which, come to think of it, may be why my daughter has yet to fully appreciate my salads. But if you'd like, you can add edible flowers: dandelions, bachelor's buttons (*Centaurea cyanus*), chickweed (*Stellaria media*), common violets (*Viola sororia*). Or other vegetables like slender green beans or asparagus, blanched for just a minute in boiling water then scooped into ice water to chill. Tomatoes are fine in salads too, but I prefer crisp peppers for sweetness. A sprinkle of toasted nuts or something crunchy like coarse breadcrumbs sautéed in olive oil. Sometimes cheese. There's a recipe for a complicated kale salad on page 78 that you might enjoy if any of these enhancements appeal to you.

A couple of dressings to play around with follow. Make these in canning jars and keep them in the fridge for a quick lunch salad (or to use as a sauce to spoon over something you find too bland). Or halve the quantities and whisk them right in a large bowl, pile lots of greens and other salad ingredients atop it, and toss just before serving.

Lemon Dressing

Makes about ½ pint (240 ml)

PRACTICE SKILLS

Squeezing lemon juice

Grating garlic

Measuring and tasting

4 tablespoons (60 ml) fresh
lemon juice

1 teaspoon mustard

1 teaspoon honey

½ teaspoon kosher salt

Freshly ground black
pepper

1 small clove garlic

½ cup (120 ml) olive oil

Add a pinch of dried herbs (oregano, basil, tarragon, parsley, savory, thyme, for example), or a few tablespoons of minced fresh herbs, if you'd like.

In a half-pint jar, combine the lemon juice, mustard, honey, salt, and a couple grindings of pepper. Grate in the garlic. Put the lid on tightly and shake well. Add enough oil to fill the jar, put the lid back on, and shake until the dressing is creamy (emulsified). Taste and add more salt, pepper, or honey if needed. Shake again just before serving. The dressing will keep in the refrigerator for about a week; shake well, and set the jar in a bowl of hot water to re-liquefy it if necessary.

Tahini Dressing

Makes about ½ pint (240 ml)

PRACTICE SKILLS

Measuring and tasting

3 tablespoons white wine
vinegar or fresh lime juice

4 tablespoons (60 ml) runny
tahini

½ teaspoon kosher salt

2 tablespoons olive oil

If you want to toss this with cold noodles and crisp raw vegetables (slivers of cucumber, carrot, scallion) and herbs (cilantro, basil, mint), grate in some garlic and fresh ginger, and add a good pinch of hot pepper flakes.

In a half-pint jar, combine the vinegar, tahini, salt, and oil. Put the lid on tightly and shake well. Add enough water to fill the jar, put the lid back on, and shake until thoroughly combined. Taste and add more salt if needed. Shake again just before serving. The dressing will keep in the refrigerator for about a week; shake well before serving.

Foraging

Learn to forage with someone who knows what they're doing. A grandparent, a teacher from the local university extension office. Carry a guidebook with you. *Leave mushrooms alone* unless you're traipsing the woods and fields with a certified mycologist.

Collect edible plants and fruits from areas that haven't been treated with herbicides, pesticides, or fertilizers. Roadsides are fine if the roads are in the country or quiet neighborhoods and not busy with traffic and the pollution it causes. Don't trespass.

Start with fruits and plants that are easy to find and identify. Dandelion leaves are mildest when picked before the flowers bloom, but if it's your first time collecting them wait until you see the tell-tale yellow blossoms. Persimmons are widespread and stand out on the trees because they ripen in autumn as the leaves are falling.

Blackberries and black raspberries, wineberries, and raspberries are pretty easy to find and identify, as are muscadines in the South and Saskatoon berries in the Northwest. Staghorn sumac, whose cone-shaped clusters of fuzzy brick-red fruits you'll see all over the eastern part of the country in late summer, are hard to miss: cut one cluster off, put it in a bowl, and cover with cool water to steep until the water is deeply colored, then strain and sweeten with honey to make a tart lemonade-like drink. Or dry and grind to use as a tart spice (sprinkle on grilled or broiled meats, or on a shallow plate of hummus, for example).

Take only what you need, and don't pull anything up by its roots (except chicory and the occasional sassafras seedling). Leave plenty of berries for the birds and bears.

On Small Kitchens

The first kitchens I cooked in that weren't in a restaurant or a dorm (apologies to any fellow students trying to nap in nearby rooms while I kneaded and pounded bread dough my senior year, but surely you tried the cafeteria rolls and found them as unappealing as I did?) were in my apartments in Astoria and on the west side of Manhattan. They were enormous by New York City standards—in other words, they were quite small.

In Queens, I had space for one (1) appliance: a hand-me-down Hamilton Beach stand mixer from my mom that was avocado green before my dad painted it black so it would look more city-chic. When I lived in a railroad flat in Hell's Kitchen, I bought a single wall cabinet at the IKEA in Elizabeth, New Jersey, took it by bus to the Port Authority, lugged it up Ninth Avenue to my fifth-floor walkup, and screwed it securely to the wall in the kitchen for a tiny bit of extra storage space. It felt ridiculously luxurious to have a clean, brand-new plywood box just for drinking glasses and a few coffee mugs. I lost my security deposit for that, but it was worth it for the lone cabinet's years of service—and my landlords, two older Italian men who had a barbershop on the ground floor from which they could observe every coming and going, would've found another excuse to keep the deposit anyway. Another kitchen upgrade from Elizabeth: a $79 pine table that served as workspace, pie-assembly area, Thanksgiving-with-friends table, cocktail party bar, sewing table, and crafting surface, then changing table when my daughter was an infant, then—thoroughly cleaned and repainted—dining table again, and now remote-schooling desk.

Our current kitchen is 99 square feet (but who's measuring?), which is smaller than average but not New York–apartment tiny. With every new kitchen—even the freakishly large one in the farmhouse in the country—I complain to myself for the first couple months. This drawer is too wide and it's in the wrong place, the sink isn't quite right, the fridge door doesn't open all the way and I'll never get used to it, the lighting is weird, the countertops are going to drive me nuts . . . *Where will I put the spices?* But I do get used to it, and as a family we figure out how to make things work—and that's exactly why, when we move to a new house, the kitchen feels so awkward. Because the most recent one, the one with all the problems, was *perfect*.

Obviously if you're cooking with more than a couple of people at a time, a slightly larger space may be preferable, but if that doesn't happen very often, a more modest kitchen, in my opinion, is ideal, especially if there's somewhere else to keep overflow pantry items and infrequently used pots and pans and dumpling-folder-sealer thingies and the backup meat thermometer. (We keep most of that in the basement here, and we have a sort of tote box we use to bring ingredients and cake pans or whatever up the stairs when we need them and down the stairs when we're finished with them.) Movements from fridge to stovetop to sink to garbage can in one or two steps are quick and efficient. Time shuffling from one side of

the kitchen to the other is time wasted. Time cleaning the vast surfaces of the modern *gourmet kitchen* is time—well, not wasted, because it has to be done, but time you could've spent doing anything else. Who on earth wants to clean more than you have to?

I also suspect that cooking with a young kid, and letting them take on more challenging tasks like using a chef's knife or the range, is easier in a small kitchen than in a large one: even if you're working too, you're by definition always close by, ready to swoop in with a guiding hand when needed.

There are ways to manage small spaces, most of which should become pretty obvious as your kitchen sees more action. Keep utensils for hot use—heatproof spatulas, a wooden spoon, metal turners, tongs—right next to the stovetop; keep potholders and a few extra side towels in a drawer nearby too. Stash appliances in cupboards or deep drawers if you can. If you know you're going to use the slow cooker the next day, try to pull it out of deep storage the night before so the hill to climb in the morning is a little less steep. Start big cooking or baking projects by clearing the decks—emptying the sink, putting clean dishes in cupboards, moving junk you're not going to use off the countertops, refilling the little cellar of kosher salt. Use vertical space as you work if you have to. Stack things! Prep bowls of chopped vegetables for a stir-fry can be nestled on top of each other if you don't have space to spread them out. Use square storage containers rather than round to maximize cupboard and fridge inches.

Many restaurant kitchens are incredibly cramped, and you can take some cues from their line cooks: When you're cooking with other people, especially kids, who may not be as attuned to the timing and rhythms of food preparation as more experienced adults, try to anticipate where they're heading and get out of the way. You see your partner holding a hot dirtied pan, don't stand planted in front of the sink. Where else could your sous chef be heading with an armload of carrot and onion peels but the compost pail or garbage can? Even better, two chess moves ahead, what are they going to do with the peels piled on the cutting board a minute and a half from now? And you'll never see, in a well-run commercial kitchen at the height of the dinner service, a flat of eggs just . . . sitting out, or a Cambro of cleaned romaine near the hot flat-top, or an open carton of heavy cream on the work surface. Put all that stuff away as soon as you're done with it. Perhaps most important—and this is something I've been forced to learn over the years—clean as you go. Wash out the cake-batter bowl right after the cake goes in the oven, before you start the frosting. Wipe up spills as soon as they happen, or you'll be working in potentially hazardous conditions you can't easily avoid by moving to another part of the room. Always point pot and pan handles to the side, not the front of the stove, where they can be snagged with disastrous results. Good practice in a kitchen of any size, but even more important in a small one.

A small kitchen keeps me honest.

A small kitchen keeps me connected to the beloved people I'm making meals with.

I'm not saying I'd intentionally shrink a too-large kitchen should I find myself in one, but I've been so very happy cooking in closer quarters I'd certainly not seek out anything else.

Vegetable Curry   Serves 4

ingredients continue

recipe continues

PRACTICE SKILLS

Stovetop cooking over medium heat

Peeling potatoes

Grating fresh tomatoes (or opening a can of tomatoes)

Chopping hard squash

Cutting corn kernels (but you can use frozen instead)

---

2 tablespoons vegetable oil or ghee

1 teaspoon whole yellow mustard seeds

½ teaspoon whole cumin seeds

3 cloves garlic, chopped

3 coins fresh ginger, chopped

2 teaspoons ground coriander

1 teaspoon ground cumin

1 teaspoon paprika

¼ teaspoon ground turmeric

1 zucchini, cut into 1-inch (2.5 cm) chunks (about 2 cups/280 g)

½ kabocha squash, seeded and cut into 1-inch (2.5 cm) chunks (about 2 cups/320 g)

So where *do* we keep the myriad spices for all the curries and such we cook in these 99 square feet? I have a simple three-level system that's transferred well from one house to the next. Perhaps it can be adapted to your kitchen and your style of cooking; perhaps it will sound patently absurd.

Level one: a trio of rectangular plastic containers with locking lids, labeled "A, P–Z," "B–C," and "D–O" (trust me on this), housing sealed heavy-duty freezer bags of spices, arranged roughly in alphabetical order—*cumin ground, cumin whole,* and so on. We have a container just for bags of various ground chiles, a large plastic container of bags of whole dried chiles, and one for dried herbs, which because they can take on unwanted strong spice smells are kept separate from them. And there's a sturdy cardboard box where I put jars and canisters of odd things like smoked salt or seldom-used spice blends and the good saffron. Fragrant asafoetida is kept in the jar it came in, sealed inside two freezer bags, off to the side. All of these are stored on shelves in the basement (the ersatz pantry), where there's plenty of room.

Level two: masala dabbas in the kitchen, a regular-sized one and a miniature one, in a shallow drawer near the stove. These are round, flat stainless-steel lidded containers, each with seven smaller cups inside and a cute little spoon. In the larger one we keep spices generally used for savory dishes; the selection varies, but it's usually something like this: ground cumin, whole cumin, ground coriander, whole mustard seeds, ground turmeric, garam masala, and sweet paprika (or hotter Kashmiri chile powder or still hotter ground cayenne—which all look similar, and yes, this is a rare flaw in the system!). The tiny masala dabba contains spices for sweet dishes, though of course there will be times when you'll tap both dabbas for a savory or sweet use: whole green cardamom pods, cardamom seeds, ground cloves, ground

2 russet potatoes, peeled and cut into 1-inch (2.5 cm) chunks

1½ cups tomato puree (see Note)

1 scant cup cooked chickpeas; or one 7¾-ounce (220 g) can, drained

2 teaspoons kosher salt, or more to taste

½ cup (85 g) sweet corn kernels (from 1 small ear, or frozen)

¼ teaspoon garam masala

allspice, whole allspice berries, whole anise seeds, and whole fennel seeds.

Level three: countertop and prime cupboard-space spices. These are the sanctified few. Black peppercorns in a brass Turkish coffee grinder, hot chile flakes in a shaker bottle, toasted chile powder (dried red Thai chiles, toasted in a dry skillet until crisp and a bit blackened in spots, then cooled and ground in a spice grinder), very good ground cinnamon in a salt shaker that can be opened for teaspooning, a canister of Goya Adobo seasoning (sin pimiento) and one of Creole seasoning, and a bottle of dried oregano.

When we need star anise or black cardamom pods or nigella or guajillo chiles or kasoori methi or all of the above, we take the box tote to the basement and load it up.

Have all your ingredients measured, chopped, and ready to go. In a Dutch oven, heat the oil over medium heat. When the oil shimmers, add the mustard seeds and whole cumin seeds and stir until the seeds start to pop, after just a few seconds. Add the garlic and ginger, then the coriander, ground cumin, paprika, and turmeric and stir for 30 seconds. Add the zucchini, kabocha squash, and potatoes and stir to coat them with the spices. Carefully add the tomato puree and 1 cup (240 ml) water, along with the chickpeas and salt. Make sure the vegetables are mostly covered with liquid. Bring to a boil, then lower the heat and simmer, stirring occasionally and adding water as needed to keep the vegetables just barely covered, for 40 to 45 minutes, until all the vegetables are tender.

Stir in the corn and garam masala and simmer for 5 minutes. Season with more salt if needed, then serve.

Note: To use fresh tomatoes, cut about 3 good-sized slicing tomatoes in half crosswise (through the equator). Hold each tomato half in your palm and rub it, cut side down, over the coarse holes of a box or flat grater; grate until you reach the skin, being careful not to cut your hand, then discard the skin. You can also just use one 14½-ounce (411 g) can crushed or diced tomatoes.

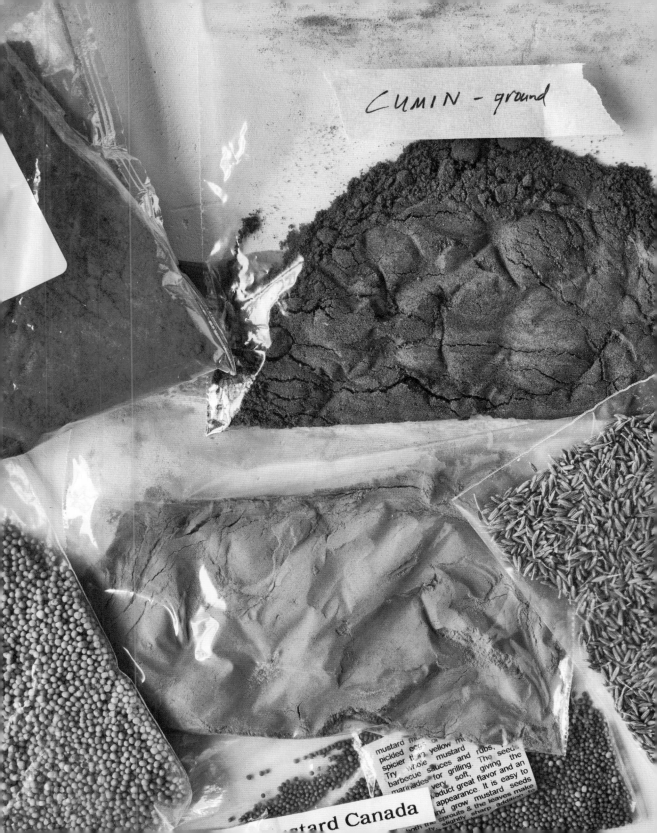

CUMIN - ground

mustard ~~~~~ or
pickled ~~~ yellow m~~
spicier ~~~ whole mustard
Try ~~~~ sauces and rubs,
barbecue ~~~ for grilling. The seeds
marinades ~~~ soft, giving the
~~~ very ~~~ great flavor and an
~~~duct ~~~ It is easy to
~~~ appearance ~~~ mustard seeds
~~~ grow ~~~ the leaves make
~~~ sprouts & ~~~ sharp additions
~~~ slightly

~~stard Canada

Keeping the Kitchen Clean

If you have a small kitchen, remembering to clean as you cook will be easy—because there's no other way to use a small kitchen.

Before you start cooking or baking, check the dishwasher, if you have one, and the sink. If there are clean dishes in the dishwasher, put them away. If there are dirty dishes in the sink, wash them now, or put them in the dishwasher, and wipe the sink clean. Now you have plenty of beautifully free space to put dirty bowls and pans and utensils while you're cooking! Clear off as much counterspace as you can. If you plan to use a cutting board, stabilize it on the countertop with a damp towel underneath.

As you work, put dirty bowls and pans in the sink, stacking them as neatly as you can and filling them with hot soapy water if they need to soak. Put used utensils (except good knives, which should never go in the sink) in the bowls or rinse them and put them in the dishwasher. Wash a few at a time and put them in a dish drainer when you have a spare minute while cooking.

Wipe countertops often with a damp, clean dish rag or paper towel. I'd advise against using sponges for countertops, as after just a couple days of use they can become pretty bacteria-ridden—and who wants to replace or re-sterilize a sponge every couple days? Dish rags,

hung up after use, will dry more quickly, prohibiting bacteria growth.

Pay special attention to your sink. Sprinkle it with baking soda, then a little white vinegar, and scrub well. Rinse with hot water. Wipe down the faucet handle often. If any raw meat juices have gotten into the sink, first rinse the sink, then spray or drizzle diluted bleach in the sink (¼ cup/60 ml bleach to 1 quart/960 ml water) and let it stand for a few minutes, then rinse again and scrub with baking soda and vinegar. It's a good idea to use a bit of bleach every now and then even if no meat has come in contact with your sink. I'll also pour some very hot water around and down the drain when I have extra in the kettle just for good measure. If you have a dish drainer, periodically clean that well too.

Clean your cutting boards. Plastic ones can go in a dishwasher, but wood and resin should be washed by hand. Rinse with a little water and scrub with a brush, then wipe them dry immediately—if wood boards stay wet they could warp or crack, and even thinner resin ones can warp a bit. I use a plastic board for cutting meat and either put it straight in the dishwasher or rinse it off in the sink, scrub it very well with very hot soapy water, rinse again, and wipe with a very weak bleach solution. Let stand for a few minutes, then wash it again. (And, of course, wash the sink well after the meat board's been in there.)

Try to wipe up spills on the stovetop as soon as it's cool enough to do so safely.

Get in the habit of using a hand towel correctly: Use it only to dry off your clean hands after you've washed them. Don't wipe dirty hands on the towel unless it's an emergency (and afterward you should toss that towel in the laundry and pull out a clean one).

Put containers of ingredients away as soon as you're done with them, or at least move them out of your workspace to keep it uncluttered.

Culture

I was about three-quarters of the way through writing a book about canning and preserving when I realized that, in fact, I should've been writing exclusively about fermentation because it's so much more interesting than pickling with vinegar and processing with heat—and the results are more healthful than preserves that are canned in boiling water to kill off pathogens. (Luckily there are lots of books on the subject that are exponentially better than mine would've been, and my daughter and husband avoided a *complete* takeover of our kitchen by jars of bubbling sour things.) Fermented—or "cultured"—foods have three big things going for them: they're healthful, they extend the useful life of produce and dairy, and they taste good ("good" as in sour).

Ferments contain live bacteria (most of them of the *Lactobacillus* species) that are beneficial to gut health and that boost immune responses. And they really are alive. My daughter walked over to the kosher grocery store in our neighborhood when we first moved to Pittsburgh and bought a jar of dill pickles from the refrigerated section. When she got home and opened the jar, the brine bubbled up furiously. When I make fermented carrots with turmeric and whole spices, they do the same after a few days or so on the counter. I've been making ferments for years, and it's still a delight every time the science experiment works the way it's supposed to. In order to experience the full health benefits of ferments, you have to keep those bacteria alive, by storing them in the refrigerator instead of heat-processing them for long-term storage at room temperature, and by using the fermented foods cool or just barely warmed: sauerkraut added to a soup after it's taken off the heat, for example.

So how does fermentation preserve food? In general, the idea is to promote the growth of good bacteria while prohibiting that of the bad bacteria that cause spoilage. You can do this in one of two ways: by adding salt or a salt brine and relying on the bacteria already present on the vegetables (sauerkraut, kimchi, pickles, and other fermented vegetables are made this way), or by adding a starter culture that contains live good bacteria (yogurt, cheeses, cultured butter, kefir, and so on are made this way). While spoilage-causing bacteria die off with exposure to salt, *Lactobacilli* and other good bacteria are more resistant to salt. They'll survive the salty environment of brine-covered vegetables and proceed to the next phase of fermentation, which is the part that makes fermented foods deliciously sour: those live bacteria convert some of the sugars in vegetables (or fruit, or whatever you're fermenting) to lactic acid. The acid produced in turn inhibits spoilage further, because the nonbeneficial bacteria that have managed to survive the salt can't survive their now-acidic environment. Your cabbage has become sauerkraut.

When you ferment with a starter culture, you're adding sufficient good bacteria to jump right to the sugar-to-acid conversion in order to overwhelm the other bacteria with acid. The culture not only sours the milk or cream, but also thickens it: lactic acid alters the structure of the milk's casein proteins so they are no longer suspended in the liquid and instead clump together in a net-like structure. Your milk has become yogurt. (You can culture nondairy milk just like regular milk to make yogurt and fresh nondairy cheeses, but it won't really thicken like dairy versions. You'll need to add a thickener like pectin or agar-agar if you want a yogurt-like or cheese-like result.)

Fermenting is easy, but it requires cooks to overcome the modern idea that certain changes in foods—the slight softening of a vegetable, the thickening of milk, the souring, the bubbling—are signs that there's something wrong. It requires some judgment and a certain amount of experience with the target food. Is your kraut sauer enough— does it taste like it should? If not, let it stand on the counter a little longer. Does your ferment smell weird, and not like what you're aiming for? It's likely that something has indeed gone wrong and it's best to compost it and start over. Has mold somehow formed? (It happens on occasion.) You can scrape off the top layer and keep going, and discard the whole batch if it appears again or if the mold extends farther into the food. For cooks who are used to achieving consistent results time after time, the uncertainty inherent to fermentation can be a difficult ask. To me, the variations from batch to batch are part of the appeal of it. The yogurt doesn't always set just right, which means my plans for it may have to change; I'll use it for smoothies or marinades rather than spooning stiff mounds of it into bowls with fruit and honey for breakfast. It challenges me to be flexible and to accept that living organisms can't always be expected to conform to a schedule and a way of being like salarymen or Twinkies that come an identical two to a pack.

Small Batch of Sauerkraut for the Fridge

Makes 1 quart, tightly packed (ferment in two jars)

PRACTICE SKILLS

Thinly slicing cabbage

Squeezing salted cabbage for an extended period of time

2 pounds (910 g) cored cabbage wedges

1½ tablespoons pure kosher salt (with no additives)

Kraut is one of the best starting points for fermenting. It is exceedingly easy and quick; it's satisfying to watch the transformation of a simple vegetable to a tender-crisp, flavorful pickle; and lasts quite a while in the fridge.

With a sharp knife, thinly slice the cabbage wedges crosswise. Put the cabbage in a large, very clean bowl or other container and sprinkle with the salt. Roll up your sleeves and wash your hands and forearms well, then start squeezing: grab handfuls of the cabbage and squeeze them hard, and keep doing so until the cabbage has reduced considerably in volume and has released enough of its liquid to cover the shreds when you pack them down very firmly with your fist. This could take as long as half an hour—take breaks when you need to and let the cabbage sit for a few minutes. It may not seem as if the cabbage will ever release enough liquid, but it almost certainly will (but see Note). You can use a very clean potato masher or meat pounder to press and pound the cabbage in the bowl if your hands get tired.

Divide the cabbage between two very clean quart-sized canning jars, pouring in the liquid as well. Use a clean wooden spoon handle (or your clean hands, if they're small enough) to press down on the cabbage so it's completely submerged in the salty liquid. Stuff a heavy-duty freezer bag into each jar, with the opening just above the jar rim (for extra security against leaks, double the bags, one inside the other). Carefully pour water (or extra brine; see Note) into the bags to weigh them down and keep the cabbage fully covered in the liquid and not exposed to air. Seal the bags closed. Set the jars on plates in a cool spot in the kitchen for about 1 week, tasting after a few days with a clean fork and letting it stand until it's as sour as you'd like. If any mold develops on the side of the bag, gently remove the bag, rinse it off, and carefully stuff it back in the jar; if there's mold on or in the cabbage, or if there are any weird non-sauerkraut, non-cabbage smells, just discard it and try again.

When the sauerkraut is as sour as you'd like it, remove the bags, put the lids on the jars (transfer all the sauerkraut to one jar, if it'll all fit), and store in the refrigerator, where it'll keep for weeks. Serve cool.

Note: Some cabbage varieties just don't have as much water in the leaves, and less-fresh heads will be drier than just-picked ones. If you've been massaging for half an hour and there still isn't enough liquid, make a brine: Dissolve 4 teaspoons salt in 2 cups (480 ml) hot water, let cool completely, then pour it over the cabbage to cover.

Variations: Stir ½ teaspoon toasted caraway seeds into the finished sauerkraut.

My friends Leda Scheintaub and Nash Patel, who own a dosa food truck in Brattleboro, Vermont, make a spectacular sauerkraut flavored with a masala of whole and ground spices; the recipe is in their book *Dosa Kitchen* and is well worth trying.

Mix some purple cabbage or shredded beet in with the green for lovely color.

Coarsely shredded carrot or radishes are fine additions for a sweeter or spicier ferment, respectively. Or mix some shredded kale, collards, or other hearty greens in with the cabbage for extra-nutritious, darker green kraut.

Good Yogurt

Makes about 3 cups (710 ml) very thick yogurt,
8 cups (2 L) very thin, or any quantity in between

PRACTICE SKILLS

Using a candy thermometer

Stovetop cooking over medium heat, or using an Instant Pot with a yogurt setting

½ gallon (2 L) whole milk

2 tablespoons already-made plain yogurt with no additives

Yogurt is cultured with a starter that already contains the relevant good bacteria. The most accessible starter is already-made yogurt, so save a little yogurt from your last batch to make the next. After a few batches, you may notice that the yogurt doesn't thicken as readily, in which case you can just buy a little container of plain yogurt to use to culture the next batch. Look at the ingredients list on the label: the best yogurt to use for culturing milk contains nothing but milk (sometimes cream) and live bacteria—no fillers or thickeners like pectin or guar gum.

If using the stovetop: Find two empty half-gallon milk jugs (the one the milk is in can be rinsed out after you pour out the milk) and two clean quart-sized canning jars with lids, and an insulated shopping bag or cooler they'll all fit in. Set aside.

Pour the milk into a large, clean pot. Attach a candy thermometer to the side of the pot (or use an instant-read thermometer) and place over medium heat. Bring to 180°F (82°C); immediately remove from the heat. Let the milk cool to 116°F (47°C).

Ladle a little of the warm milk into a bowl and stir in the yogurt until smooth, then stir back into the milk in the pot. Set a funnel in a clean quart-sized canning jar and ladle in the milk mixture, then fill another canning jar. Put the lids on.

Fill the empty milk jugs with hot tap water and put the lids on. Nestle the water-filled jugs and the milk-filled canning jars in the insulated bag, close it up tight, and set aside for about 8 hours to culture and thicken. Halfway through, without jostling the canning jars, quickly refill the milk jugs with hot water and replace them in the bag. At this point the milk should be thickened to the consistency of runny yogurt. If it isn't, let it

158

culture in the warm bag for up to another 4 hours. Transfer the jars to the refrigerator to chill completely—8 hours or overnight. You can use the yogurt as is, or spoon it into a sieve lined with four layers of rinsed and squeezed cheesecloth set over a bowl in the fridge to thicken (use the whey that collects in the bowl in bread doughs or smoothies).

If using an Instant Pot with a yogurt setting: Different models have different buttons and readouts; check your instruction booklet. Our model is the Duo, and this is how it works for yogurt: Make sure the inner pot is very clean, put it in the Instant Pot, and pour in the milk. Put the lid on and set the vent to "venting." Press "yogurt" and then "adjust" until the readout says "boil." When the pot beeps, open the lid and use potholders to remove the inner pot to a folded towel on the countertop. Put a candy thermometer in the milk (or use an instant-read thermometer) and let the milk cool to 116°F (47°C).

Ladle a little of the warm milk into a bowl and stir in the yogurt until smooth, then stir back into the milk in the inner pot and return it to the Instant Pot. Put the lid on and set the vent to "venting." Press "yogurt" and then "adjust" until the readout says "8 hrs." Let the milk culture. Check after 4 hours to see if the milk has thickened; if not, keep going for up to another 8 hours.

Remove the Instant Pot lid and let the yogurt cool to room temperature without disturbing it, then transfer the inner pot to the refrigerator to chill completely—8 hours or overnight. (Or gently spoon the cooled yogurt into another container or two for refrigerating.) You can use the yogurt as is, or spoon it into a sieve lined with four layers of rinsed and squeezed cheesecloth set over a bowl in the fridge to thicken (use the whey that collects in the bowl in bread doughs or smoothies).

Preferences

I have a cornbread problem. The problem is that I've genuinely enjoyed every single cornbread I've made or eaten, and as a food writer with some ties to the South, however tenable they may be, that is unacceptable. I know I'm expected to have strong opinions about it, inflexible preferences that no one, no new recipe, no nonconforming version of the stuff, can possibly make me question. There are people out there, I'm certain, who've read my cornbread recipes—or who might even have noticed that I've published more than one of them in print, and that they're each quite different!—and thereafter refused to take me seriously as a cook, as a writer, or as a person. I don't blame them, really.

The main areas of debate when it comes to cornbread are the following: sugar or no, and yellow or white. But there are still more disagreements to be had: fine or coarse, wheat flour or none, skillet or baking pan, butter or bacon grease? Are add-ins like cheese and corn kernels and chiles at all acceptable? And if sugar is allowed, how sweet should cornbread be, exactly? Like a muffin or cake, or just sweet enough to offset the slight bitterness of the cornmeal? My mom and dad didn't make cornbread all that often—we were more of a fried cornmeal mush family, I guess—and so no one type of it had imprinted itself in my consciousness. Until recently I thought I didn't much care about any of it, as long as the result was something that could be called "cornbread."

Since moving back north of the Mason-Dixon line, though (just north of it, from just south of it, but still), and noticing that regular grocery stores here in Pittsburgh tend to offer only one kind of cornmeal, the generic degerminated yellow, I've discovered that I do, in fact, have cornbread opinions! When presented with only one option, I am sure it's the incorrect one, at least for cornbread. I grumble and sigh theatrically in the baking ingredients aisle at the Giant Eagle, and it gives me an odd sort of pleasure. *Finally*, I think, *I'm disgruntled.* I can claim cornbread partisanship.

But when I realized I missed stone-ground whole cornmeal, preferably (I think?) the white variety, I'd satisfied only one of the controversies involved. So I decided to mail-order several kinds of good cornmeal from South Carolina and work a little harder on the latest iteration of my cornbread recipe to figure out precisely what I really wanted. As I was pulling yet another batch out of the oven one morning, my daughter came into the kitchen.

"Making cornbread?"

"Yep, trying out some different things."

"Well, I like it with *coarse* cornmeal and *no* sugar."

What was this?

By the age of fourteen she'd developed a very clear opinion about cornbread, despite the fact that the ones I'd made throughout her lifetime were, literally, all over the map. And she'd *lived* all over the map. How had this happened? Maybe I'd made more of the crunchy-edged unsweetened variety than I thought I had? More likely, she probably just, well, preferred it.

The conventional wisdom is that northern cornbread is sweet with sugar, made with yellow cornmeal, often in a regular baking pan. Southern cornbread is made with no sugar, white cornmeal, in a skillet. Modern versions in each category usually contain some wheat flour to lighten it. There are, of course, finer distinctions and copious exceptions. Kathleen Purvis, in a fascinating article in the *Charlotte Observer*, delineates a sugar/no sugar divide between Black- and white-owned restaurants in the South.

Purvis writes that modern corn varieties and industrial milling techniques had a role in solidifying the split. A piece by Robert Moss at *Serious Eats*, which draws on the expertise of heirloom grain grower and miller Glenn Roberts, of Anson Mills in Columbia, South Carolina, explains: older published cornbread recipes—from before the turn of the twentieth century—rarely contained sugar or wheat flour, but with the increasing prevalence, especially in the North, of large-scale steel roller milling over more time-consuming water-powered stone milling, sugar crept in. Industrial milling strips a lot of the character from the grain by grinding off the germ and by narrowing the range of particle sizes in any given handful of cornmeal. The modern corn varieties that take to steel roller milling are harvested when still unripe and not as sweet as the old dent corns that were allowed to ripen on the stalk before they were harvested, dried, and milled. Cane sugar stands in for the ripe corn's sugar, and I'd suggest that wheat flour in the mix replaces some of the floury particles present in coarse stone-ground meal, to make a lighter, finer crumb.

African Americans who moved north during the Great Migration, Purvis writes, had to make do with the cornmeal available there, which was less naturally sweet and needed a bit of sugar to make cornbread taste the way they remembered it. And then they brought those sugar-enhanced recipes with them when they moved back South. But take a look at the "flight" of cornbread and adjacent recipes in Toni Tipton-Martin's essential cookbook *Jubilee: Recipes from Two Centuries of African American Cooking*: There you'll find sugarless cornbread, cornbread with just as much wheat flour as cornmeal, cornbread with cheese and canned corn and chiles, and so on. And the cornbread traditions of Appalachia, the mountain South, complicate things even further.

Being vehemently attached to a certain style of a certain food is a way of maintaining a very physical connection with your family, your homeplace and history. Reading Meredith McConnell's heart-rending ode to the Three Rivers brand of cornbread mix, which she says was used to make her Tennessee family's three-times-a-week staple bread, and the desperation she and her extended family felt when it was discontinued, I felt a visceral longing—not only for a taste of her grandma's cornbread, but also for a sense of belonging and deep food history as publicly meaningful as McConnell's. I know I have this history in other ways, with other, less-widespread foods, but those foods are either less well known or less controversial. Who knows from "ballpark sandwiches," which are kind of like boureki, or maybe more like runzas, with a slightly sweet, soft yeasted dough and wildly different fillings, one mild with sausage and spinach, one spicy beef and apple? Who really cares if there's a half peanut embedded in the top of one's peanut cookie or not? I don't get to argue— or reminisce—about those foods with anyone outside my family.

I won't pretend, now, at the age of forty-seven and living in Pittsburgh, that I'm truly a zealous defender of one style of cornbread. I will undoubtedly continue to enjoy all the others I'm likely to encounter. But apparently my daughter has a stake I didn't even know about in the cornbread debate, and I'm happy to keep making nothing but unsweetened cornbread with coarse cornmeal in our cast-iron skillet for her.

Johnnycakes

Makes about 12 small johnnycakes

PRACTICE SKILLS

Pouring boiling water from the kettle

Stovetop cooking over medium heat

Spatula work

1 cup (120 g) cornmeal (coarse-ground yellow is particularly good, but even the degerminated canister variety works well here)

½ teaspoon kosher salt

1½ cups (360 ml/g) boiling water from the kettle, or more if needed

1 tablespoon unsalted butter

In the winter of 2018, teachers in West Virginia went on strike, and my daughter was happily out of school for a solid week and a half. She joined teachers picketing on the corners in the cold drizzle, came with me to drop off hot coffee for them, and otherwise stayed home and read whatever books she wanted to read—a luxury for a middle-schooler. On one of her days home, she looked up a recipe and made johnnycakes because she'd read about them in *Pax*, a sweet novel by Sara Pennypacker in which, among other important events, a stack of sizzling, just-out-of-the-skillet johnnycakes and a slice of fried ham are "flooded" with syrup. I'd have wanted to make them immediately too if I'd read that, and flood them with syrup.

The recipe my daughter landed on by chance that day is lost to a cleared browser history, but it was one whose batter consisted of just a few ingredients and was close to what I know from reading a similar recipe at *Leite's Culinaria* is the Rhode Island version. So that's how she and I think of "johnnycakes." Spreading out dollops of thick batter in a butter-slicked skillet this morning, I realized that this kind of johnnycake is basically fried mush that's skipped a grade or two, and that as such it fits quite nicely into my own family's food story.

In a medium bowl, combine the cornmeal and salt. Pour in enough boiling water, stirring until smooth, to make a thick batter that can be dropped from a spoon.

In a cast-iron skillet over medium heat, melt some of the butter. Drop large soup-spoonfuls (about 3 tablespoonfuls) of the batter into the skillet, spread to ¼ inch (6 mm) thick, and cook until nicely browned on the bottom, 3 to 4 minutes. Use a thin metal spatula to turn the johnnycakes over and brown the other side. Remove to a plate and cover loosely with foil to keep warm while you cook the rest of the batter in more butter. Turn down the heat if the skillet starts to smoke.

Buttermilk Cornbread (Final Version)

Serves 6

PRACTICE SKILLS

Measuring dry and liquid ingredients

Cracking eggs

Moving a hot skillet in and out of the oven (remembering to use potholders)

2½ cups (285 to 295 g) fine or coarse stone-ground cornmeal (see Tips)

2 teaspoons baking powder

½ teaspoon baking soda

1 teaspoon kosher salt (a little less if using bacon grease)

¼ cup (½ stick/55 g) unsalted butter or bacon grease

1½ cups (355 ml) buttermilk (see Tips)

2 large eggs

A cast-iron skillet with a smooth patina of seasoning is the best cooking vessel for cornbread, but the method may be tricky for younger cooks who aren't yet comfortable moving very hot pans in and out of the oven. Feel free to simply melt the butter in a microwave and use some of it to grease a regular 9-inch (23 cm) cake pan before pouring in the batter. The cornbread won't be as crisp on the bottom and sides, but if it means a child has been able to make a pan of it without much help it's worth the small sacrifice.

Put a well-seasoned 10-inch (25 cm) cast-iron skillet in the oven. Turn the oven on to 425°F (220°C) to preheat the oven and skillet.

In a medium bowl, whisk together the cornmeal, baking powder, baking soda, and salt.

Use a potholder and carefully remove the hot skillet from the oven and set it on the stovetop. Add the butter and swirl it around in the hot skillet to melt it and coat the bottom and a little up the sides, then pour the melted butter into a glass measuring cup. Return the buttered skillet to the oven.

Add the buttermilk and then the eggs to the melted butter and whisk with a fork to combine. Pour into the cornmeal mixture and stir gently just until the dry ingredients are evenly moistened.

Use a potholder to carefully set the skillet on the stovetop. Scrape the batter into the hot skillet and spread it evenly, then return the skillet to the oven. Bake for 20 minutes, until golden brown at the edges. Cut into wedges and serve warm from the skillet, or flip it out, bottom up, onto a cutting board and slice.

Tip: If you don't have buttermilk on hand, use plain yogurt thinned with milk, or stir a squeeze of lemon juice into regular milk and let it stand on the counter for 15 minutes to thicken a bit.

Home Work

A little before midnight, ten days after our daughter was born, Derek and I loaded up the car with our infant daughter, two large dogs, and some miscellaneous lampshades and such and drove through the night from Florida to our new home in Athens, Georgia, and just beat the movers' truck there. It must have been the unsettled nature of those early weeks as a mom, in a new town, a new house, forty or fifty boxes of books piled three deep against the walls making them seem as if they were closing in on us in a very disturbing way, a need for some sort of normalcy between crying jags (the baby cried a lot too), that led to one of the most laughably poor decisions of my cooking life. On Derek's first day back at work outside the home, I decided to prepare supper—it'd be nothing fancy, just meatloaf and a little pan of green peas, but it'd be comforting and homemade. Even with a newborn in the house, good old meatloaf would be a piece of cake. Speaking of which, maybe I'd put a little cake in the oven after the meatloaf, so it'd be ready for dessert.

You can probably guess how my morning trip to the grocery store and my evening in the kitchen went, and whether there was cake for dessert that night. Or any night for the next several months. I didn't even make meatloaf again for a very long time afterward—it had become the opposite of comfort food. In fairness, I could've decided to cook just about anything and the scene would've been the same: a woman, collapsed to the floor in exhaustion, sweat dripping onto soft baby or dog head depending on which being needed to be held at any given moment, probable cross-contamination events that miraculously didn't result in actual illness, and a haphazard supper with no vegetables.

I learned that day what the shape of my life would be like for the time being, but still I kept trying to push the edges out in awkward ways, and it bulged and kinked like a cheap Hula-Hoop. I baked an upside-down plum cake that didn't go very well, and I reminded myself that upside-down cakes often don't. (It tasted good, though.) Simply because I didn't know any other way to be, I was still taking on a lot of editing work. Too much of it. At one point I resorted to the unthinkable: I sent an unfinished free-lance job back to the publisher because I couldn't handle the complicated workflow for the project while also holding a baby who refused to sleep or lie quietly on her own for more than a few minutes at a time. I didn't want to hold up the book's schedule, and thought I was doing the responsible thing.

My contact at the publishing house, an older woman, sighed into her phone somewhere in Manhattan. "Well, fine, but back in my day, we'd just get one of those playpens for the baby so we could actually do our work." I never corresponded with her again. I was too busy doing my work.

The shape would crack like this many times over the next few years, the angles and curves I tried to force on it refusing to meet up in geometrically plausible ways. When

it did, I'd hunker down and turn inward for a while, declining to go out to meet the knitting group or the short-story reading group who'd welcomed me so enthusiastically when we first moved to Georgia (and who welcomed me back after these absences). I'd need and have to ask for more help than usual from other people. I'd take my daughter blackberry picking, then fill up a kiddie pool to cool off, and decide we'd had enough of *doing things* for the day, work deadlines falling behind me like the bits of scrap paper that fluttered to the floor as we cut snowflakes. For as long as I could, I'd try not to notice the mess. Then I'd sweep up hastily, in a brief episode of intense focus, getting projects out the door one after another and letting the late blackberries rot in the patch up the road, the snowflakes go uncut. I'd hand my now-two-year-old my purse to empty, one linty bobby pin or uncapped ballpoint at a time (which got me a solid ten minutes), or let her use tiny fingers to slip stiff papery peels off the stash of shallots she happened to find within her reach. I'd work at my screen fixing other people's books, one eye on the child sitting splay-legged on the floor in the sun playing with bobby pins and pens and alliums. I didn't know it at the time, but soon—it's a cliché, sure, but almost comically soon—my daughter would be making the meatloaf.

Sewing a Nice Apron

This makes a sturdy, finished-looking half-apron, but you could also just fold under and finish all four sides of a square of fabric and attach lengths of twill tape to two corners for ties. Add a patch pocket to the front if you'd like.

1 For the main apron piece, cut a rectangle of linen, quilting cotton, lightweight cotton canvas, or seersucker:

> about 24 by 30 inches (61 by 76 cm) for an adult
>
> or 20 by 18 inches (50 by 46 cm) for a young child

2 For the waistband and ties, cut a long strip of the same or a different woven fabric, or sew several strips together end to end to make one long one:

> 4 inches (10 cm) wide and long enough to go around the waist once or twice and tie comfortably (in the back or front)

3 On the two short sides and one long side (the bottom) of the rectangle piece, fold up ½ inch (12 mm) of the edges toward the *wrong* side of the fabric and press with an iron.

4 On the bottom of the rectangle piece, fold up 2 inches (5 cm) toward the *right* side of the fabric and press with the iron.

5 Sew the two side edges of the folded-up section, close to the raw edge. Trim off the corner, cutting close to but not through the stitching.

6 Turn the bottom of the apron right side out and press with the iron. Press the sides to enclose the raw edges.

7 Sew each side, close to the folded-in edge.

8 Sew across the bottom hem, close to the folded-up edge. This should leave you with a rectangle with three finished edges and one raw edge at the top.

9 Pin the long strip of fabric to the raw top edge of the apron, right sides together, with the center of the long strip at the center of the top edge of the apron. Sew the strip onto the apron ½ inch (12 mm) from the edge. Press the strip up, with the seam allowance pressed up.

10 Turn the unsewn long edge of the strip under ½ inch (12 mm). Fold the strip lengthwise, right sides together, and sew across the short ends. Trim the corners, turn the strip right side out, and press.

11 Pin the long edges of the strip together, aligning the folded edge with the line of stitching along the apron's rectangle piece, and stitch all along the folded edge, attaching the strip to the apron to make the waistband and ties. Press again, tie it on, and go cook something messy!

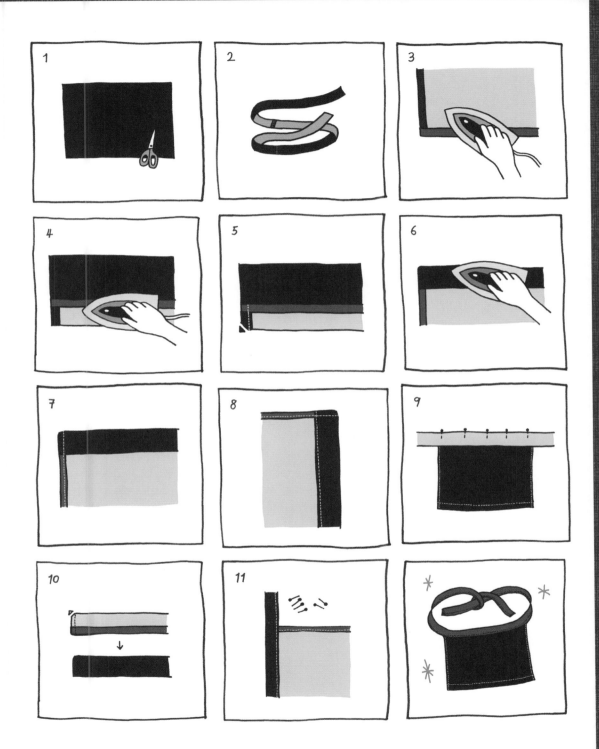

Basic Meatloaf with a Few Vegetables

Serves 6

PRACTICE SKILLS

Cracking an egg

Chopping hard vegetables, with a knife and/or food processor

Working with raw meat

Moving a full baking dish in and out of the oven

Using a meat thermometer

½ cup (50 g) dry breadcrumbs

½ cup (120 ml) milk

1 large egg

½ cup (50 g) grated Parmesan or cotija cheese

½ bunch parsley, stems removed

½ onion

1 carrot

½ (12-ounce/340 g) bag frozen chopped spinach, thawed and squeezed dry

1½ teaspoons kosher salt

½ teaspoon freshly ground black pepper

1½ pounds (680 g) ground beef (chuck)

½ pound (225 g) ground turkey

My mom always spread a little red pepper relish over the top of the meatloaf in the last 30 minutes or so of baking time for a nice sweet-and-sour crust; you can do this too, or just serve the slices with relish (or ketchup or tamarind chutney—same concept) on the side.

Preheat the oven to 350°F (175°C). Set out a baking dish—at least 7 by 11 inches (17 by 28 cm).

In a large bowl, combine the breadcrumbs, milk, egg, and cheese.

Coarsely chop the parsley and onion, put them in a food processor or blender, and pulse to mince them. (Alternatively, mince them together on a cutting board with a chef's knife.) Very finely dice the carrot (see Note). Add the parsley and onion, the carrot, spinach, salt, and pepper to the bowl with the breadcrumb mixture and stir well with a rubber spatula to combine.

Pinch bits of the beef and turkey into the bowl, then use your hand or the spatula to thoroughly combine the meat with the vegetable mixture—don't overmix, but be sure that the vegetables and seasonings are evenly distributed throughout the meat. Dump the mixture into the baking dish and shape it into a compact loaf about 9 inches (23 cm) long and 4 inches (10 cm) high. Bake for about 1½ hours, until the internal temperature registers at least 165°F (74°C) on a meat thermometer. Set the baking dish on a potholder or trivet on the counter and let the meatloaf rest for 5 minutes. Use a wide metal spatula and tongs to transfer the meatloaf to a carving board. Use a sharp chef's knife to slice and serve.

Note: You want the carrot to be in tiny, relatively even-sized pieces so they become tender but still retain their carroty character in the meatloaf. Here's an easy way to do that: Cut the carrot into thin slices on the diagonal, then stack the slices and cut them into thin strips (these are called julienne). Line up the strips and cut them crosswise into cubes.

An even easier way to deliver diced carrots is to leave it out of the meatloaf altogether, and warm up some frozen mixed vegetables in a covered saucepan with a little water to serve on the side.

Scarcity Mode

For many people, the stay-at-home orders during the early months of the coronavirus pandemic were an opportunity to learn to cook and bake new foods. I'll remember locked-down March and April 2020 especially as a nonstop stream of social media posts featuring seared this and lightly braised that and truly gorgeous breads and cakes and pies. It was exhilarating—and sent me into a kind of peevish depression. I had entered full scarcity mode as soon as the schools closed, but all I really wanted to do was grill a couple of fresh red snappers like the ones I'd seen pictures of online, make a tangy salad and top it with a new-to-me cheese, bake a kind of frosted layer cake I'd never made before, like *that one, right there, the one with toasted hazelnuts and cream and coffee liqueur and fresh raspberries and—*

I couldn't do it.

There was some bolognese in the back of the freezer and I'd have to use that first, freezer-burned and dried-out as it was, because I hadn't thought carefully about the future when I'd stashed it improperly years ago. There was also a freezer bag of frosty shreds of roast pork, and half a bunch of celery that had partially frozen in our poorly calibrated fridge's crisper drawer, and small amounts of many kinds of dried beans and lentils and grains in the pantry.

There would be no fresh fish or anything like it until all of that had been gotten through. Sweets would be made with whatever was already in the house, and I wouldn't even consider breaking into the bag of chocolate chips or the boxed cake mix I'd tucked into the large box of "emergency" food in the basement when I started gradually filling it on my trips to the grocery store in late February and early March, weeks before the governor shut down nonessential businesses.

On my daughter's birthday, she and I made a full-sized Russian honey cake, something she'd been asking to make for at least a year, and while a special dessert was so very deserved, I still felt a twinge of guilt as I made space for the many-layered thing to chill in the fridge next to the stack of eighteen-packs of eggs. Cake felt decadent to me—almost deviant. (If I'd known my daughter wouldn't see her friends or even the inside of a school building for the next year, and that her next birthday would be a pandemic one as well, and that everyone I loved would get through the year reasonably unharmed, I'd like to think I would not have felt that cake to be extravagant at all. I hope I would've made another one for her the next week.)

I recognized this feeling even then as an unhealthy one, and that this wasn't a level-headed way to think about food during that time. We went to the grocery store every week and a half or two weeks, some ingredients were hard to come by but we're resourceful enough that we could easily do without them, and I could have grilled some nice seafood or made a salad with delicate fresh greens on grocery-shopping day. I could have been inspired by my friends' pictures of beautiful meals, put the necessary ingredients on a shopping list—at that time I was compiling "wish lists" rather than shopping lists for those infrequent trips outside the house—and cooked whatever I wanted. I could have tried new dishes, and if they failed it wouldn't have been devastating, and we absolutely would not have suffered in the least.

We ate very well, despite my feeling that I was missing out on food that seemed more fun. We cultured cream with piimä and made fresh butter with some of it (to spread on all the home-baked bread, natch). I used the rest of the cultured cream to make gelato, scooping the soft frozen custard into labeled single-serving containers and stacking them neatly in the freezer to be pulled out one at a time and eaten on the porch in the evenings. We made chewy brownies from a tried-and-true recipe with just a little flour in the batter, we made eggless Depression-era wacky cake with cold coffee in one well instead of water and a splash of cream sherry instead of vinegar in another well, and my daughter found some half-full bags of frozen blueberries and sour cherries we'd picked the year before and made little saucepans of jam (to spread on the bread). A couple of our neighbors commissioned her to make loaves of challah, and she'd put on a mask and drop them off on their porches in exchange for locally roasted coffee (which Derek in turn exchanged for cash, because she doesn't drink coffee). I had dal and idli rice in the pantry so I fermented them and we had dosas for breakfast for a week or so, and I took a bottle of the dosa batter to another neighbor's porch. I learned to use leftovers more creatively, and how to securely pack meat for the freezer rather than just throwing it in a freezer bag and tossing it in—and how to plan ahead and pull the packages out to thaw in the fridge the night before.

Given my own reactions to seeing other people's food on social media during that time, it would've felt indecorous to share what I was cooking myself, much less recipes for any of it. How could I know what other people had in their pantries, how could I encourage people to go out and find a special ingredient (one I happened to have on hand already, for whatever reason) at a time when initiating any unnecessary contact by shopping or even getting grocery delivery could have serious consequences? Instead I turned inward, cooked and baked with my daughter, fed my family, and shared as much food as possible, as safely as I could. And mostly tried to stay away from food-related social media.

I'd considered myself a decent home cook, but over that year I realized that a lot of what I'd been doing was mechanical: see an interesting recipe or luscious photograph or think of something specific to cook, gather up the ingredients, cook it. Repeat with a different food the next day. This robotic way of cooking didn't require a whole lot of skill. It was simply cooking one food after the next, following whims. My habits during the height of the shutdown—which I've more or less maintained since then—aren't less extravagant, exactly, but do have a more homely sensibility. Most of the meals I've made in the last year (there are certainly exceptions, like the frost-flavored bolognese) are ones I'll probably keep making for the rest of my life. Even the new-to-me dishes—jollof rice and beef suya, for example—will stick around. Maybe because I gave the dishes more thought before committing to them, and because more care went into their preparation than might have been the case before. When grocery trips were most severely limited, I came to better appreciate the old standbys, those dishes I've made well for years, ones I knew wouldn't let me down.

We still have that big box of "emergency" food supplies in the basement (it moved with us, intact, from West Virginia to Pittsburgh), and I have yet to touch that boxed cake mix at the very bottom of it. I may no longer be thinking in terms of preparing for societal collapse on a week-to-week basis, and I often do just go out and get whatever special ingredients sound appealing to me on a given day, but my cooking style has permanently changed—for the better, I think.

Classic Pot Roast

Serves 3 to 4, with leftovers

PRACTICE SKILLS

Working with raw beef

Stovetop cooking over medium-high heat

Turning and moving a large beef roast with tongs

Chopping carrots and potatoes (peeling is optional)

One well-marbled 3-pound (1.4 kg) beef chuck roast

Kosher salt and freshly ground black pepper

1 tablespoon olive oil

2 tablespoons tomato paste

4 cups (960 ml) beef or vegetable broth or water

1 bay leaf

1 heaping teaspoon dried savory, or 2 sprigs fresh rosemary (optional)

4 carrots

4 russet potatoes

Good old pot roast, naturally, has held a solid spot in the rotation throughout the pandemic, even as the weather warmed and humidified, and I'm sure that when this period is finally, fully over I'll continue to make it much more often than I did before.

Pot roast leftovers practically come up with their own ideas: hash, of course; tacos with crisped meat plus minced onion and cilantro and lots of lime juice; a small meat pie or a few Cornish pasties with scraps of leftover piecrust dough I'd gathered and put in the fridge or freezer; beef and vegetable stew with some broth and barley or rice added; and so on.

Season the meat all over with about 2 teaspoons salt and several grindings of pepper. In a large Dutch oven, heat the oil over medium-high heat. When it shimmers, add the roast and cook until deeply browned on one side, 5 to 7 minutes; use tongs to turn it over and cook on the other side for 5 to 7 minutes. Remove the meat to a plate.

Turn the heat down to low, add the tomato paste, and cook for 20 seconds, stirring with a wooden spoon. Immediately add the broth, stirring to scrape up all the browned bits from the bottom of the pot and incorporate the tomato paste. Carefully return the meat to the pot, then add the bay leaf and savory (if using). Turn the heat to high, bring to a boil, then lower the heat to a simmer and cover the pot. Cook, covered, at a very low simmer for 2 hours.

Peel the carrots and potatoes, if you'd like, and cut them into big chunks (1½ to 2 inches/4 to 5 cm). Nestle the carrots and potatoes around and over the beef in the pot, nudging them into the broth so they're mostly covered. Cover the pot again and cook at a low simmer until the vegetables and meat are very tender, about 1½ hours longer.

Use a large spoon to skim off and discard the clear fat from the top of the liquid, then season with salt and pepper and serve.

Enough for a Pie

I stepped out onto the back porch on a dark, socked-in morning in late summer, coffee mug warming my hands, and saw bats flitting and swooping around low over the yard, in and out of thick fog bolls. We had loads of *Myotis lucifugus* in our neighborhood in Morgantown, West Virginia—I suspect many of them hole up in the rock outcroppings along Deckers Creek, down the hill from where we lived—and nearly everyone I knew there had a bat-trapped-in-the-house story. Our own resident bats, thankfully, had been outdoor creatures, first hanging out in the sliver of space between our porch roof and the house's brick wall and then, after I built a beautiful bat box to the exacting specifications of various bat conservancy nonprofits and blocked off the porch sliver with strips of foam, who knows where—not in the bat box, of course, no doubt because it was too ideally suited to bats.

I'd never seen bats in the morning, though, and I thought that was as good a sign as any that today was the day we would do something momentous. We would pick all the apples—all the apples!—from our trees, and my daughter would make a pie all by herself for the first time. (It was also the last day of summer vacation before sixth grade, and I thought the task would help distract her from worries about things like locker combinations and where to put her trombone before the first bell rang.) Pulling the trigger on a yard's worth of apples was not to be taken lightly, and I guess I needed the bats and the county school calendar to make the decision for me.

The fog was almost all burned off a couple hours later. I handed over the colander and we went out to the trees we'd planted the first spring after moving to West Virginia two and a half years ago. The trees had together borne exactly two apples last summer; my daughter and I had stood in the yard and eaten them, tossed the cores over the fence, and that was apple season. This year, there were more—I'd finally grown enough fruit for a pie. Just barely.

The first fruit tree I ever planted was a Celeste fig at our farmhouse in Georgia. It never had a chance to get large enough that it wouldn't be mistaken for an interesting-looking weed and run over by a lawnmower, which is precisely what happened to it. In retaliation, I planted eight or ten red currant bushes in an even more exposed part of the yard. They died when I threw out my back and gave up wrestling the hose all the way out to them during a drought, and then we gave up on rural Georgia altogether and moved to a rental house in town. I planted two cherry trees, a sour and a sweet, as soon as we settled down in Lincoln, Nebraska, which I quickly learned is home to many more rabbits per capita than you'd expect—rabbits that absolutely adore tender young fruit tree bark. Those trees succumbed to their adorable predators and I planted two more in their place, plus a good-sized plot of raspberry canes, and almost immediately thereafter we moved to West Virginia, having harvested two child-sized handfuls of berries and zero cherries.

By the time I was in middle school, my family had moved five times and lived in four states, but it sure seemed like I was the only one of my friends who was moving. Maybe the kids who befriended me did so because they'd been in place for a while and

felt confident enough to bring the new girl into the fold. Maybe I was just too self-centered to pay attention to my friends' back stories, and they too had moved a few times. In any case, my parents did what they could to put down roots wherever we were: my dad became fast friends with the neighbors; my mom planted fruit trees.

In Virginia, she had plums, pears, Winesap apples, sweet cherries, and sour cherries. The sour cherry tree was installed late in the Virginia period, and when my parents were considering retiring to Washington State the only hesitation I remember from my mom, who has always said that at any given time she could be ready to load a moving van in less than two weeks, was that she had yet to get enough sour cherries for a pie. (It's small consolation that the current owner of the old house now has so much fruit each year she doesn't know what to do with it. In summer I see a slew of posts on Facebook about being swamped with sour cherries, filling the freezer and pantry with sour cherries, pitting pound after pound of sour cherries . . . It's probably a good thing my mom is not on Facebook.)

The apple trees we planted in Morgantown are Golden Delicious (for boosterish reasons; the famous variety was developed in Clay County, West Virginia), Winesap (for sentimental reasons; see above), and Cox's Orange Pippin (for placating-my-daughter reasons; she got hold of the Stark Bro's catalog and was taken with its description of the early-nineteenth-century apple as tasting of orange and mango—and I couldn't say no even though our yard was getting crowded). For her bat day pie, she'd have a few Golden Delicious and a bunch of Winesap to work with.

It would be inaccurate to say that these trees had it easy since being sunk in the ground in Morgantown. Year one: They shared the yard with a puppy who liked to chew living twigs and chase soccer balls that would regularly crash into their upper branches and scatter leaves everywhere, and there was a very early warm period in spring followed by a very late frost. But year one was a piece of cake compared to year two, which featured Brood V, the cicada emergence to end them all (for the next seventeen years, anyway). The WVU extension agent told me to cover my trees with cheesecloth *before May 15*, so that's what I did, even though the instruction was baffling: where do you find that much cheesecloth, and how do you go about draping the narrow, clingy, snaggy fabric over the branches in such a way that it'll protect them from insects so determined to destroy them that they've spent almost two decades underground preparing their assault? The answers, respectively, are: *by mail order* and *with much profanity*.

On May 15, the cicadas emerged and basically dominated every aspect of life in north-central West Virginia for the next four or five weeks. We'd wake up in the morning to a gentle high-pitched hum. At eleven o'clock, the hum would quite suddenly shift into a wall of sound so loud we couldn't talk on the phone if we were outside or standing near an open window. Occasionally the wall would seem to fall slightly and then rise again, a wavering and almost electronic sound, a fifties sci-fi alien spaceship lifting off in black and white. Our dog snarfed the

newly emerged nymphs by the dozen as they came up from the earth, but wasn't interested in the fully matured ones who'd shed their exoskeletons, either because the day-old ones didn't taste as good or because she'd already indulged too enthusiastically.

The thumb-sized insects—red-eyed, lacy-winged—climbed up our fruit trees, clinging to the cheesecloth and in many cases wheedling their way underneath it to the soft bark of the tenderest twigs. I'd make the rounds several times throughout the day to reach in through the gaps in the cloth and pick cicadas off the branches and fling them into the grass, but of course I couldn't be everywhere at once. By the time Brood V was gone a few of them had left their telltale marks on our trees: deep gashes where the females had slit the bark with their sharp legs and laid their eggs; their offspring would hatch and then drop to the ground and burrow into the soil to feast on tree roots.

Brood V left another, somewhat more charming legacy: our apple trees developed branches that were bent and growing at more or less precise right angles. Their cheesecloth shrouds, applied just before the spring growth on the young trees started up, and I suppose draped not loosely enough, trained the new growth sideways, horizontally. When I carefully lifted the exoskeleton-covered cloth away, meticulously detangling the delicate leaves, the branches were free to continue growing—vertically. That late summer of the apple pie, a year and change after the brood emergence, the trees had survived their various trials, bends and all, and they were as strange and beautiful as the unexpected bats.

Apple Pie

Makes one 9½- or 10-inch (24 or 25 cm) pie

PRACTICE SKILLS

Cutting butter into flour mixture for shortcrust dough

Rolling out dough

Peeling and slicing apples (or using a peeler-corer-slicer contraption)

Moving a pie in and out of the oven

FOR THE DOUGH:

3 cups (390 g) all-purpose flour

1 teaspoon kosher salt

1¼ cups (285 g) cold unsalted butter, cut into cubes, or shortening, leaf lard, or a combination

1 large egg

1 tablespoon Marsala, apple cider vinegar, or sherry

Ice water

FOR THE FILLING AND TOPPING:

6 crisp apples the size of an adult's fist

Squeeze of lemon juice

½ cup (100 g) sugar, plus more for sprinkling

1 teaspoon ground cinnamon

¼ cup (35 g) all-purpose flour

1 tablespoon unsalted butter, cut into cubes

2 tablespoons milk or half-and-half

It's taken me decades to figure out how to make a very good apple pie. Or, rather, to make very good apple pie *consistently*. I'd happen to make one excellent pie, then I'd somehow forget what I'd done that was so right and the next attempt wouldn't go as well—an incorrect crust, or too-firm apples, or not enough juice-thickening action, or not sweet enough for the rest of the family. But that day three years ago I felt confident that I could guide my almost-sixth-grader to a more-than-acceptable apple pie. She put the colander of sweet Golden Delicious and tart-sweet Winesap apples aside—you need about six adult-fist-sized apples or the equivalent in smaller or larger apples, and this is about what she'd picked, with a few extra for lunchboxes when school started.

Make the dough: Lay out two sheets of plastic wrap. (I've finally learned to do this *before* starting the dough and getting my hands floury.) In a large bowl, combine the flour and salt. With a pastry cutter or your fingertips, cut in the butter until the pieces are the size of raggedy peas.

Make a well in the center of the mixture and crack in the egg. Add the wine and 6 tablespoons ice water to the well and beat the liquids together gently with a rubber spatula, then continue with the spatula to lightly toss the liquids and the flour mixture together, until the dough holds together when you squeeze some of it in your palm. Sprinkle in a little more ice water if it seems too crumbly.

Gather the dough into a ball in the bowl and use one palm to smoosh it. (This is called *fraisage*.) Gather it up again, smoosh, and form it into a ball again. Divide into two balls and wrap each one tightly in plastic wrap, smoothing the

recipe continues

dough out through the plastic and flattening each ball into a thick disc. Refrigerate for at least 1 hour and up to 1 day.

Make the filling: Peel, core, and thinly slice the apples—we do this with a crank-operated apple peeler-corer-slicer gizmo to make slices about ³⁄₁₆ inch (5 mm) thick, but use whatever tools you have. Toss the apples in a large bowl with the lemon juice, sugar, about half of the cinnamon, and the flour and set aside.

Preheat the oven to 425°F (220°C). Put a rimmed baking sheet on the bottom rack to catch any drips.

Remove one of the dough discs from the fridge and use a rolling pin to roll out to about ⅛ inch (3 mm) thick, then transfer it to a 9½ or 10-inch (24 or 25 cm) glass pie dish. Scrape in the apple filling, sprinkle with the remaining cinnamon, and distribute pieces of the butter over the top. Roll out the second dough disc and lay it over the filling. Fold and crimp the rim of the crust to seal it tightly. Cut a few small slits in the top crust, brush with milk, then sprinkle lightly with about 1 teaspoon sugar.

Bake on the center rack of the oven (over the baking sheet) for 15 minutes, then lower the oven temperature to 350°F (175°C) and bake for about 1 hour longer, until the crust is deeply browned and the filling is bubbling and possibly leaking—according to family lore, overflowing means it's a Good Pie. Remove to a wire rack to cool for at least 2 hours, then slice and serve.

Rolling Out Pastry Dough

In general, handle the dough as little as possible and work quickly so the warmth of your hands doesn't melt the fat in the dough prematurely. A nice heavy rolling pin is good for beginners and younger bakers. If your countertop is tiled, find a big wooden board to roll out on instead.

1 Remove the disk of chilled dough from the fridge and set it on a flour-dusted counter for about 10 minutes before starting to roll it out. Have a bench knife (aka dough scraper) or a wide metal spatula handy. Dust the dough with flour. Flour the rolling pin, too, and have a little cup of flour handy for dusting again if the dough sticks.

2 Whack the dough disk firmly with the rolling pin, then rotate the disk 90 degrees and whack it again to flatten it a bit.

3 Set the rolling pin in the center of the dough disk (parallel with the edge of the counter) and firmly roll it away from you, almost to—but not over—the edge. Return the pin to the center and firmly roll it toward you. Apply even pressure as you roll.

4 Use the bench knife to loosen the dough from the counter and rotate it 90 degrees. Flour the counter underneath it if necessary.

5 Repeat the rolling from the center to the far edge, then from the center to the near edge. Rotate again and repeat until you have a rough circle. As the circle widens, you can roll out from the center at 45-degree angles rather than rotating the dough each time. Keep everything well floured, and frequently loosen the dough from the countertop so it doesn't stick. Work as quickly as you can, so the dough doesn't soften and melt. For piecrust dough, roll until it's about ⅛ inch (3 mm) thick.

6 To transfer a round of dough to a pie dish, set the dish right next to the dough. Place the rolling pin on the round at the edge closest to you. With one hand, loosen the dough from the countertop with the bench knife, and hold the rolling pin with the other while you roll the dough onto it—gently, and not tightly. Scoot the pie dish underneath, and unroll the dough into it. Tug with your fingers to get it centered in the dish and nudge it into the corners. If there are cracks or tears, repair them by smudging with your fingertips or pinching off a bit of the excess dough at the edge and sticking it over the hole.

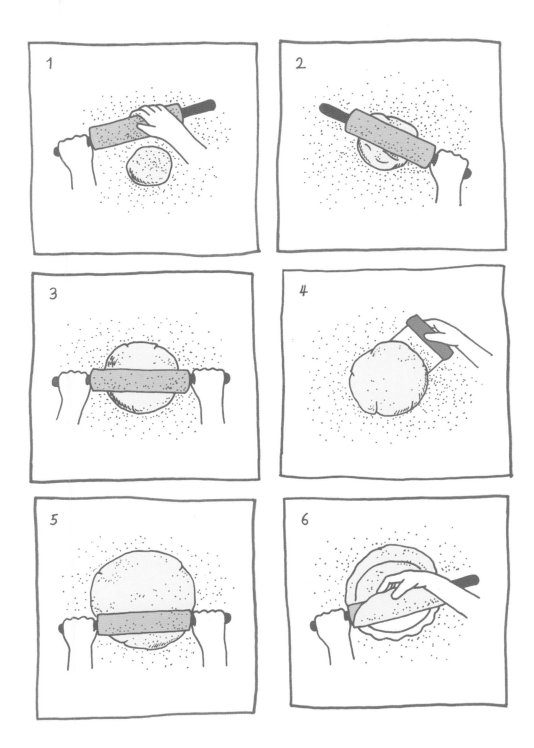

Using Piecrust Dough Scraps

Gather dough scraps into a ball; either roll out the dough and use it right away or wrap in plastic and refrigerate for up to a few days or freeze for a few months.

IF YOU HAVE A LITTLE

Cinnamon pinwheels: Roll out the scraps into a rectangle ⅛ inch (3 mm) thick, spread with soft butter, and sprinkle with cinnamon and sugar. Roll up from a long edge, then slice into ½-inch (12 mm) rounds. Bake on a small pan lined with parchment paper alongside a pie—and remember to take them out when they're golden, in 10 minutes or so.

Nut rolls: Roll out the scraps into a round ⅛ inch (3 mm) thick, spread with soft butter, and sprinkle with sugar and finely chopped nuts, as well as a spice—ground cardamom or cinnamon or even crushed fennel seeds. Use a knife or pizza cutter to cut into thin wedges, then roll each wedge up from the outside. Bake on a small pan lined with parchment paper alongside a pie—and remember to take them out when they're golden, in 15 minutes or so.

A small galette: Roll out the scraps into a round ⅛ inch (3 mm) thick and transfer it to a small rimmed baking sheet lined with parchment paper. Find a couple pieces of stone fruit and slice them thinly, or put some berries in a bowl. Toss with sugar, a few pinches of cornstarch, and a spice if you'd like, maybe a squeeze of lemon juice, and pile the fruit in the very center of the dough. Fold up and pleat the edges of the dough so it partly covers the mound of fruit. Brush the dough with milk and sprinkle with sugar. Bake alongside a pie until the crust is deeply golden and the fruit is tender, maybe 20 to 30 minutes.

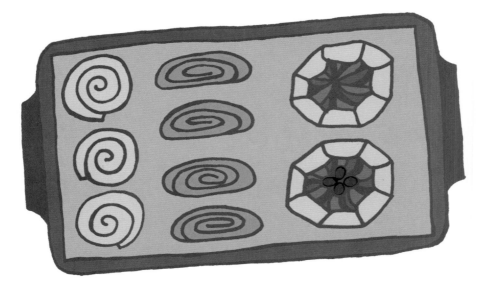

IF YOU HAVE MORE

Butte-style pasties: Mix raw finely chopped beef, diced potatoes, and diced onion and season with salt and pepper. Divide dough into 2½-inch (6.5 cm) balls and roll each out into a round. Pile the meat mixture on one side of each round, fold the dough over to make a half-moon, and seal the edges tightly. Brush with beaten egg and bake at 350°F (175°C) for about 1 hour, until deeply browned and cooked through.

Chicken pot pie: Roll out the dough between sheets of plastic wrap into a round ⅛ inch (3 mm) thick and as wide as the top rim of a cast-iron skillet; slide the round into the refrigerator to chill while you make the filling. In the skillet, sauté diced onion, carrots, celery if you like, and some diced potato (for maximum heartiness) in about 3 tablespoons butter until just starting to get tender,

then sprinkle in 3 tablespoons flour and cook, stirring, for a minute. Pour in about 2 cups milk and 1 cup chicken stock and stir well. Bring to a boil over medium heat and cook for 2 minutes. Add several handfuls of diced cooked chicken, salt and pepper, and a handful of frozen peas. Cook for a few minutes, until everything is heated through and the sauce is thickened. Remove from the heat.

Unwrap the dough round and set it atop the skillet, quickly and carefully pressing the edges to the rim of the hot skillet. (If you think that will be difficult, scrape the filling into a pie plate or round casserole instead and then top it with the dough.) Bake at 400°F (205°C) until the crust is deeply browned and the filling is bubbling through it (put a baking sheet on the rack underneath to catch drips), about 45 minutes. Let cool for a few minutes before serving.

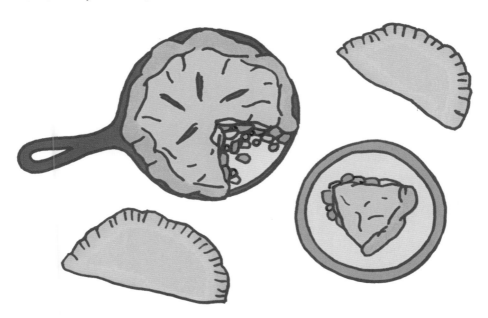

A Thing of Its Own

If I were running a Home Ec class, which as a parent I kind of am, one of the first things I'd put on the syllabus would be hash, that old standby of the frugal American cook. At its most basic, it's simply chopped onion, chopped cooked potatoes, and chopped cooked meat of some sort—the word comes from the French *hacher*, or "to chop." It may seem incredibly dull, but it's a dish that, if prepared with patience, adds up to far more than the sum of its parts. It should be more than just "many chopped ingredients cooked together in a skillet." It should be a thing of its own. The potatoes should break down and meld with the bits of meat, the onion soften and become indistinct, and, most important in my opinion, there should be lots of browning.

When I lived in Hell's Kitchen in New York I identified as the kind of person who would order corned beef hash in diners late at night and ask for it "well-done," as if it were a T-bone (and I an idiot who hadn't learned that steaks ought to be medium-rare). It was cool to be discriminating about a food that had almost certainly been scooped straight out of a #10 can onto a dubious griddle on the far West Side. Now that I'm no longer a resident of the ever-shrinking diner belt of the Northeast, my hash consumption habits tend more toward a very different, home-style version, the kind my mom would make often to stretch leftover pot roast or pork. But I still insist (to myself, usually) that all hash be cooked well-done. The crisp browned bits are why one makes hash, after all; otherwise you might as well just put meat-and-potatoes leftovers in the microwave and relive the night before.

If you search through today's stylish food blogs and hotel restaurant brunch menus you might come across hashes that are gorgeous and surely delicious (pancetta, asparagus), but maybe too perfectly diced, the ingredients too distinct from one another in the pan, to be quite what I think of when I hear the word. And that's fine. I think that's always how it's been, in fact: flip through an old cookbook—an early *Joy of Cooking*, say, or the indispensable multivolume *Woman's Day Encyclopedia of Cookery*—and you'll see page after page of "hash" recipes, and many of them don't resemble my own nostalgic ideas of the dish at all. One involves a béchamel; another, marshmallows.

Hash can be pretty much whatever you want or need it to be, and sometimes—no judgment—that may mean a hash featuring candied cherries.

Home-Style Hash   Serves 2

PRACTICE SKILLS

Dicing an onion

Chopping cooked potatoes, shredding cooked meat

No raw meat handling—it's already cooked

Cast-iron skillet is best; use a potholder on the handle

Stovetop cooking over medium heat

Seasoning to taste

1 tablespoon olive or vegetable oil

1 onion, diced

Salt and freshly ground black pepper

2 cooked russet potatoes, diced (about 3 cups/420 g)

1 to 1½ cups (195 to 290 g) finely shredded cooked meat (the pot roast on page 175, for example)

This hash is a great dish to teach younger kids to make, because it doesn't really matter if the onions are properly diced or if the ratios of ingredients are a little off. There's no way to include exact salt and pepper quantities in a recipe like this—the seasoning of whatever leftover meat you use will determine that—so kids will learn to season and taste, season and taste, until it's just right. The end product can be a complete breakfast or lunch for two people, and that's a legitimately satisfying accomplishment for a beginner cook.

Cooking up a skilletful of home-style hash like this one is a classic way to stretch a bit of leftover meat, but also a good way to use up random vegetables—that bit of shredded cabbage you couldn't fit in the pan when you were making haluski the week before, a stray half sweet pepper, the bottom of the bag of sweet corn kernels you put in the freezer over the summer, and so on.

In a cast-iron or other not-nonstick skillet, heat the oil over medium heat. When it shimmers (or ripples when you tilt the pan), add the onion and a pinch of salt. Cook, stirring with a metal spatula, until the onion is softened and the pieces are translucent at the edges, about 5 minutes.

Grind in some pepper and stir in the potatoes and meat. Spread the ingredients out evenly in the pan and let cook without stirring for about 5 minutes, then use the spatula to turn everything over; the undersides should be golden. Cook for another 5 minutes, then turn the ingredients again and continue cooking for about 5 minutes longer, turning as needed until most of the hash is nicely browned; taste and season with salt and pepper as you cook. It's okay if the ingredients stick to the pan a bit, but don't let them burn: use the spatula to scrape all those browned bits up. Serve hot.

Variations: Replace some or all of the meat with vegetables: thinly slice a wedge of cabbage and add it with the onion to make the dish more substantial. Or add a diced bell pepper or some fresh or frozen corn kernels with the potatoes and meat for sweetness and color.

Serve a fried egg (page 21) on top.

Experiment with adding different spices and flavorings toward the end of cooking. Try a Cajun spice blend; curry powder; berbere or another North African spice blend; or a mix of dried Italian herbs like parsley, basil, and oregano.

Diner-Style Corned Beef Hash Serves 4

PRACTICE SKILLS

Coarsely chopping onion

Peeling and chopping cooked potatoes, pulsing in a food processor

No raw meat handling—it's already cooked

Cast-iron skillet is best; use a potholder on the handle

Stovetop cooking over medium-low heat

---

1 small onion, coarsely chopped

One 12-ounce (340 g) can corned beef, or 2 cups (390 g) chopped home-made corned beef

2 tablespoons half-and-half or heavy cream

2 cooked russet potatoes, peeled and chopped (about 3 cups/420 g)

Freshly ground black pepper

1 tablespoon vegetable oil

Corning a brisket over the course of days or a week, then cooking it for hours until it's perfectly tender: absolutely worth the time and effort, and if you have leftovers, by all means use it here instead of the canned stuff; you'll need about 2 cups coarsely chopped corned beef to put in the food processor. But if not, I'm happy (and, to be honest, a little relieved) to report that canned corned beef is a perfectly fine product—no less so than, say, canned tuna. Plus it comes in a fun trapezoidal container that you have to use a special key (included with the can!) to cut open—I felt like I'd stepped right into the efficiency kitchen of a girl Friday in a late-forties film noir the first time I opened one.

I have also made this hash with deli corned beef, which is often lean top round instead of brisket; it's fine, but doesn't work nearly as well as the canned—and it costs about three times as much. Home economics for the win.

Put the onion in a food processor with the metal blade and pulse to finely chop it. Add the corned beef. Pulse to combine with the onion. Add the half-and-half and pulse a few times to combine. Take the food processor blade out and fold in the potatoes and several grinds of pepper.

In a cast-iron or other not-nonstick skillet, heat the oil over medium-low heat. When it shimmers (or ripples when you tilt the pan), scrape in the corned beef mixture and spread it evenly in the pan. If there are any large pieces of potato, cut them up in the pan with a metal spatula. Cook over medium-low heat, turning the hash over with the spatula every 4 to 5 minutes, for 25 to 35 minutes, until the minced onion bits are tender and there are lots of crisp, golden-brown parts. If the hash starts to darken too quickly, lower the heat and turn it more frequently. Serve hot.

Taking Care of Cast Iron

A cast-iron skillet is one of the easiest pieces of cookware to maintain, and it'll last several lifetimes. If you're shopping for used ones, look for those with a very smooth interior surface rather than pebbly-textured. Don't worry if a skillet has a little rust on it; you can scrub it off and revive the finish with a round or two of seasoning. If it's in very poor shape, look up instructions online for how to remove the old seasoning entirely before re-seasoning.

TO SEASON A NEW SKILLET, OR REVIVE AN OLD ONE

1 Scrub with warm soapy water, rinse, and wipe dry.

2 Use a paper towel to lightly coat the skillet all over, including the outside and the handle, with vegetable shortening or a neutral vegetable oil. Rub the shortening in well so that there's just a bare sheen of it on the surface—not enough to even rub off very much with your finger.

3 Put it in a 400°F (205°C) oven, upside down on the rack, with a baking sheet on the rack below it to catch any stray drips of oil. Cook for 1 hour, then let cool in the turned-off oven.

TO WASH AFTER USING

1 Rinse with hot water and scrub with a plastic scrub brush, a steel scrubber, a chain mail–type scrubber, or a scouring pad to remove crusty bits. Scrape with a metal spatula if you need to.

2 If it's super crusty, fill it with warm water and let it soak for a couple hours, then scrub.

3 It's okay to use a little bit of mild dish soap to remove extra-greasy residue that doesn't come off easily even in very hot water. Just keep old-fashioned lye-based soaps away from it, as they can cause deterioration of the seasoning on the surface.

4 Wipe dry and put it away.

Ordinary Chicken

We couldn't actually smell the chicken farms from our house in Madison County, Georgia, about half an hour outside Athens. But if the wind was right and we were driving anywhere—west into Athens, east to Elberton, and I'm not even sure what was directly north or south of us because those roads were small and confusing—it would be very clear that we lived in the top chicken-producing state in the country. In our six years in Georgia, we learned what a chicken farm smells like, and what a strawberry farm newly sprayed with chicken fertilizer smells like, and what a chicken-feed plant smells like. Trucks full of live chickens, feathers streaming out the back, would pass us one after another on the highway, headed to the processing facilities in Athens and beyond. (If you followed one to its destination, you'd almost certainly end up across the road, or down the block, or in any case only a stone's throw from an excellent Mexican grocery store or taquería—or both.) In 2020, a staggering 37 percent of the country's shipborne frozen poultry exports moved through the Port of Savannah. The Peach State is no such thing.

Those farms and processing plants weren't necessarily producing chicken for local consumption, but it was always disconcerting to me that chicken didn't occupy a more vaunted place in the Athens culinary landscape—unless you're talking fried chicken, of which there was plenty in the area, though I honestly can't remember ever having an extraordinary rendition when we lived there (cue the emails reminding me of Weaver D's Automatic for the People, which I'm ashamed and sorry I never managed to visit). Hugh Acheson's high-end Five & Ten restaurant served Bell & Evans, which is excellent chicken . . . from east-central Pennsylvania. I once made the mistake of buying an expensive locally raised French heritage-breed chicken from a small farm on the far side of Elberton; it was inedible. I should've slowly braised it or put it in a stew pot with a bottle of red wine, but I was naïve enough to believe that a fancy young chicken, raised on an idyllic-seeming farm my family and I had actually visited, could be lovingly *roasted*.

I didn't learn to use chicken more thoughtfully until we moved to Nebraska. The state is not exactly known as an important producer of non-red meat, but it probably should be even if its numbers remain miniscule compared to those of the Deep South states. In Lincoln, I bought inexpensive locally raised chicken of shockingly good quality at the co-op a half mile from our house, as well as packs of something called "Smart Chicken" at the chain grocery stores. The dry-air-chilled Smart Chicken was a revelation, better than any supermarket chicken I'd cooked before—and it was also local, grown nearby and processed in Waverly, Nebraska, just outside Lincoln. This was chicken I couldn't mess up, no matter how much I experimented with challenging-for-chicken cooking techniques like smoking and high-heat grilling. It had a nice dense texture after cooking, and the flavor of chicken and nothing else I hadn't added myself.

Air chilling was part of the reason it worked so well for me as a not-especially advanced cooker of chicken. The vast majority of poultry plants in the United States use an immersion chilling process, dunking the chickens in super-cold chlorinated water to lower their temperature quickly right after slaughter. Air chilling cools the meat with, well, just air (and sometimes, in the case of evaporative air chilling, a fine mist). It takes longer, but results in meat that is less waterlogged, more tender, and more flavorful.

Another check mark in the "pro" column for air chilling is that it uses less water than immersion chilling. A year or so ago, Costco opened the Lincoln Premium Poultry in Fremont, Nebraska, about an hour north of the Smart Chicken operation. The chicken plant and associated verticals, including a hatchery and feed mill and scores of independent growers on fifteen-year contracts with Costco, was designed solely to supply Costco stores in the western states with air-chilled chicken—and to leverage control of the entire production process to keep their hugely popular rotisserie birds under five bucks each. I know people love Costco, and I do too, but I wouldn't trust the motives of any company that size as far as I could throw a $1.99 hot dog and refillable soda combo. Many residents of Omaha and Lincoln and the towns around them have been apprehensive about the turn toward chicken farming in the southeastern corner of the state, pointing to the problems Des Moines, in neighboring Iowa, has had with livestock waste runoff into the river that supplies the city's drinking water, as well as the possibility that chicken plants would deplete water supplies in the area. The Ogallala Aquifer, which underlies a huge swathe of the Great Plains, including almost all of Nebraska, has long been a plentiful source of water for drinking and crop irrigation, but the aquifer is shallow and vulnerable to contamination and overuse. Conventional chicken farming and processing together have a pretty large water footprint: chicken meat requires more water per kilocalorie to produce than, for example, corn or soybeans (though much less than beef). Nebraska communities that draw drinking water from the aquifer and surface sources are absolutely right to be concerned when any waste-generating, water-intensive industry moves in. It'll be instructive to see how the Costco plant and its many components deal with those pressures, and how effective local regulators can be in the face of massive political pressure to allow the company ever freer rein. Water use is a big issue for poultry mass-producers in Georgia, too: processing plants have at times been forced to cut back on the number of birds running through their facilities when water became scarce during droughts. The expensive conversion to dry air chilling in the South could eventually become cost-effective in addition to being more environmentally and socially responsible, but I'm not holding my breath.

My feelings about the possibility of ethical meat consumption, as you might imagine from my contradictory thoughts in these few pages alone, are complicated— and have changed considerably since the days when I might've considered a Poulet Rouge to be worth its well-over-$20 price tag because it came from a small farm just a few miles from where I lived. Local doesn't always mean better quality, of course, but it also isn't a guarantee that the production and transport of those foods have a smaller footprint. S. Margot Finn, in *Discriminating Taste,* for example, summarizes studies estimating gallons of fuel per pound of food used in different models of production, and thoughtfully pushes back against the admittedly appealing idea that local farms are more efficient.

The three big companies I've mentioned here—Bell & Evans, Smart Chicken, and Lincoln Premium Poultry—all use some form of air chilling, and all employ a method of incapacitating the animals that's considered to be more "humane" than those used in the majority of poultry plants and on small farms (if you can consider any method to be humane at all). Most of us don't care to think very hard or often about how the animals we consume are killed, much less talk in detail about those issues with young kids, which is why marketers for chicken producers large and small tend to focus on how the sweet goofy birds lived and what they ate and how much sunlight and ranging they enjoyed each day. (And, no surprise, Costco's chicken farms have come under fire since they began production for deplorable living conditions. Execs say they're working on it.) I'm not sure that how an animal lives is more important than how an animal dies, and I don't know how to explain my daily meals in a way that would make sense to every person who might read this, and that includes my sharp and compassionate daughter and my future—I hope at least slightly smarter—self.

I do have serious doubts that the "natural" husbandry practices at small farms like the one outside Elberton (which is no longer extant) are by default any more humane than those at companies operating at a larger scale, or that exponentially more small farms producing enough calories to "feed the world," as they say, will necessarily strain resources less than vertical integrators like Costco. A comprehensive set of policy priorities—a New Deal, say, that is "green"—that alleviates the costs of transitioning to more humane, less-resource-intensive production and distribution methods and guarantees income floors for farmers would reduce the barriers to entry for smaller farms.

Farm sector workers across the country, from giant meatpacking and poultry plants in right-to-work Nebraska and the South to small family dairy farms and apple orchards in ostensibly more progressive states like New York, are highly susceptible to exploitation and unsafe, unhealthy conditions. Too many consumers, I think, take it on faith not only that animals raised and processed by small farmers have lived and died in more pleasant ways than those raised and processed by larger operations, but also that workers at those farms are treated fairly because the commodity they produce costs more than the supermarket versions. As Margaret Gray discusses in *Labor and the Locavore*, ethical consumption requires taking into consideration labor practices and worker welfare as well as animal welfare and the environmental and economic impacts of the farms that stock your kitchen.

When you're just trying to cook a healthful, relatively affordable meal, all of this is a lot to reckon with. I've come to believe that truly ethical consumption is impossible without, at the very least, a much more robust and punitive regulatory apparatus that applies to businesses of all sizes, and strong international unions to ensure democratic control of the workplace by workers. Supporting activists' efforts to solidify worker, environmental, and animal-welfare protections in law, addressing inequalities of access to food as well as the resources to produce food, and in general asking more questions about all the farms producing our food is essential as we try to make individual day-to-day choices.

Very good ordinary chicken was one of the foods I missed most when we left Nebraska. The chicken of Lincoln, Nebraska, occupied, for me, a rare space on the graph: a relatively high point at the intersecting lines of affordability, quality, and socio-environmental responsibility (at least as I understand that slippery concept). I adjusted after moving by essentially eliminating every part of the bird except thighs from my repertoire, and by just doing my best to make what I thought were reasonably sound purchases that worked for the way my family cooks and eats and what we can afford to spend on ingredients. It's worked fine: we ate well in West Virginia, and we've eaten well since moving to Pittsburgh and within a few minutes' walk of a Sunday farmers' market and a few minutes' drive of a Costco that sometimes stocks chicken with "air-chilled" on the packages. I've thought about branching back out to such wild and crazy cuts as chicken breasts. But I keep going for the thighs, and I haven't regretted it yet.

Honing a Knife

Honing is different from sharpening. I have my one good chef's knife professionally sharpened every once in a while, but I hone it often with a honing steel. When you hone a blade, you're not actually removing any of the steel (or not as much, anyway, as you would when sharpening it). You're simply straightening out the cutting edge of the blade, which can get a tiny bit bent or folded over with use.

Different cooks use different techniques, and you can find them online if you'd like. This is the way I taught my daughter to do it because it involves sliding the blade away from you rather than toward you (but I reverse it when I do it myself):

1 Make sure there's plenty of space (and no other people) in front of you. Hold the knife in your usual knife hand and the steel in the other. Form an X with the steel and knife blade, the heel of the knife resting atop the end of the steel closest to your hand so that the bottom part of the X is very small. The blade edge should be touching the steel at a slight upward angle.

2 Smoothly swipe the blade up the length of the steel while pulling both the steel and blade outward so the blade slides along the length of the steel all the way to the blade's tip. Put just a bit of pressure on the blade as you do this.

3 Reposition the blade in an X, but this time with the blade underneath the steel, with the blade edge touching the steel at a slight downward angle. Again smoothly swipe the blade up the length of the steel, all the way to the tip of the blade.

4 Repeat the top and bottom swiping several times, then check the edge for sharpness and repeat if needed.

 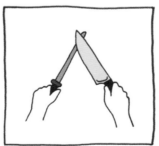 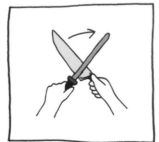

Yogurt-Marinated Spiced Chicken

Serves 3 or 4

2 limes

1 cup (240 ml) plain yogurt

1 tablespoon grated or minced fresh ginger

1 tablespoon vegetable oil

1½ teaspoons paprika

1 teaspoon ground cumin

1 teaspoon ground coriander

½ teaspoon ground turmeric

1½ teaspoons kosher salt

6 boneless, skinless chicken thighs

The keys to tender but still juicy chicken thighs: marinate with plenty of salt, and cook them just past the point where they're technically cooked through. When thighs are at the USDA-approved minimum internal temperature of 165°F (73.9°C), they're not quite ready, in my opinion. Give them time to sizzle and brown, and for the excess fat to melt away.

Cut the limes in half. Cut one half into pieces and set aside for serving. Juice the remaining three halves into a large bowl. Stir in the yogurt, ginger, oil, paprika, cumin, coriander, turmeric, and salt.

With a sharp knife, carefully trim any large areas of fat from the chicken thighs—use the knife to scrape the crumbly solid fat off the top (smooth) side of the thighs, and don't worry too much about the fat on the rough underside, which will mostly melt away in the oven. Put the thighs in the bowl with the yogurt mixture and turn to coat them thoroughly. Cover the bowl with plastic wrap and refrigerate for 2 to 4 hours.

Position the oven rack in the center of the oven and preheat the oven to 450°F (230°C) (see Note). Arrange the thighs, spread out flat in a single layer, on a rimmed baking sheet, keeping most of the yogurt marinade on them. Roast for 25 minutes, then turn the broiler to high. Broil for 5 to 7 minutes, until the thighs are blackened in spots. Carefully remove the baking sheet from the oven and set it on the stovetop; use tongs to flip the thighs over; return the sheet to the oven and broil for 5 minutes, or until the other side is blackened in spots and sizzling. Serve with the lime pieces for squeezing.

Note: If your chicken thighs are quite small, you can skip the roasting step and simply broil (with the rack in the center of the oven) for about 10 minutes per side.

Tangy Sumac Chicken   Serves 3 or 4

Juicing lemons

Slicing an onion

Working with raw chicken

Moving a full baking sheet in and out of the oven (using two small baking sheets—quarter-sheet pans—instead of one large one will make this easier for younger cooks)

2 tablespoons lemon juice, plus lemon wedges for serving

1½ teaspoons paprika

½ teaspoon ground cumin

Pinch of ground cinnamon

1½ teaspoons kosher salt, plus more for the onion

¼ cup (60 ml) plus 1 tablespoon olive oil

6 boneless, skinless chicken thighs

1 onion, sliced ½ inch (12 mm) thick

1 teaspoon sumac, or more to taste

Fresh parsley

On North 27th Street in Lincoln, amid a dozen or more Asian and Middle Eastern and Mexican grocery stores, there was a small Iraqi restaurant. (Lincoln is a refugee-relocation center, and has a fairly large number of Yazidi residents.) In that restaurant, sadly just once, I had the most delicious shawarma I'd ever had in my life, and I've been chasing it in my own kitchen since. Its main characteristic was lots and lots of lemon juice and tangy sumac. Head out to the country to collect staghorn sumac in late summer (or hit up a local Middle Eastern grocer or Penzeys) and try this, adding sumac until you shiver just looking at it. Serve with pitas, sumac- and olive oil–dressed yogurt for dolloping, maybe some sliced cucumbers and fresh herbs on the side.

In a large bowl, use a fork to whisk together the lemon juice, paprika, cumin, cinnamon, salt, and ¼ cup (60 ml) of the oil.

With a sharp knife, carefully trim any large areas of fat from the chicken thighs—use the knife to scrape the crumbly solid fat off the top (smooth) side of the thighs, and don't worry too much about the fat on the rough underside, which will mostly melt away in the oven. Put the thighs in the bowl with the lemon mixture and turn to coat them thoroughly, poking some holes in them with the fork so the marinade permeates the meat more thoroughly. Cover the bowl with plastic wrap and refrigerate for 2 to 4 hours.

Position the oven rack in the center of the oven and preheat the oven to 450°F (230°C) (see Note, page 200). Arrange the thighs, spread out flat in a single layer, on one side of a rimmed baking sheet. Scatter the onion slices on the other side of the pan, drizzle with the 1 tablespoon oil, and sprinkle with a pinch of salt. Roast for 25 minutes, then turn the broiler to high. Broil for 5 to 7 minutes, until the thighs are lightly browned in spots.

recipe continues

Carefully remove the baking sheet from the oven and set it on the stovetop; use tongs to flip the thighs over; return the sheet to the oven and broil for 5 minutes, or until the other side is browned in spots and sizzling. Sprinkle the chicken with the sumac. Serve the chicken and onion with the lemon wedges and parsley. (If you'd like, transfer the chicken thighs to a carving board and use a chef's knife to cut them crosswise into ¼-inch [6 mm] slices before serving.)

Note: If your chicken thighs are quite small, you can skip the roasting step and simply broil (with the rack in the center of the oven) for about 10 minutes per side.

Lemon–Thyme Roasted Chicken   Serves 4

PRACTICE SKILLS

Slicing a lemon

Trimming raw chicken

Moving a loaded baking sheet
into and out of the oven

1 lemon

8 large bone-in, skin-on
chicken thighs

2 teaspoons kosher salt

1 teaspoon dried thyme

Freshly ground black
pepper

Line a large rimmed baking sheet with parchment paper. Thinly slice the lemon and scatter the pieces on the prepared baking sheet.

Using a sharp chef's knife, trim any excess flaps of skin or fat from the chicken thighs and save for schmaltz or discard. Sprinkle the chicken on both sides with the salt and thyme, grind some pepper over it, and place the thighs, skin side up, on top of the lemon. (Wash your hands in hot water after touching the chicken, and wash the knife and cutting board as well.) If you have time, set the pan aside on the counter for 1 hour, or put it in the refrigerator, uncovered, for about 4 hours.

Preheat the oven to 425°F (220°C).

Roast for about 1 hour, until the skin is golden and crisp and the meat has shrunk back from the end of the bone a bit. Serve, or let cool, shred the meat, and refrigerate it for other uses.

Tip: To roast a whole chicken rather than just thighs, first spatchcock it so the skin on the thighs, which would normally be underneath a whole bird as it roasts, gets nice and crisp: Carefully, using a sharp chef's knife or a pair of poultry shears—special heavy-duty scissors—cut through the small bones along either side of the backbone to remove it. (Save the backbone for stock, if you'd like.) Turn the bird over so the breast side is facing up, and use the heel of one hand to press down in the center of the breast to flatten it—you'll crack that bone a bit, which is what you want to do. Season all over, top and bottom, with salt and pepper (or any other seasonings you'd like). Lay the chicken out flat, breast side up, on top of the lemon slices; roast as above.

Bliss Point

The fluffy blanket pulled straight from the dryer in winter. The toeing-off of wool socks in the middle of the night because you're now warm enough without them, your feet on cool sheets. Your favorite movie on a rainy afternoon, dog chin resting heavy in your lap. This is homemade pudding. A balm.

Scientists and processed-food developers studying the physiology of taste perception talk about the "bliss point," that Goldilocks spot on the curve where a subject—or consumer—perceives that a food is neither too sweet nor not sweet enough, neither too salty nor not salty enough. The idea, for those who want to sell as much of a food as possible, is to concoct such a bliss-inducing combination of flavors and mouthfeels and visual impact that the food in question will not only seem to satisfy our deepest sensory desires but also keep us coming back for more and more, forever seeking—never finding—satiety. These foods promise joy and comfort, but always fall just short of providing the latter, and that's by design, of course.

An evil project!

It has a powerful antidote, though, in the humblest puddings. Those that are just sweet enough, and made with full-fat ingredients, and that are dominated by a single main flavor, not complicated by layers or toppings or too much variety of texture: coconut, chocolate, vanilla, lemon, one of these at a time. Why is that simplicity important? Food scientists also talk about "sensory-specific satiety." As Michael Moss explained in a fascinating and influential 2013 piece in the *New York Times Magazine*, sensory-specific satiety is "the tendency for big, distinct flavors to overwhelm the brain, which responds by depressing your desire to have more." Plain vanilla pudding signals *vanilla* (and *fat* and *pillowy smoothness*) over and over as you dip the spoon, and then at some point you decide you're satisfied. Enough with the vanilla! I'm over this pillowy smoothness! It's done its work, and you're both joyful and comforted.

That's my theory of pudding.

My mom would make a pot of vanilla custard pudding when one of us was having a hard time in some way. A difficult math test, a social disappointment, a sore throat. We'd have a small bowl of it warm from the stove, and then ice-cold from the fridge if there was any left the next day. It might have been that dreaded and maligned thing "emotional eating" (except in the case of a sore throat, a physical problem that pudding objectively soothes), but I suspect it's not quite the same as digging into a bag of lab-engineered Doritos and still feeling sad as you shake the last crumbs into your palm.

I've never regretted making pudding. As I was working on fine-tuning these recipes we had an awful lot of it in our fridge, but even the misses were welcome at the ends of long days, and the nearer-misses were enjoyed well enough by friends. (One whose young son, upon subsequently being offered quinoa, complained—poor kid—that *quinoa was not double-chocolate pudding*.) I sometimes have too much cake or too many cookies or too much leftover mac and cheese. Never have I felt that way about real homemade pudding.

At points in my life I've tried to make fancier versions, but it's mostly unnecessary fuss. The beauty of a well-made pudding is that you know what you're getting. Pudding as part of a trifle, or between layers of a Brooklyn blackout cake—fine. If I want any more excitement than that in my comfort food I'll make a Shaker lemon pie.

Coconut Rice Pudding

Makes about 4 cups (960 ml)

PRACTICE SKILLS

Stovetop cooking over medium heat

One 13½-ounce (400 g) can unsweetened coconut milk

½ cup (65 g) coconut sugar

¾ cup (145 g) jasmine rice

Tiny pinch of kosher salt

This ridiculously easy three-ingredient recipe makes a barely sweet dessert—feel free to add a little more sugar at any point in the cooking process if it seems to need it. You can of course use any kind of sugar, but if you have it coconut sugar gives the pudding a slight butterscotch flavor and, I don't know, seems correct here. You can also use any kind of white rice, and 5 cups (1.2 L) regular milk instead of the coconut milk and water. If you just need something sweet and satisfying and carby, this will do nicely as is, but if you're looking for a fancier presentation, by all means top the pudding with some mango or kiwi or stone fruit slices or a handful of berries, and maybe some coconut flakes toasted in a dry skillet, and add an extra sprinkle of sugar.

Pour the coconut milk into a heavy 3-quart (3 L) saucepan and add 2 cansful of water. Stir in the coconut sugar, rice, and salt. Place over medium heat and bring to a boil, stirring frequently with a wooden spoon or heatproof spatula and watching the pan carefully so the liquid doesn't boil over. As soon as it boils, lower the heat to medium-low and cook, stirring frequently, for about 15 minutes, until the rice grains are tender and you can see some of them on the surface of the liquid even when you're not stirring. Remove from the heat and let cool—the pudding will thicken as it cools. Serve warm, or transfer to a container, cover, and refrigerate until chilled, at least 2 hours—it will thicken further in the fridge.

Simple Chocolate Pudding

Makes about 4 cups (960 ml)

PRACTICE SKILLS

Whisking and stirring in a saucepan over medium heat (taking care if some of the hot pudding plops out of the pan as it cooks—use a long-handled wooden spoon or heatproof spatula)

1 cup (200 g) sugar

½ cup (50 g) cocoa powder

¼ cup (30 g) cornstarch

½ teaspoon kosher salt

4 cups (960 ml) whole milk

2 tablespoons unsalted butter

1 teaspoon vanilla extract

Here the thickener is cornstarch, and while some may frown on a pudding that isn't truly custardy, I prefer this style for chocolate because it allows the main ingredient to dominate. No egg yolk custard flavor muddying the waters.

In a heavy 3-quart (3 L) saucepan, whisk together the sugar, cocoa powder, cornstarch, and salt. Whisk in a little of the milk until smooth, then whisk in the remaining milk. Place over medium heat and bring to a boil, stirring frequently with a heatproof spatula or wooden spoon and whisking occasionally (I like to switch back and forth between spatula and whisk to be sure the thickening pudding from the bottom and corners of the pan get mixed in evenly). Boil for 2 minutes.

Remove from the heat, add the butter and vanilla, and whisk to thoroughly incorporate them. Scrape into a container. Place a piece of plastic wrap directly on the surface of the pudding, then refrigerate until cold, at least 3 hours. Serve cold. After a night in the fridge, the pudding leftovers will release a little liquid; just drain it off or stir it in.

Variation: For double-chocolate pudding: Add 3½ ounces (100 g) chopped dark chocolate with the butter and vanilla and whisk well to melt it all.

Vanilla Custard Pudding

Makes about 3½ cups (840 ml)

PRACTICE SKILLS

Whisking and stirring in a saucepan over medium heat (taking care if some of the hot pudding plops out of the pan as it cooks—use a long-handled wooden spoon or heatproof spatula)

Pouring hot liquid from a saucepan while whisking (use a pan with a rolled lip for easier pouring)

3 large egg yolks

3 tablespoons cornstarch

⅔ cup (135 g) sugar

½ teaspoon kosher salt

2 cups (480 ml) whole milk

1 cup (240 ml) half-and-half

2 tablespoons unsalted butter

2 teaspoons vanilla extract

This is the ur-pudding, an egg yolk–based custard that's further thickened with cornstarch to help it set as it cools. There's not much to making a custard, but it does take some practice and care. I'd made vanilla pudding countless times before I knew quite what I was doing, and I think what finally solidified the process in my mind was showing my daughter how to make it. Explaining to her what she should be doing—and why—helped me approach the whisking and tempering and watching of the pot with much more care.

In a large bowl, whisk the egg yolks to loosen them, then whisk in the cornstarch, sugar, salt, and a splash of the milk. Keep whisking until the mixture is very smooth.

In a large, heavy saucepan, heat the remaining milk and the half-and-half over medium heat, occasionally stirring with a heatproof spatula or wooden spoon, until it's just about to boil: Bubbles will form and pop at the edge of the pan, a little steam will rise, and the surface of the milk will just start to tremble. Remove from the heat and use a ladle or a measuring cup with a handle to *very slowly* scoop out and pour about ⅓ cup (75 ml) of the hot milk mixture into the egg yolk mixture a tablespoon or so at a time, whisking constantly. Whisk very well, then ladle in another ⅓ cup (75 ml), whisking very well.

Again whisking constantly, slowly pour the egg mixture into the hot milk mixture in the saucepan. Return the pan to medium heat and cook, whisking, until the mixture comes to a boil and has thickened to the consistency of a sauce or heavy cream—this should take about 5 minutes. Switch from whisk to spatula occasionally so you can scrape the custard from the bottom and sides of the pan. Boil for 1 minute.

Remove from the heat and whisk in the butter and vanilla until the butter is melted.

Scrape the custard into a wide bowl (if there happen to be any lumps, pour it through a fine-mesh sieve into the bowl to strain them out) and let cool to room temperature. To speed up cooling, set the bowl in a larger bowl of ice water and whisk frequently. When it's no longer warm, transfer the custard to a container and lay a piece of plastic wrap directly on the surface to prevent a skin from forming. Cover the container and refrigerate until cold, at least 2 hours. It will thicken as it cools. Spoon into small bowls and serve cold.

After a night in the fridge, the pudding leftovers may release a little liquid; just drain it off or stir it back in.

Unless it's a rainy day or you've accidentally gotten some egg yolk in with the whites while separating the eggs, use the extra egg whites to make almond meringue cookies: With an electric mixer fitted with a whisk attachment, beat 3 egg whites and a pinch of kosher salt until very foamy, then very gradually, a tablespoon at a time, beat in ½ cup (100 g) sugar, beating for at least 30 seconds between each addition. Keep beating until the whites are bright white, glossy, and thick. Take a dab of the whites and rub them between your fingertips: if you can feel only a couple undissolved grains of sugar, they're ready. Stir in ½ teaspoon vanilla extract, then use a rubber spatula to fold in about 1¼ cups (150 g) almond meal. Spoon 2-tablespoon blobs of the mixture onto a parchment paper–lined baking sheet, put a pinch of sliced almonds on top of each, and bake in a 350°F (175°C) oven for about 15 minutes, until dry and just starting to brown at the edges. Let cool on the pans.

If it's a rainy day, etc.: Save the whites to add to scrambled eggs the next morning, or cook a little no-cheese egg-white omelet for the dog, who surely deserves it.

Lemon Pudding-Soufflé

Serves 6

Using an electric mixer

Folding beaten egg whites into a yolk mixture

Baking in a hot water bath (a bain-marie)—setting it up on the hot oven rack and pouring boiling water into the larger pan. Removing the bain-marie from the hot oven

5 tablespoons (70 g) unsalted butter, at room temperature

1 cup (200 g) sugar

3 large egg yolks, plus 6 large egg whites

⅓ cup (75 ml) lemon juice

2 teaspoons finely grated lemon zest (from about 2 lemons)

¼ cup (45 g) all-purpose flour

1 cup (240 ml) half-and-half

Pinch of cream of tartar

This was my mom's go-to pudding-like dessert for a long time, and probably one of my all-time favorites. Fluffy "soufflé" topping a tart warm custard; it isn't beautiful or fancy, but if you love lemon there are few better ways to enjoy it.

Preheat the oven to 350°F (175°C). Find a deep 8-inch (20 cm) square baking dish (or a 2-quart round soufflé dish) and a larger baking dish or pan that the smaller dish fits into—a 9 by 13-inch (23 by 33 cm) one works well. Use about 1 tablespoon of the butter to very generously butter the smaller baking dish all the way up the sides. Set the small baking dish inside the larger dish. Put a kettle of water on to boil.

In a deep bowl, using an electric mixer with the beater attachments, beat the remaining butter and the sugar together until thoroughly combined. Beat in the 3 egg yolks one at a time, then continue beating until the mixture is pale yellow. Gradually beat in the lemon juice and zest, then the flour and half-and-half, scraping the side of the bowl a couple times so everything is smooth and well incorporated. Set aside.

Switch to a whisk attachment on the electric mixer. Put the 6 egg whites in a clean, dry, deep bowl. Whisk until foamy, then add the cream of tartar and continue to whisk until firm peaks form (when you lift the whisk, the whites should stand up straight in a peak and not flop over). Use a rubber spatula to stir about one-third of the whites into the egg yolk mixture, then add half of the remaining whites and gently fold them in until mostly combined. Fold in the remaining whites until just combined and no large clumps of whites remain in the batter. Scrape the batter into the buttered baking dish.

With potholders, carefully pull the center rack partway out of the oven. Place the small baking dish (in the large dish) on the rack and carefully pour hot water from the kettle into the large

dish until it comes about 1 inch (2.5 cm) up the sides of the
small dish. Gently slide the rack back into the oven and close
the door. Bake for about 50 minutes, until puffed up and evenly
browned on top. Remove both baking dishes from the oven,
taking care not to spill the hot water, then lift the small dish
onto a wire rack and let cool for 20 minutes. Scoop portions of
the soufflé (and the soft pudding underneath) into dishes and
serve warm.

Groceries in a Small Town

The day after arriving at our new house in Morgantown, West Virginia, following a lengthy midwinter cross-country move from Nebraska, my daughter and I went for a drive to see just what we'd gotten ourselves into.

The closest grocery store was in a neighborhood called Sabraton (pronounced like the curved sword), nestled tightly in the narrow, steep-sided valley along Deckers Creek to the west of Morgantown proper, so we headed there first. Sabraton was an early settlement that saw its first big push of industrial development around the turn of the last century. Immigrants from Hungary, Greece, Italy, Poland, Ukraine, Czechoslovakia, Austria, and throughout eastern Europe worked in the tin plate mill (later a faucet factory) right by the creek, and a glass factory (later a shirt factory) a bit downstream—and, of course, in the coal mines in the area. The mine a few miles outside Sabraton that would eventually become known as the Richard Mine opened in 1903 to fuel coke plants on site; the coke would be taken by rail to steel mills in Maryland, and in the 1940s, when steel (and the coke used to make it) was in especially high demand, it employed five hundred West Virginians.

The Richard Mine closed in the early 1950s. The tin plate mill and the glass factory had closed around twenty years before. The faucet factory hung on until the mid-nineties. The Morgan Shirt Factory, having survived dramatic strikes and contentious labor disputes in its sixty or so years as union workers won and lost raises, health care benefits, and paid time off, closed around that time too, and if you search for it on the internet your results will be dominated by the obituaries of many of the hundreds of women who'd worked there to produce garments for Brooks Brothers and Ralph Lauren and Calvin Klein. The once-gorgeous hip-roofed brick building was razed in 2001.

One of the most distinctive early-twentieth-century buildings still remaining in the neighborhood is St. Mary's Holy Protection Byzantine Catholic Church, where the liturgy is still delivered partially in Slavonic. The church, founded in 1918, hosts an annual Slavic food festival in the low-ceilinged basement in summer: kielbasa, sauerkraut, pierogies, cabbage rolls, cake, loaves of sweet bread heavy with poppyseeds or walnuts. The construction of I-68 from the east in the 1970s severed a large chunk of the community, forcing parishioners to other parts of Morgantown and beyond (a tidy example of Robert Byrd's interstate system in the state making it easier for people to leave it), and now the church sits at a dead end hard by exit 4, from which you can spy its small domed steeple glinting gold.

Sabraton was annexed to Morgantown starting in around 1949 and today is a pretty standard commercial strip: AutoZone, Dollar Tree, Dollar General, Sheetz, that kind of thing. The most exciting development in its recent history was the opening of a Popeye's— the lines of cars heading toward the drive-thru, that first week, stretched the equivalent of at least a city block down the main drag.

The Kroger, backed right up to Deckers Creek, was small, with smoked-glass windows angled back from the facade at the entrance. You could probably fit three or four Sabraton Krogers in any Hy-Vee in Nebraska. I was, frankly, a little concerned as my daughter and I picked up a small hand basket just inside. We wandered around, assessing the situation. Produce: not bad at all; the herbs were in big bunches and seemed fresh. Meats: well, we weren't expecting a Nebraska-style meat department, with a full-service butcher counter, and our expectations were realized. Mexican, Asian, and otherwise "international" foods: we'd find better places to shop for those ingredients— no worries.

And then we came to the pasta-and-tomatoes section. I knew that north-central West Virginia had a large Italian American population whose ancestors had come to work in the glass factories and as masons and (as always) in the mines, but I could not believe what I was seeing. Was I gawking? Row after row of glorious imported canned tomatoes, some in those tiny shelf-stable cartons, some of them *yellow* tomatoes in tiny shelf-stable cartons, more than a couple brands of passata (luxuriously smooth strained tomatoes in beautiful tall glass jars I'd save to use as vases), fancy tuna in olive oil, and a selection of dried pastas that would not have been surprising if we'd been in a grocery store in, say, the Bronx but was totally unexpected in this tiny neighborhood in Appalachia with a Byzantine church at one end of it. My daughter and I just stood there and took it all in.

Oh, this is going to be good, I thought. We may have to drive the hour and change to Pittsburgh for whole fish or esoteric cuts of meat or big bags of dried guajillo chiles or that one brand of fish sauce I liked best, but I was eager to cook with everything we could find here, just a few minutes from our house. This little grocery store would do.

When Derek got home from work that evening, he asked if we'd been to the Kroger in Sabraton earlier. A coworker had told him she'd seen us there.

"How did she know it was us? We haven't met anyone yet!"

"She said you looked like you weren't from around here."

Apparently I had, indeed, been gawking. And apparently we'd just moved to a very small town.

Pasta e Ceci   Serves 2

PRACTICE SKILLS

Peeling garlic

Stovetop cooking over
medium-high heat

2 cloves garlic

2 tablespoons olive oil

2 tablespoons tomato paste

½ teaspoon dried oregano

Pinch of chile flakes
(optional)

2 cups (150 g) dried small or
flat pasta (ditalini, malfada
corta, and farfalle have
worked best for us)

About 1 cup (185 g) cooked
chickpeas (straight from
the freezer or from a can)

Kosher salt and freshly
ground black pepper

Grated Parmesan cheese

When I open a can of good-quality tomato paste only to use just a little of it, I spoon the rest into mounds on a piece of parchment paper and freeze them; I peel them off the paper and put them in a freezer bag in the freezer door. Making this classic quick pasta dish myself, I use a couple of those lumps, still frozen. But my daughter likes to use the tomato paste that comes in a toothpaste-style tube that we keep in the fridge door. It's even more convenient—please: squeeze it straight into the pan in blobs that look approximately tablespoon-sized and don't bother with a measuring spoon—and, importantly, it doesn't splatter as much as lumps of frozen paste.

Smash each garlic clove with the flat side of a chef's knife (lay the knife on the clove, bang the heel of your hand down on the knife), lift the clove by the "tail" of the peel, and use the back of the knife to tap the clove gently out of the peel. Coarsely chop the garlic, or just smash it so it falls apart into several pieces.

Put the garlic and oil in a skillet and cook over medium heat, stirring frequently with a wooden spoon, until it's softened and golden, about 3 minutes. Add the tomato paste, oregano, and chile flakes (if using), and cook, stirring, for just 1 minute, until the tomato paste is darkened a bit. Add the oregano and 3 cups water, then the pasta and chickpeas. Stir in 1 teaspoon salt and a few grinds of pepper. Make sure the water just covers the pasta; if it doesn't, add more water.

Raise the heat to medium-high and bring to a boil, then lower the heat and simmer, stirring frequently, for 8 to 10 minutes, until the pasta is cooked al dente—tender but firm, not soggy or floppy—and the sauce has thickened from the pasta starch. If the pasta starts to stick to the pan at any point, add a little more water and keep stirring. Season with more salt and pepper, if needed, then top with cheese and serve.

Lemon-Pepper Pasta Serves 4

1 teaspoon whole black peppercorns

Kosher salt

1 pound (455 g) dried pasta (any shape except orzo or lasagna or the like)

¼ cup (60 ml) olive oil

Grated zest of 1 lemon

½ cup (50 g) grated Parmesan or pecorino romano cheese, plus more for serving

This bright, peppery-sharp pasta with a creamy built-in sauce is one of those simple, satisfying dishes I make when the fridge is low on fresh vegetables and meat—or when my stores of creativity are running on fumes.

Using a mortar and pestle (or the side of a chef's knife or bottom of a heavy pot on a cutting board), coarsely crack the peppercorns.

Bring a large pot of salted water to a boil, add the pasta, and cook until almost al dente—cook for about a minute less than it says to on the package. Ladle out about 1½ cups (360 ml) of the pasta water.

A few minutes before the pasta is ready, place a deep skillet over medium-high heat and add the oil and cracked peppercorns; stir for 30 seconds, then add 1 cup (240 ml) of the reserved pasta water.

Drain the pasta in a colander and add it to the skillet (or use a spider strainer to transfer it), along with the lemon zest and 1 teaspoon salt. Stir and cook for 1 to 2 minutes, until the pasta is al dente and the water and oil have boiled together and emulsified to make a thin sauce that just barely coats the pasta. Add a little more pasta water if needed. Sprinkle in the cheese, toss, and serve with more cheese on the side.

Tip: If you're a person (or cooking with a person) for whom draining a full pot of pasta in a colander is not stressful or difficult, simply reserve some of the pasta water in a glass measuring cup and drain the pasta in a colander when it's done. Return the same pot to the heat and make the sauce in that pot instead of using a second pan.

Haluski

PRACTICE SKILLS

Chopping an onion

Coring and chopping cabbage

Stovetop cooking

Draining cooked noodles in a colander (or use a spider skimmer to scoop them out of the boiling water)

In the refrigerator in the back of the Polish grocery in Pittsburgh (and I think in several of the Russian and generically international markets, too) you'll find not only pierogies and kishka but to-go containers of haluski ready for the microwave. It's offered as a side dish at Lenten fish fries, and generously spooned out of hotel pans in church basements during the frequent food festivals across western Pennsylvania. I wasn't familiar with haluski before we moved here, but I've found that it's my kind of comfort food—and my daughter adores anything cabbage related, so it's a no-brainer for a simple, easy lunch.

In a large saucepan or deep skillet, cook chopped onions in lots of butter—like, half a stick—until tender but not browned, and add some chopped garlic if you'd like (it's not necessary, but it's good). Pile in a ton of chopped cabbage. Don't worry if you fill the pan; the cabbage will wilt and shrink as it cooks down. Sprinkle with salt and pepper (and a little caraway?) and stir and cook for maybe 15 minutes, until the cabbage is silky and tender, adding a little water to help it steam and wilt.

Meanwhile, bring a large pot of salted water to a boil. When the cabbage is ready in the other pan, add dried egg noodles to the pot of water. Cook until the noodles are al dente—not too soft—then drain and stir them into the cabbage. (Or use a spider skimmer to scoop the noodles from the water into the cabbage pan.) Season again and serve. I like to sprinkle some coarsely cracked black peppercorns and grated Parmesan or pecorino Romano over my haluski, but I would never suggest you do such a thing.

Free to Read

*O**n our honeymoon in the Cinque Terre ... The kids licked
their plates! ... I don't make this very often, but when
I do ... When I was growing up ... An easy weeknight
meal ... Perfect for Sunday dinner ... How to make lasagna: How
to layer lasagna: How to cook lasagna: What you'll need to make
lasagna: Skip to recipe.*

One of the easiest jokes you can make on the internet, one
that is sure to get those laugh reacts and inspire engagement
(of a predictable sort), is any joke made at the expense of food
bloggers. *Just get to the point already. I don't want to read a
novel, I just want to know how to make lasagna! Yes, so true! I get
all my recipes from Pinterest, and it drives me crazy! We don't care
about your honeymoon. Thank god for the "skip to recipe" button
lol!* Some people seem angry about excess copy to an unhealthy
degree: *It pisses me off, I don't care about you and your family.*
Then, from the knowing cynic in the thread: *It's all about ad
revenue, SEO phrases.* Or from the even more knowing among
us: *Google searches are more sophisticated now, search engine
optimization is useless anyway.* But few people respond the way
I do (*usually* silently, as I tend to prefer seething internally to
arguing on social media): food blogs are free to read. They are

a hell of a lot of work to produce, and if you don't like what you're reading you can either mash that scroll button, check out a cookbook from the library for free, or navigate your way to a recipe website whose format is more palatable to you. Why complain about food blogs that don't have to affect you at all; that provide some income to their creators, most of them women; that offer information that may or may not be useful to you as a home cook; and that serve as meaningful creative outlets for many people—again, mostly women?

Recently someone in a cooking group I'm in on Facebook shared a cartoon mocking wordy food bloggers, and the example in the cartoon was a post about lasagna that delved into the blogger's experience on a trip to Italy to such an extent that the reader had become a cobwebbed skeleton by the time they arrived at the recipe. Out of morbid curiosity, I searched for "lasagna recipe" on Google, and clicked through to actually read every single personal food blog post—twenty-two of them—on the first page of results. Only two posts mentioned a trip to Italy in the copy preceding the recipe itself, both of those covering the trip in a sentence or less, and most of the posts went into no significant personal detail at all. Yes, they were pretty repetitive, both in content and in format, but that's a separate issue from the wordiness and navel-gazing that irritate so many readers. It took maybe a minute and a half of reading, on average, to get to each recipe. I don't know about you, but my time isn't so valuable that the lost income due to the minutes I spend reading a blog post can even be meaningfully measured.

So why are readers so annoyed, so *put out*, by food blogs (of all things)? Some of it has to do with a misunderstanding of the amount of time and labor that goes into blogging about food. I let my own website go fallow years ago because it was simply too much work—and I wasn't even including recipes or remotely decent photographs in many of my posts. The bloggers that appear in search results post early and often, and the pressure to come up with relatively new content week after week must be unbelievably intense. One complainer on the post I mentioned above said that because recipes are "very easy" to write, we as readers should expect to be given them for free. I wonder if that person has ever been burned by a poorly written recipe, or posted a recipe in a public place that others have used and found lacking in some way. Recipe writing isn't the hardest kind of writing, but writing them well is a skill that must be acquired and honed, and that labor should be valued and respected as much as other kinds of labor. I wonder if that person demanding free labor routinely does his own professional work for no pay.

All those beautifully lit photographs don't come without material costs, either. For example, a dish of basic lasagna using store-brand ingredients costs more than $35 to make—once. That's not counting staples like dried herbs and a bit of wine in the sauce, and it's not counting the expense of testing that recipe several times, or trying out different techniques and ingredients to make sure you're posting the best possible version of the recipe (though obviously not every food blogger does a whole lot of recipe development).

Yes, but you can feed it to your family, so it's practically free. A hearty lasagna recipe posted in winter and photographed in lovely natural light indicates to me that unless the blogger is thinking months in advance or working in the Southern Hemisphere it was likely assembled and cooked early in the day, which means the family is getting artfully forked-into leftovers for dinner—which is fine for lasagna but not for other dishes, and it doesn't mean it's free. Neither is Photoshop, camera equipment, a cabinet full of stylish props, a workable kitchen, web hosting services, or internet access.

Even among readers who understand and respect the labor of food writing, and those who are aware that they can scroll straight to the recipe if they please, there's an undercurrent of contempt for the writers who dare to discuss their personal experiences with the dishes at any length. It's hard to imagine that this attitude doesn't have roots in a general disdain for the work that takes place in the domestic sphere—like cooking and child-raising (see also: the amount of disgust it's socially acceptable to express when "mommy blogging" comes up). The idea seems to be that bloggers selling visitors' data and clicks to advertising networks—with more or less financial success—should try to do so in a way that doesn't call attention to the fact that they, like most of us, are not living extraordinary lives that the public deems worth memoir-izing. Maybe we don't like being reminded that even if advertisers were handing us wads of cash to write about lasagna and such we, too, might have a hard time coming up with interesting things to say about what we're cooking, the meals we're having, our daily lives. It's healthy to be critical of food blogs and recipes, but we could also stand to bring some introspection to that criticism. What is it, in fact, that makes us uncomfortable about long-winded blog posts? Is it that we feel as if no one cares about *our* trip to Italy, or that *our* kids licked their plates for once? That we aren't selling our accounts of those experiences for clicks?

My daughter often says to me, when I put food on the table that she hasn't helped make, "Thank you so much." She says it, sincerely, when we bring home takeout pizza, too. I think that when she starts going to sit-down restaurants on her own with her friends she'll tip well, and I hope she'll be as considerate of the workers behind the food and material goods and content she consumes—or scrolls quickly past on the way to the content she came for.

And I hope, most of all, that she finds people who do care about her day-to-day life and whatever experiences are special to her, whether she writes them up for acquaintances or strangers to read about or not.

Draining Pasta

Until the first time I got to the pasta-draining point while making supper with my daughter, I didn't realize how difficult this simple-sounding task would be for her. I wanted her to be able to make pasta for herself sooner rather than later, though, so we came up with some solutions. We cook pasta in a wide stainless-steel Dutch oven rather than a tall pasta pot—it's easier for shorter people to reach into when stirring or scooping out pasta.

THE STRAINER BASKET

We don't have room for one of these in our kitchen, and it's a little more awkward than using a spider, but lifting a perforated basket from the pasta pot to drain it is much easier than carrying a full pot of boiling pasta water to the sink and draining it in a colander, hotter-than-boiling steam rising from around the edge of the pot as the water flows out. Use potholders to lift the basket, carefully let the water drain out, then dump the pasta into the pan with the sauce.

THE SPIDER

Pick up one of those wide, shallow wire strainer-scoopers from an Asian food store. They look a little like a spider web, with a wooden handle (or sometimes it's all stainless steel). Instead of draining the pasta, just scoop it out of the boiling water with the spider and into the pan of sauce. It's more efficient than a slotted spoon, which doesn't drain the water off as quickly and whose small size requires a dozen scoops to the spider's two or three.

AVOID DRAINING ALTOGETHER

Look at the pasta e ceci recipe on page 212, where the pasta is cooked with the sauce in the pan. My daughter makes this on her own all the time, because there's so little fuss involved. You can do this with other kinds of sauces, letting the excess water evaporate as the pasta cooks, and stirring frequently so it cooks evenly.

Baked Rigatoni with Sausage and Ricotta

Serves 6

PRACTICE SKILLS

Stovetop cooking over medium-high heat

Working with raw meat

Chopping garlic

Opening a can

Cracking an egg

Draining pasta (or using a spider strainer)

Moving a large baking dish (or two smaller ones) in and out of the oven

1 tablespoon olive oil

1 pound (455 g) loose Italian sausage

2 cloves garlic, chopped

One 28-ounce (794 g) can whole peeled tomatoes

1½ teaspoons kosher salt, plus more for the pasta water

Freshly ground black pepper

8 ounces (225 g) ricotta

¼ cup (25 g) plus 2 table-spoons grated Parmesan cheese

1 teaspoon dried basil, or ¼ cup (10 g) chopped fresh basil or parsley

1 large egg

1 pound (455 g) dried rigatoni or similar pasta

1 cup (110 g) shredded mozzarella cheese

I worked in an Italian American restaurant in a small town in Virginia for a while during and after college that attracted a number of New York, New Jersey, and Long Island expats. Chef had baked ziti—a dish I'd never in my life heard of, much less eaten or cooked—on the menu just for them, and they went bananas for it. On days when I suspect the chef was just burned out on ideas for dinner specials, we'd throw some sausage in half of the oval bakers of pre-assembled ziti portions.

When I make baked pasta at home, I prefer a heftier, less slippery shape like rigatoni or penne rigate over smooth ziti. And because usually I make it when I'm craving lasagna but don't want to futz with layering, I dollop the top with a ricotta-and-egg mixture to simulate that creamy layer. You can certainly omit the ricotta dollops or the sausage here; both in one dish is almost overkill. (Delicious overkill.) At the restaurant we added lightly sautéed strips of red bell pepper and onion to fill out the dish, and if you have the bandwidth you can add a couple handfuls of those vegetables when you sauté the garlic for the sauce—it'll all still fit in the large baking dish.

Another improvement to this basic recipe that you might want to make: Just before pouring the juice from the can of tomatoes into the skillet to deglaze it, add a splash of red or white wine, stir well to scrape up browned bits and let it boil almost all the way down before adding the tomatoes—it provides a nice depth to the sauce.

Preheat the oven to 350°F (175°C). Have a 9 by 13-inch (23 by 33 cm) baking dish (or two smaller ones) ready.

Heat about half of the oil in a skillet over medium heat. Quickly pinch the sausage into rough 1-inch (2.5 cm) bits and add them to the pan in a single layer (though a few bits will have to sit atop others, and that's fine). Cook for 3 minutes without disturbing the sausage, then use a thin metal spatula to turn it. Continue to cook the sausage, turning frequently now, for about 7 more minutes, until no longer pink—cut into a piece to make sure it's cooked all the way through. Remove from the heat and scoop the bits into the baking dish, leaving as much of the fat behind as possible. Use a paper towel to wipe out most of the fat in the pan.

Return the pan to medium heat and add the remaining oil and the garlic and cook, stirring, for 1 minute. Pour in the juice from the can of tomatoes, then crush the tomatoes with your hand and add them to the pan, stirring up any browned bits from the pan with the spatula. Add 1 teaspoon salt and several grinds of pepper. Bring to a boil, then lower the heat and simmer for 15 minutes.

Meanwhile, in a medium bowl, whisk together the ricotta, ¼ cup (25 g) Parmesan, ½ teaspoon salt, the basil, and a few grinds of pepper until smooth. Set aside.

Bring a large pot of water to a boil over medium-high heat, add a few teaspoons of salt and the pasta, and cook uncovered, stirring the pasta occasionally, for about 2 minutes less than the time indicated on the package—just until you can bite into a piece and chew it and it's not crunchy but still quite firm.

Drain the pasta, or use a spider strainer to quickly transfer the pasta to the baking dish with the sausage. Spoon in the simmered sauce and stir everything together until all the pasta is coated with sauce and the sausage is evenly distributed. Spoon big dollops of the ricotta mixture on top, sprinkle with the mozzarella and 2 tablespoons Parmesan, and bake for 30 minutes, or until the cheese is melted and the ricotta mixture is set. Serve with a big spoon.

After-School Special

What food did you make for yourself when you got home from school and the adults were busy or at work (not to say they weren't busy there, too) and you were hungry because your lunch period was at the ungodly hour of 10:15 a.m.? I poured myself some cold cereal—and it was a bonus if I could find my dad's stash of Corn Pops. My brother microwaved nacho cheese sauce for tortilla chips. Nothing too spectacular.

I've recently become fascinated by—okay, slightly obsessed with—a certain kid-friendly food my West Virginia friends have told me about that would have seemed outrageously sophisticated to me at, say, thirteen. Apparently, if you lived within a radius of Charleston that included part of Ohio but *not* central or northern West Virginia and certainly neither of the panhandles, you might have slapped a frozen Buzz Buttered Steak in a hot pan as an after-school treat. The Buzz meat company, which had been producing them for decades, discontinued them for a while, then resurrected them a few years ago in a limited way. They're square, and thin enough to cook through directly from the freezer, and each has a pat of butter stuck to the center of one side—a nice touch, having the cooking fat right there attached to the meat. I'd received conflicting information about what they actually are: some people described them as tenderized pieces of beef (like a cube steak), some said they were formed patties of chopped beef (like a burger). The pictures I found online seemed as if it could've gone either way.

As I've done countless times with foods I've read or heard vague things about but never eaten, as soon as I learned of them I decided to make my own version of Buzz Buttered Steaks. I studied the pictures and read descriptions of them on defunct message boards and old posts on nostalgia blogs. I had a box of waxed paper squares for separating formed burgers for food-service purposes—not sure why I bought those, but they've come in handy. I had a big tray of ground turkey, which, I figured, would be close enough. And I had butter, of course—I always have butter. I seasoned the turkey meat, made four-ounce pucks and flattened each as thinly as possible on a square of paper, then pressed a nice thick slice of butter into the surface. They were round, not square, but they looked pretty good! They looked like factory-made convenience food, which was precisely the goal. I stacked them in a tall column and wrapped it carefully in plastic and freezer paper. My daughter, I imagined, would be able to open the freezer, pull out a "buttered steak," and cook it up in a skillet by herself whenever she needed a reasonably healthful, no-fuss hot food.

When I was sure the meat had had time to freeze, I retrieved the package for a test run. The whole column of meat, butter, and waxed paper had frozen into a solid mass. A minor setback. I crowbarred one off the top with a dull knife and preheated a skillet. I pinched a corner of the waxed paper still frozen to the pried-off patty and peeled it off in five or six pieces, then scraped off the stubborn stuck strips with my thumbnail. So far, so good. I put the turkey burger in the hot pan, butter side down. I knew almost immediately what was going to happen, and indeed I watched helplessly as a disturbing hole in the shape of a pat of butter formed and then widened in the center of the meat and the butter sizzled up to the pink uncooked surface. I scraped up the turkey donut—the edges around the butter hole stuck to the unbuttered pan, of course—and tried to spread the butter around in the skillet before flipping the meat and putting it back in the pan to finish cooking. This hadn't gone well. I had a couple dozen of these

things to get through. I did cook them all eventually, but it wasn't the kind of experience I'd hoped for.

But I couldn't get the real buttered steaks out of my mind. Finally I called up Buzz and started asking questions. Dickinson Gould, third-generation Buzz president, got on the line and explained that the buttered steak is not a steak, per se, but ground beef: "It's just a hamburger patty," he said. I asked if they're seasoned in any way. Nope: "They're pure beef." With a pat of salted butter. That's it. I wondered to myself why mine had been such a disaster; maybe the turkey, maybe there was too much butter or not enough?

Gould confirmed that in southern West Virginia, which is the only place you can buy them, people remember them as the first food they learned how to cook as a kid—or, he said, as a newlywed. He said that when people first come to work for Buzz Food Service, which in addition to being the producer of now-niche Buzz Buttered Steaks is a substantial-sized fresh meat and seafood purveyor in the Charleston area, they're surprised by all the folks who come up to them when they're out and about wearing their company shirts to wax nostalgic about the beloved frozen patties.

There's nothing else on the market quite like the Buzz Buttered Steak, in southern West Virginia or beyond, as far as I can tell. And it's too bad, because it's not a product I'm going to try to DIY again anytime soon. In any case, my daughter's old enough by now to stop at the grocery store on the way home from school, buy a package of ground beef (or turkey), and make her own burger from scratch if she really wants to.

Burgers
Makes 4

PRACTICE SKILLS

Working with raw meat

Stovetop cooking over medium heat

Spatula work

1 pound ground beef (I like 85% lean ground chuck, but 80% is fine too)

¾ teaspoon kosher salt or other salty seasoning

Freshly ground black pepper

Tiny bit of vegetable oil

Sliced cheese (optional), toasted buns, and whatever other fixings you'd like

A crusty burger cooked in a heavy skillet to medium doneness is one of those beautifully simple foods that drive cooks to develop all kinds of hacks to achieve. I've tried many of them myself: the smash burger, where you shape seasoned meat into a ball, place it in the hot pan, then quickly smash it down with a spatula to a thin patty (great if you're making only one or two burgers at a time); the burger that's shaped around a pat of butter for extra juiciness; a dash of Worcestershire sauce, the grated onion, and shreds of cheese worked into the ground meat; the meticulously home-ground blend of sirloin and chuck for the ideal mix of tender lean and fat.

I'm pretty sure none of them makes a measurably better burger than the simplest of all possible techniques, using a convenient store-bought grind. I don't even season the ground beef before shaping it into patties—though I do like to season the outside of the patties well in advance of cooking so the salt can start to penetrate the meat on its own and draw some of the protein-rich moisture to the surface, where it will first evaporate a little, allowing the proteins to brown nicely in the hot pan. Sometimes instead of plain salt I'll use a spice blend like Goya Adobo seasoning (which is fine salt, onion and garlic powder, and a minuscule quantity of dried oregano and maybe another spice or two) or a low-salt Cajun spice blend designed for blackening (definitely open up the window for that).

If you can, shape and season the meat up to 1 hour before cooking: gently shape the meat into four patties about ½ inch (12 mm) thick. Remembering to wash your hands well after touching the meat and before touching anything else, season the patties on both sides with the salt and several grinds of pepper. Set aside on the counter.

Heat a large, heavy skillet (preferably cast iron) over medium heat. Add a few drops of oil and spread it out on the surface of the skillet, then place the patties in the pan without overlapping them. Cook without disturbing them for 3 minutes. Turn on the exhaust fan over the stove or open a window if it gets too smoky.

Using a thin metal spatula so you pick up all the browned crust on the bottom, turn the patties over. Cook for another 3 minutes or until cooked to your desired doneness. If you'd like, lay a slice of cheese on top of each burger and cover the pan with a lid until it's melted. Serve on toasted buns with toppings.

Here's a burger I personally like: Burger patty seasoned with a Cajun spice blend before cooking, so it blackens in the pan and makes anyone nearby cough as chile fumes fill the air; toasted soft bun spread with a thin layer of Duke's mayonnaise (tangier and less sweet than other brands) and a squiggle of sriracha; topped with copious pickled jalapeños. No cheese necessary, but try a semi-firm Gouda if you've got it, melted on the burger in the pan or on one of the bun halves in a toaster oven if you have one.

Patience

The ability to step back and let heat and time do their work is not an easy skill to develop as a young cook, but it's one of the most important and rewarding. It took me years to learn to just . . . leave food alone—in a skillet, in the oven, in the backyard smoker. And forget about letting things cool or freeze or thaw or rest properly before moving to the next step: I was always—often still am—jumping the gun.

In the very early days of food TV, when it was slower and more methodical than it is now, I saw one episode of a show in which a famous chef would cook food for friends while telling them what he was doing (really high-concept stuff). I don't remember what he was cooking—osso bucco, maybe—but he imparted one lesson that truly changed the way I cooked. It was about how to brown meat, for a stew or anything else: don't move it around in the pan too much, he said, and *brown it longer than you think you need to*. It's golden on the bottom? Keep going, because "golden" is not *brown*. One side is nice and crusty? That's great, now brown the other sides. I'd worked in an Italian restaurant, but I hadn't learned about browning like this in any serious way, perhaps because long-cooked dishes like roasts and stews were started early in the day by the actual chef, not punk line cooks and sometime dishwashers like me—when I was cooking, it was mostly quick made-to-order pastas tossed high in sauté pans and on their way to the dining room within a few minutes. And if we had a fancy steak special on the menu, the chef cooked that expensive cut of meat himself.

I knew about the Maillard reaction, in which proteins (strings of amino acids) react with simple sugars (like glucose) when exposed to high temperatures—which also serve to drive off surface moisture that might otherwise steam a food—to create new molecules that result in flavor, aroma, and color changes. In other words, the substances that make a nicely seared New York strip or an Extra Toasty cheese cracker or a roasted marshmallow so appealing. I just hadn't realized how important it was for long-cooked, braised dishes, or how to achieve the ideal level of browning. And even if I had understood it fully, I was impatient.

Letting time pass without *doing anything* is not easy for me. I might get this from my dad, who is always, always doing something (except when he's taking his afternoon nap). He jumps up right after lunch and goes out to the garage to replace a part on his old truck and then chainsaws half a dead apple tree and then does something involving ladders. I'll check the progress of the rising bread dough for the fourteenth time in half an hour and then try to distract myself by tightening one (1) loose screw on a doorknob (my projects are less-intense than Dad's).

The periods of downtime that are so ubiquitous in cooking are tough to manage as an adult, and even more so when you're cooking with a kid: you want to sustain their interest, get them excited about the food, and then you're asking them to wait? For possibly *hours*? It's tempting to give up and dive back in too soon, lest you and your kitchen partner lose the thread altogether. I've watched my daughter spend half an hour cheerfully mixing cookie dough, put a panful of cookies in the oven, set the timer magnetized to the fridge for eight minutes, and then head straight up to her room to become engrossed in listening to music through *noise-canceling headphones*. And I'll admit to doing similar things myself.

Even when you're just supposed to let some meat cook without touching it, so it browns well and doesn't release too much moisture as it cooks, and so its crust loosens from the pan readily with a nudge, it can be hard to keep from futzing with it. I know of no psychological tricks to play on myself when cooking a steak, for example, except to try to remember the best one I've ever cooked and keep telling myself that I can re-create that experience if I can manage a bit of patience. When the dish is made up entirely of vegetables, the urge to pull the pot from the heat before they've reached absolute silky tenderness is powerful, but I do have one neat trick for that: it's at least a little easier to leave it be when it's stashed in the oven with a lid on it.

A Nice Steak or Pork Chop

PRACTICE SKILLS

Working with raw meat

Stovetop cooking over high heat

Tong work

Generously season a New York strip, ribeye, or bone-in pork chop, at least ¾ inch (2 cm) thick, on all sides with kosher salt. Set aside on a plate for 1 hour, or put it in the refrigerator, uncovered, for several hours or overnight. Even longer than overnight is fine too. The time in the salt is essentially a dry brine; it'll draw water to the surface, where it will form a salt solution that will be partially absorbed back into the meat. Go do something else while the meat and salt take their time.

Pat the meat dry with a paper towel and season with pepper.

Heat a heavy skillet over high heat with a slick of vegetable oil. Carefully add the steak or pork chop, turn down the heat to medium, and cook for about 4 minutes *without disturbing it*. Turn it over with tongs (it should release from the pan easily and be nice and brown on the bottom) and cook the other side for 4 minutes. Use the tongs to hold the steak or chop vertically so that the edges are against the skillet and some of the fat browns and melts.

Add some butter and aromatics (fresh herbs like rosemary and thyme sprigs and whole garlic cloves or quartered shallots) to the pan and turn the steak to coat it in the butter while it continues to cook. If the pan is really smoking, lower the heat and tong the aromatics onto the top of the meat. A thick steak should be medium-rare after 13 to 15 minutes total, or 125 to 130°F (52 to 54°C). A thick pork chop should be 145 to 150°F (63 to 65°C). Remove the meat to a carving board and let rest for 5 to 10 minutes before serving—patience!

Oven-Braised Vegetables

Serves 4 to 6

PRACTICE SKILLS

Coarsely chopping an onion

Peeling garlic

Stovetop cooking over medium-high heat

Chopping a pepper, eggplant, and summer squash

Opening a can of tomatoes (or use chopped fresh ones)

Moving a heavy pot in and out of the oven

1 onion

5 cloves garlic

1½ teaspoons kosher salt, or more to taste

4 tablespoons (60 ml) olive oil

1 large eggplant

1 large or 2 small summer squash (zucchini and/or yellow squash)

One 14½-ounce (411 g) can diced or whole tomatoes; or 1½ cups (250 g) ripe fresh tomatoes, chopped, plus a little water

Fresh basil and/or parsley leaves

Cooking a ratatouille (which is essentially what this dish is) slowly on the stovetop can be a drag; I tend to pull the pot from the heat too soon because I get tired of tending it and miss out on the pillowy-soft, heat-sweetened eggplant. If I put it in the oven, though, I'm less likely to undercook it.

Preheat the oven to 350°F (175°C). Position the top rack in the lower third of the oven so you'll have room to safely remove the hot lid from the Dutch oven that'll be in there later.

Chop the onion and spread it in the bottom of a Dutch oven. Smash and peel the garlic cloves and add them to the pot. Sprinkle with ½ teaspoon salt and drizzle in 1 tablespoon of the oil. Place over medium-high heat and cook, stirring frequently, until the onion is tender and beginning to brown, 5 to 7 minutes.

Cut the eggplant and squash into 1-inch (2.5 cm) chunks and add them to the pot with the onion and garlic. Sprinkle with about 1 teaspoon salt and drizzle in the remaining 3 tablespoons oil. Let cook without disturbing the vegetables for 3 minutes to brown some of them on the bottom, then toss well and continue to cook, stirring occasionally, for another 7 minutes, or until the vegetables are softened somewhat. Stir in the tomatoes (breaking up canned ones with your hands) and their juices. Bring to a boil, cover, and transfer to the oven.

Bake for 30 minutes, without stirring, until the vegetables have released a lot of their liquid and have reduced in volume considerably. Uncover (carefully) and continue to bake for another 30 minutes, or until the vegetables are very tender, their expressed juices have reduced somewhat, and the whole thing is starting to brown at the edges of the pot. Season with more salt, if needed, tear some fresh herbs over the dish, and serve warm or at room temperature.

A Fortnight
of Cake

You need thirty-five different layer cake recipes tested, tasted, and edited, and they're all due in two weeks? Sure, I can do that—send them on.

Oh god, what have I done?

The kitchen in our house in Lincoln, Nebraska, was small, but I knew it could handle a few cakes in progress at a time, with overflow into the mudroom by the back door and the dining room on the other end. What I needed was an assistant. Someone with a well-developed palate, some experience baking unusual cakes, and a lot of flexibility in her schedule. As it happened, it was June, and my daughter had just finished up second grade and had a lot of as-yet-unstructured free time on her hands. We agreed on a fair wage, put fresh batteries in the kitchen scale, and dove in.

The first four or five cakes went slowly as we adjusted our technique and tried different quantities of leaveners. By around cake seven, we'd gotten into a groove and for the most part knew what we were doing and how to fix any errors we might come across before they happened. Most of the cakes followed the basic batter-making process: beating butter and sugar until light and adding eggs one at a time (wet ingredients), then stirring in whisked-together flour and baking powder and/or baking soda and salt (dry ingredients), and finally milk or another liquid. Before starting each batter, I'd ask, "Wet or dry?" and my daughter would either head to the stand mixer (for wet) or grab a whisk (for dry). After cooling, frosting, and decorating (luckily these particular cakes didn't require much in the way of fancy décor), we'd cut a slice and taste. At the end of the baking day, we'd wrap leftovers of the successes and take them to neighbors.

It was a whirlwind, those two weeks, a slog, and an absolute delight. I loved working side by side—or rather, in our galley kitchen, back to back—with my kid, getting a sense of how she might be as a colleague in a real job someday. She was cheerful and funny and supportive and always game.

She was also only eight, and I hadn't expected her to last through all thirty-five cakes. The tasting slices got thinner and thinner as the project went on. At cake seventeen, my aproned coworker hit a wall. She declined to take even one bite, apologized, and asked if she could make a bowl of instant ramen for lunch (because I'd forgotten we needed actual meals). Then she went out into the yard to hang out with the dog for the rest of the day while I moved on to cake eighteen.

Perfect Chocolate Cake

Makes two 8-inch (20 cm) round cake layers

PRACTICE SKILLS

Boiling water in a kettle

Measuring dry ingredients

Cracking eggs

Using an electric mixer

Moving hot cake pans out of the oven

¾ cup (6 ounces/1½ sticks) unsalted butter, at room temperature (see Notes, page 232), plus more for the pans

¾ cup (70 g) cocoa powder (regular, not Dutch-process)

2 cups (480 ml) boiling water

2¾ cups (360 g) all-purpose flour

1½ teaspoons baking powder

1 teaspoon baking soda

¾ teaspoon fine kosher salt

1¾ cups (350 g) sugar

3 large eggs, at room temperature (see Notes, page 232)

1 teaspoon vanilla extract

I've made a lot of chocolate cakes, but this one, adapted from a recipe I tested (and tested . . . and tested) for Yolanda Gampp's book *How to Cake It!* a few years ago, has been the best. The hot-water technique makes a thinnish batter that bakes up exceedingly tender and light.

Preheat the oven to 350°F (175°C). Butter two 8-inch (20 cm) round cake pans and line the bottoms with parchment paper.

Put the cocoa powder in a heatproof bowl and pour the boiling water over it. Stir to combine, then set aside.

In a medium bowl, whisk together the flour, baking powder, baking soda, and salt and set aside.

In a large bowl, using an electric mixer with the beater attachment (or in a stand mixer fitted with the paddle attachment), beat the butter and sugar on medium-high speed until light and fluffy, at least 5 minutes. One at a time, crack the eggs into a small bowl or cup and add them to the butter mixture, beating until smooth after each. Beat in the vanilla. With the mixer on low speed, alternately add the flour mixture and cocoa powder mixture, beginning and ending with the flour (that is, add about one-quarter of the flour mixture and mix until it's incorporated, then add about one-third of the cocoa powder mixture, and so on). Mix just until everything is combined; don't overmix or the cake will be tough.

Divide the batter between the prepared pans and bake on the center rack of the oven for 30 to 35 minutes, until a toothpick inserted in the center comes out mostly clean, with just a few crumbs clinging to it. Transfer to cooling racks and let cool for a few minutes, then loosen the edges of the cake layers with a dull knife and invert them onto the racks, peel off the parchment, and let cool completely. If you have time, wrap the cooled layers

recipe continues

in plastic wrap and refrigerate overnight before frosting—the cake will be firmer and less likely to tear as you work with it.

Notes: Leave the butter on the counter for a few hours before you start, or put the sticks on a plate in a microwave oven on low power for just 10 seconds at a time to soften them slightly without melting.

To warm eggs straight from the fridge, put the uncracked eggs in a bowl and cover with hot water while you prepare the other ingredients, then drain them.

You can also bake this batter in one 9 by 13-inch (23 by 33 cm) baking pan to make a sheet cake. Bake for about 40 minutes. The frosting below will cover it generously.

Perfect Cream Cheese Frosting

Makes about 6 cups (1.4 L), plenty to fill and frost a two-layer 8-inch (20 cm)

PRACTICE SKILLS

Using an electric mixer

1 cup (2 sticks/225 g) unsalted butter, at room temperature

16 ounces (2 blocks/455 g) cold cream cheese

Up to 32 ounces (1 bag/ 907 g) confectioners' sugar

2 teaspoons vanilla extract

Another precious keeper from my work as a recipe tester—this one adapted from Amirah Kassem's book *The Power of Sprinkles*. I'd struggled with cream cheese frosting (which *should* be so simple!) until I read her game-changing piece of advice: *Use room-temperature butter and cold cream cheese.* That's it. That's pretty much all you need to know. I generally err on the side of less sugar, preferring a tangier, softer frosting, but if you want it to hold its shape with a little more definition (though it won't be as stiff as a buttercream by any means), use the full amount.

In a large bowl, using an electric mixer with the beater attachment (or in a stand mixer fitted with the paddle attachment), beat the butter on medium-high speed until smooth. Add the cold cream cheese and beat until thoroughly combined. Gradually add the confectioners' sugar, with the mixer on low speed; scrape down the side of the bowl with a rubber spatula to get everything mixed in well.

Frosting a Layer Cake

1. If you have one, a spinning lazy Susan makes frosting a round cake easier: tape a cardboard cake round to the center. If you don't have one, just work with the cardboard on the counter or directly on the cake platter. Dab a little frosting on the cardboard round (or the platter) and place one cake layer, bottom (flatter) side up, on it. The frosting dab helps hold it in place. If working on a serving platter, tear several strips of waxed paper or parchment and arrange them on the platter in such a way that they'll extend out past the edges of the cake layer—when you're done frosting, you'll tug them out from underneath the cake and the platter around the cake will be clean.

2. If your cake layers are pretty domed on top, no worries: Just use a long serrated knife to shave off the dome a bit. Place one cake layer, bottom (flatter) side up, on the dab of frosting and use an offset spatula to slather frosting on top all the way to the edges.

3. Top with the second layer, bottom side up. Spread frosting on the second layer. If you want to be more meticulous, put the frosting in a pastry bag fitted with a large plain round tip, and use that to lay frosting evenly down on the layers, piping in a spiral, then offset-spatula it smooth.

4. Spread a thin coating around the sides, reserving plenty of frosting for a second coat later. (This thin layer of frosting is called the crumb coat; it'll seal in the crumbs as it firms up.) Be sure to keep crumbs that stick to the spatula out of the bowl of frosting: scrape the crumby frosting off the spatula into a separate small bowl as you work before plunging it back into the bowl of clean frosting. The cake may look pretty rough at this point, or the bare look of the sides may be appealing to you— either way, place the thinly frosted cake in the refrigerator for about 1 hour, until the frosting is firm. If you'd like, apply a clean, crumb-free coat of frosting to the chilled cake and tug out the strips of paper.

5. Decorate however you please. Serve right away, or cover loosely and refrigerate until ready to serve.

6. Slice with a knife dipped into hot water and wiped off between cuts.

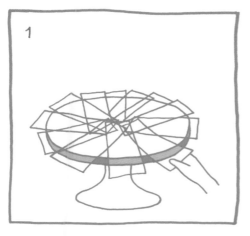

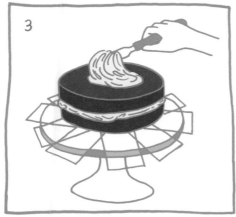

No Recipes, No Masters

Cook without a book (there's a cookbook for that), cooking without recipes (there's a *Bon Appétit* website recipe tag for that), no-recipe recipes (there's a *New York Times* regular recipe feature *and* a cookbook for that). There seems to be a market for published programs of culinary study that promise to empower us to produce delicious food of our own, with no guidance from the written word. We want so much to cut our ropy tethers to staid recipes that we're willing to literally buy in to the idea that if a recipe claims *not* to be a recipe, that's what we're doing. We want to believe that we're artists working in the malleable media of produce and proteins and heat and cold and time, and we're free.

But we are not, exactly, free. The ingredients list albatross yet hangs about our necks, and we can douse the carcass with cook-without-a-recipe sentiment but it will still be a recipe. And that's fine, because in truth the only way to learn to cook "without recipes" is to cook, and cook often, *with* recipes in some form. A person won't become stronger without exercising regularly, as onerous as that may be for many of us, and

though it's sometimes difficult to use recipes, to feel constricted and uncreative and beholden to expertise, using recipes thoughtfully is one of the best ways to learn how *not* to need them. Standing next to an elder as she cooks and absorbing her knowledge and practicing alongside her day after day until we've memorized what is essentially a "recipe" is another, but not all of us have daily access to that kind of passed-down wisdom, and so we're left with the lowly cookbook—or newspaper Dining In section or what have you.

M. F. K. Fisher, in her famous skewering of antique and vintage recipes, spoofs: "a little of this, some of that, baked long enough, and then served forth." As she explains, "obviously it was assumed that the cooks knew basic principles to be followed in preparing any dish, whether baked or boiled." And there it is, though Fisher doesn't make the point explicitly: those cooks of olden days knew their stuff, all right, but it was only either baked or boiled. There's so much more they could've been doing with their pheasants and currants and brandy and spice, if only they had a modern recipe, with standard measures and wordy instructions, to show them how.

I don't use recipes for most meals I make, but most of what I cook in an average week is simple stuff. I'm not a restaurant chef, and have no illusions about my own artistry in the kitchen. I'm capable. I can be creative enough to get reasonably nutritious food on the table that tastes very good (with the occasional exception). I can bake cakes and breads and pastries on the fly, and they'll rise and brown and generally do what they're supposed to do in the oven. (Cookies are another story. They're *difficult*.) If that's all there was to it, I'd never need to use a recipe again. (Except for cookies.) With practice, you could certainly do the same. Any of the recipes in the volume you're holding now, foods I've attempted to describe in a mostly standard recipe format, are ones you could probably make a second or third time pretty easily without even cracking the book. But of course that's not all there is to cooking.

I need recipes. Not because I wouldn't survive without them, but because I'd be less happy. When I can identify the feeling of bouncing up against the limits of my creativity, I make a point of finding a recipe for a food I've never cooked or even eaten before, a new ingredient, or a technique I've never encountered. And I try very hard to follow the recipe as closely as possible. My work as a recipe tester has helped me immensely here: given a testing job, I'm essentially forced to cook and bake foods I might not otherwise have been drawn to, and to hew to each recipe exactly as it's written. Often those as yet un-tried-and-true recipes lead me to dark places I'd rather not revisit,

but even more often I find myself delighted to have been dragged out of my quiet, cozy reading chair to a party full of interesting people I'd never met before.

Relying on recipes is not a failing, as Laura Shapiro at *The Atlantic* points out in her smart commentary on the *New York Times* no-recipe cookbook. It doesn't mean you're not also using judgment and drawing on your own experiences. Professional chefs consult cookbooks and recipes all the time when they're dreaming up ideas for "new" dishes, and in turn write down those ideas, sometimes in the form of recipes, sometimes as vague (too-vague?) notes, for their staff or for the people they hire to write their cookbooks for them.

When someone says their grandma never used a recipe, what I hear is that their grandma's food was delicious and that a lot of care went into making it. I also, perhaps unfairly in some cases, assume that Grandma didn't stray too far afield in the kitchen— which is a prudent way to cook, especially when resources are limited. It would be foolish to risk total failure, wasting ingredients and time, on a whim. I'd argue that reliable recipes allow us to broaden our experience while alleviating some of the risk involved in trying new foods. My mom doesn't use recipes very often either, but there's no way in the world she would've come up with something like b'stilla or kouign-amann without at least reading about them in glossy issues of *Sphere* (RIP) or *Gourmet* (RIP) or *Saveur* (RIP). She now makes kouign-amann with sourdough starter, and it's weird and wonderful and entirely her own, and in its family tree is a recipe.

Stock

I always feel a little like a tenth-grader padding an English paper with long block quotes when I include recipes for different kinds of stock in my books. Stocks really don't benefit much, in my opinion, from rigid ingredients lists or baroque explanations. You put a bunch of flavorful things in a pot with water, simmer gently for a long time, then strain out the solids. If you plan to make a fancy consommé that must be sparkling clear and serve it to a picky great-aunt or a famous philosophy professor or someone like that, find a copy of *Mastering the Art of French Cooking* (volume 1) and look for the instructions—the recipe— for clarifying broth with egg whites.

For chicken stock you need some chicken bones, and for beef or lamb or pork stock you need bones from those animals, either already cooked—a roast chicken stripped of its meat, for example, or beef rib bones that have been roasted alongside something else until deeply browned—or raw. Some meat attached is fine, but not necessary. (If you're making vegetable stock, obviously leave out the bones and use lots of vegetables in their place.)

You'll also need some roughly chopped vegetables or their collected peels and trimmings, usually onions (keep the peels on for a broth with more color), carrots (with or without tops), and celery (say, the ends you've cut off when using the nicer parts of the stalk in other dishes). Other vegetables will impart different flavors to a stock, but are totally acceptable; for example: fennel, parsnips, tomato peels and seeds, leeks (the dark green tops you can't use for other purposes), mushrooms (or the dried parts of mushroom stems you've cut off), de-kerneled corn cobs. Some vegetables that don't really work are asparagus, broccoli and cauliflower and other crucifers, and artichokes, all of

recipe continues

238

which have too-assertive aromas and flavors, in my opinion, and greens and delicate quick-cooking vegetables like peas, which would be wasted in a stock.

Put all of these in a large pot, along with aromatics like a bay leaf, some peppercorns or other whole spices, parsley stems, a thick slice of ginger, the tops of lemongrass stalks, makrut lime leaves, or whatever you want your stock to taste like. If you're not sure how you're going to use the stock, keep it simple: bay leaf, peppercorns, parsley stems. Cover everything with water and simmer gently for at least a couple hours. Skim off foam and any scum that rises to the surface. Strain in a fine sieve. You can use it as is, or let it cool then chill it overnight so you can scrape the layer of solidified fat from the top then transfer the defatted stock (which will keep longer) to containers and freeze for up to several months.

Sweet Onion–Thyme Soup Serves 3 or 4

PRACTICE SKILLS

Peeling and slicing a lot of onions

Stovetop cooking over medium heat

Shredding cheese

Broiling cheese toast in the oven

4 sweet onions (about 1½ pounds/680 g total)

2 tablespoons olive oil

1 bay leaf

Kosher salt

½ teaspoon dried thyme

Freshly ground black pepper

4 cups (960 ml) homemade beef stock

Squeeze of lemon juice (optional)

2 or 3 slices of bread

½ cup (55 g) shredded cheese (Gruyère or sharp cheddar)

An old-fashioned version of this recipe might go something like this: Cook a large quantity of sliced onions slowly in oil in a pot until very soft and golden, with bay leaf, thyme, and seasoning. Pour in good beef stock and season with lemon juice and salt and pepper. Serve (or "serve forth") with thick slices of bread topped with aged cheese and broiled to melt it.

With a freshly honed chef's knife, cut the tops and bottoms off the onions, then cut them in half vertically and peel them. Thinly slice the onion halves.

Heat the oil in a Dutch oven over medium heat. Add the onions, bay leaf, and ½ teaspoon salt and cook, uncovered, stirring frequently with a wooden spoon, for 35 to 40 minutes, until very soft, golden, and considerably reduced in volume. If the onions start to stick to the pan or brown too quickly, lower the heat and/or add a couple tablespoons of water to the pot and scrape up the browned bits. In the last 5 minutes of cooking the onions, stir in the thyme and several grindings of pepper.

Pour in the stock and scrape up any remaining browned bits on the bottom of the pot. Bring to a boil over medium heat, then lower the heat and simmer, uncovered, for 5 minutes. Season with salt and pepper, and add a squeeze of lemon juice if you'd like. Cover and keep the soup warm while you make the cheese croutons.

Preheat the broiler to high and set a rack about 8 inches (20 cm) from the heat source. Put the bread slices on a small baking sheet and broil until golden on top—watch closely so they don't burn. Remove from the oven, flip the slices over, top with the cheese, and return to the oven to broil until the cheese is melted and bubbly and the edges of the toast are deeply browned—again, watch closely. Remove the toasts to a cutting board and cut them into bite-sized squares. Ladle the soup into bowls, top with the cheese croutons, and serve.

Being Curious, a Brief Example

On a cold winter Sunday my daughter roasted two whole chickens (they'd come in a two-pack), and we'd been eating the leftovers in various delicious formats for days when my mom invited us over for lunch and a chilly bike ride. She was making chicken soup, she said, nothing fancy. I'm sure I sighed unappreciatively. I had a pot of chicken stock simmering with the carcasses at that very moment and had planned to make a soup with it of the basic carrots-celery-onion variety and put leftovers in single-serving containers in the freezer— flipped out when solid and tossed in freezer bags—for easy lunches for my daughter.

So I had nothing against chicken soup, in fact very much enjoyed it, but wasn't especially looking forward to more of it that day.

"How do you know how far up the lemongrass stalk to keep slicing?" my mom asked as soon as we got to my parents' house.

Lemongrass? "When you don't see the purple ring in the slices anymore," I said. "Or when you *do* see it, I don't remember." It'd been so long since I'd used lemongrass! (Slice from the bottom until the purple disappears.)

Why had it been so long? For months I'd been making plain old pot roasts, meatballs in marinara, the occasional tikka masala or dal, burgers. I hadn't sliced lemongrass, much less pounded a Thai curry paste in my granite mortar, in ages. I couldn't even remember the last time I read a recipe and used it to make something new.

My mom set my daughter to work chopping a huge pile of fresh ginger. I was suddenly looking forward to this meal.

We went out on the bikes until our hands got too cold, then came inside where the fire in the woodstove was roaring and soup was ready. My mom ladled out chicken soup with all the usual vegetables but also swimming with tender slices of fragrant lemongrass and minced ginger, bright green sweet peas, and crisp, nutty, ever-so-slightly bitter, half-sprouted mung beans she'd dropped into the broth at the last minute to just warm through. It was not fancy, as she'd said, but it was the best chicken soup I'd ever eaten, and I vowed to cook a dish that was new to me the next time I made a meal at home. I'd just needed to be reminded to do that.

Chicken Soup   <small>Serves 6</small>

PRACTICE SKILLS

Working with raw chicken

Coarsely chopping vegetables

Stovetop cooking

Fishing chicken out of a pot of broth, then straining broth (while warm or cool)

One 3- to 4½-pound (1.4 to 2 kg) chicken, or the equivalent of mixed bone-in chicken parts (see headnote)

5 ribs celery

3 large carrots, peeled if you'd like

2 small onions

Stems from 1 bunch parsley

¼ teaspoon whole black peppercorns

1 bay leaf

Good pinch of dried savory or tarragon (optional)

1 tablespoon olive oil

Kosher salt and freshly ground black pepper

You'll have to remove the chicken from the pot of broth, which can be tricky tong-work if you're using a whole bird. Less-experienced cooks will find individual parts easier to fish out with a spider strainer or slotted spoon, but be sure to use bone-in, for better flavor and a richer-in-collagen broth.

If you're using a whole chicken, use scissors to cut off any large flaps of fat and skin around the cavity (save them for making schmaltz, if you'd like), and pull the giblets out (save the liver and sauté it in a little olive oil or butter with some fresh tarragon and have it as a snack).

Put the chicken in a Dutch oven. Coarsely chop 2 of the celery ribs, 2 of the carrots, and 1 of the onions and put them in the pot too, along with the parsley stems, peppercorns, bay leaf, and savory (if using). Add cold water to cover the ingredients. If you're using a larger whole chicken and you can't get it quite fully covered with water, either (a) find a larger pot; (b) turn it breast side down and let the backbone part stick up out of the water; or (c) cut out the backbone with poultry shears or a chef's knife and flatten the bird out a bit so it's submerged. Bring to a boil over high heat, then lower the heat and use a large spoon to skim off the foam from the surface and discard it.

Cover the pot and cook for 45 minutes to 1 hour, adjusting the heat as needed to keep the water at a simmer; try not to let it boil, as that can make for a cloudy broth. Remove from the heat when the chicken is cooked through—if you grasp a drumstick with tongs, you should be able to twist it in its socket without much effort; the meat will have pulled back from the ends of the drumsticks. Let stand for a bit, until it's cool enough that you feel comfortable removing the chicken (or chicken parts) from the broth, then use tongs or a spider skimmer to

recipe continues

transfer the chicken to a large bowl. Pick all of the meat off the chicken. Either discard the bones, skin, and any large pieces of fat, or set them aside (or freeze them for later) to make a batch of stock (see Tip). Shred the chicken into bite-sized pieces with your fingers.

Put a fine-mesh sieve over another large bowl or pot and ladle the broth into it; discard the solids in the sieve. Rinse out the Dutch oven. Chop the remaining celery ribs, carrots, and onion. Return the Dutch oven to medium heat and add the oil, celery, carrots, and onion and a pinch of salt. Cook, stirring frequently, for 5 to 7 minutes, until the onion is translucent but not browned. Add the broth (you should have 8 or 9 cups/2 L or so; if you have less than that, make it up with water), 2 teaspoons salt, and several grindings of pepper. Bring to a boil, then lower the heat and simmer, uncovered, for about 10 minutes, until the vegetables are just tender. Add the shredded chicken meat and cook to just heat through. Season with more salt and pepper if needed, then serve.

Tip: The chicken carcass will at this point still have a lot to give, flavor- and nutrition-wise. To make a second batch of stock—for the freezer, say—put the picked-over bones and skin in a pot with a couple of chopped carrots, a halved onion, some celery (or the washed vegetable trimmings from making this soup), a few peppercorns, and a bay leaf. Cover with water, bring to a boil, skim off the foam from the surface, then lower the heat and simmer for a couple hours, until the stock is very flavorful. Strain, season with salt if you'd like, and save for another soup.

Variation: When you add the strained broth to the sautéed vegetables, go ahead and add 2 or 3 very thinly sliced stalks of lemongrass (remove the tough outer leaves before slicing), and as much minced or julienned ginger as you'd like. Bean sprouts and a handful of frozen peas added with the shredded chicken just before serving are also welcome. I like to use diced parsnips in place of the carrots for this soup.

Sprouts

Home-sprouted beans and seeds are an excellent source of nutrition, especially in times when fresh vegetables are harder to come by.

To make mung bean sprouts, find dried "high-germination" mung beans that are harvested specifically for sprouting by a store with a lot of turnover. (Old beans won't sprout as readily.) You can also use a sprouting mix of mung beans and lentils, peanuts, dried peas, and so on. Rinse them very well in several changes of cold water, until the water runs clear, draining well each time. Put them in a clean canning jar, filling it no more than one-third full, as they expand quite a bit. (I use a quart-sized jar for 1 cup/200 g mung beans.) Fill the jar with cold water. Put the lid on the jar and let the beans soak for about 12 hours. Replace the flat lid with a few layers of cheesecloth, securing it with the lid ring, and drain off all the water. Set the jar on the counter for 1 to 2 days, rinsing with water and draining it off twice each day. The mung beans should have started to sprout after about 1 day. You can use them raw or lightly cooked. (If there's any mold in the jar or if the sprouts smell or look off in any way, toss them out.) Put the regular lid on the jar and store in the refrigerator for up to a few days.

Mom's Potato Salad   Serves 6

4 large ribs celery with leaves

1 small sweet onion

Something odd (optional); for example: ½ cup chopped lovage stalks with leaves; or 1 bunch (14 g) tarragon, minced

1 teaspoon kosher salt, plus more if needed

Freshly ground black pepper

½ cup (120 ml) cider vinegar

2 pounds (910 g) russet potatoes

2 hard-cooked eggs, cooled and peeled

¼ cup (60 ml) mayonnaise, plus more if needed

I suspect my mom has never made potato salad the same way twice, but it's always interesting, always tangy, and always unlike any other person's potato salad. She'll usually add something odd and unexpected, and I encourage you to try that with this base recipe. Fresh or pickled peppers? Sprouts (blanch them by putting them in a sieve and pouring boiling water from a kettle over them)? Sweet cherry tomatoes?

Wash the celery well, cut the ribs lengthwise into thin strips, then cut the strips crosswise to make a fine dice. Put in a large bowl.

Dice the onion and add it to the bowl, along with the odd ingredient (if using), salt, lots of pepper, and the vinegar. Toss to combine, then set aside.

Put the potatoes in a large saucepan and cover with cold water. Bring to a boil and cook until tender, about 20 minutes for child's-fist-sized potatoes. Remove to a bowl and let cool for a few minutes—just until cool enough to peel them with your fingers. Wearing rubber gloves if necessary to protect your hands from hot-potato heat, slip the peels off. Roughly chop the potatoes and add them, still hot, to the bowl with the celery and onion. Toss well, letting the potatoes get broken up a bit as you do.

Using the coarse holes of a grater, grate in the hard-cooked eggs. Add the mayonnaise and toss to incorporate it. Taste and season with more salt, pepper, or mayonnaise if needed. Serve warm or transfer to the refrigerator to chill before serving.

To Catch and Release

It was only a couple of years ago that I learned that not every adult with a young person in their care frequently imagines the worst possible thing happening, spooling out the disastrous events in vivid detail, like a Walter Molino illustration. The envisionings can arrive at any given moment—while driving across a bridge, leaning out a third-floor window to brush some detritus off the roof, while watching my young daughter out in the backyard taking some practice casts with a fishing rod with a lead weight at the end of the line . . . as a thunderstorm approached. Okay, in that latter case, anticipating a freak lightning strike and calling her to the porch when the first drops of rain started coming down could be thought of as just good parenting.

It wasn't until recently that I had an actual experience that would fuel those brief but nightmarish thoughts.

For years my daughter has wanted to learn to fish. She fished a couple times in Georgia (caught a sunfish once), and on a first-grade field trip to a reservoir in Nebraska (a few bluegills found the worms on her hook). In West Virginia, when she was twelve or so, her grandpa, from across the country, arranged for a daylong fly-casting lesson with a guy he found on the internet. She and I drove out to Arthurdale (the New Deal subsistence community founded by Eleanor Roosevelt) and met a very sweet grandfather-like man with a lovely hunting dog. When we arrived, he pulled out a gorgeous old clothbound book and reverently set it before us on the patio table in the backyard: a first edition of *Modern Fly Casting*, by John Alden Knight. No reason for the book to be there; he just wanted us to see it, and I felt I understood that impulse very well. He was about to teach my daughter a skill that people wrote whole books about. The lesson began with knot tying, and within a few hours my daughter was fly casting into a nearby pond with such grace and delicacy I was practically in tears watching her, the brilliant fall sunlight catching on the line arcing over and behind her before the line settled lightly on the water's surface.

Over the next months she practiced casting a real fly into a fast-running section of Deckers Creek, where it cuts through a steep-sided gorge upstream from the old coal mine that's turned the rocks at the water's edge below it rust-red. We'd fasten a rope to a tree at the top of the gorge and hold on to it as we climbed and slid down to the rocky creek with all our gear—her rod and reel and a few flies, our Friends of Deckers Creek–issued water-testing equipment. No trout. She practiced in our own yard, exciting our dog. No trout there, either. She cast for a couple of hours into a small lake at Coopers Rock State Forest just outside Morgantown. No fish of any kind.

By the time she was fourteen my daughter had been fishing a fair number of times and had even caught a couple of little releasables, but nothing that would make a meal—and the meal, for her, is the main point.

My dad says fishing's no fun if you're not catching anything. That's not necessarily true for me. I appreciate any excuse to just zone out, and generally consider myself to be—like Sheridan Anderson, the author of *The Curtis Creek Manifesto*, a delightfully weird book on trout fishing the Arthurdale fly fisher recommended to us—an "eternal foe of the work ethic." But as Anderson also writes, "Despite rumors to the contrary, the paramount objective is: TO CATCH FISH."

So when my dad suggested a morning on a chartered boat on Lake Erie as a good way to practically guarantee that we came home with something to eat, I began to think of all the ways I'd like to cook fresh fish. My daughter was thrilled, of course, literally jumping up and down with excitement as we set out to meet the boat at the marina in the dark before sunrise. My mom had packed sandwiches for an easy breakfast on the lake, and there was a cooler in the back of the car ready to be filled with ice and fillets. At least

a dozen rods were slotted into holders along the sides of the boat. This was going to be serious fishing.

After quick introductions to the captain and his mate, we settled in and found handholds for the fast, choppy ride out to where there might be walleye, maybe even salmon. The sunrise was spectacular. The captain had warned us the night before that the forecast was calling for rough waters, and here they were. Our boat was part of a sprawling line of commercial and chartered trawlers heading out that morning, and it was unnerving to see those other boats in the distance flying up into the air with each wave and pounding violently back down and realize that's what we were doing too. I risked a short one-handed phone video that's breathtakingly beautiful and almost impossible to watch (or delete) now, months later.

I still have sudden, powerful, catastrophizing flashbacks to what happened about half an hour after the captain opened up the throttle. Sometimes the flashbacks include events that didn't happen but could have, that are more extravagant, Walter Molino–style, than the actual events.

I'd say this is my daughter's story to tell, but she doesn't remember most of it.

She appeared to be having trouble holding herself steady on the too-high backward-facing bench seat, so the first mate switched places with her so she could sit more comfortably next to her grandpa in the stern, facing forward. My dad held on to her tightly as she leaned into him and looked toward me and then up at the sky; a couple minutes later I saw her expression suddenly change. She'd lost consciousness.

I rushed back to help my dad move her to the floor of the boat so she wouldn't tip out over the back. Her body was stiff and difficult to maneuver. The mate yelled to the captain to stop the boat, call the Coast Guard, turn around. My mom fell down hard on the boat's floor as she tried to reach me and the trawler changed course with a lurch. I wasn't used to seeing my own parent unsteady.

I held my daughter propped up as well as I could and tried to get her to acknowledge me. I shouted her name directly into her ear through the roar of the boat motor and lake spray, I felt for her pulse, her eyes were partly open but she wouldn't respond, I put my cheek next to her face to better feel her breath. Someone slid a couple of life jackets to us across the wet floor of the boat, and I don't know why we hadn't been wearing them before. I heard frantic radio calls being made at the front of the boat, and at one point I looked up across the water and saw that we were passing another trawler, which was stopped dead still in the water, its passengers all standing and watching us pass—I realized they'd heard our distress calls, and that somehow made me more frightened, not less. The sandpapery nonslip surface of the floor was bloodying my bare knees, but I didn't notice until hours later.

The captain's calls didn't sound frantic enough. I yelled to him, "We need a medic, now!" as loudly as I could, then turned back to my daughter and shouted her name, then "Medic—now!" over and over and over.

For maybe twenty minutes, or my entire lifetime, we crashed and sped back toward shore. As we slowed and reached the dock, my daughter blinked a few times and looked at me with what seemed like recognition. Half a dozen firefighters swarmed onto the boat and lifted her onto a gurney and into a waiting ambulance, and I clambered after her.

My daughter would be fine, she was fine, the EMTs told me, the doctors told me. She was just . . . *extremely* seasick in a way no one on the boat or in the ER had ever seen before. She apologized a lot—too much—to me, to the EMTs, to the nurses and doctors, to her grandparents. She was sorry we hadn't gotten to fish.

The boat's first mate met our car on the side of the highway as we were heading out of town, and into the cooler in back he dropped several pounds of walleye he'd caught and filleted the day before.

"How're you doing, sport?" he asked my daughter.

"I'm fine. I'm sorry. I'm okay now."

When we got home, I dunked a few pieces of the walleye we hadn't caught into a beaten egg, then patted them into a pile of breadcrumbs seasoned with salt and pepper to coat them all over. I fried them until golden in butter and olive oil. I wondered if I'd ever go a day without remembering that change in my daughter's expression, imagining the many ways everything could've been so much worse.

We'll go fishing again, from the banks of a still pond, and maybe we'll catch some fish and build a fire to cook them over. In the meantime I've been seeking out whole fish in the markets in Pittsburgh and doing my best to help my daughter imagine they're fresh from her own line.

Serving a Whole Cooked Trout

1 If you want to remove the skin, pull it off the top fillet with your fingers or scrape it off with a thin metal spatula.

2 Insert the spatula underneath the top fillet, starting from the backbone. Slide the spatula right over the rib bones and lift the fillet off the bones. The flesh may break apart a bit, but that's fine—just get all of it off the top layer of bones and onto serving plates.

3 With your fingers or the spatula, lift the now-exposed backbone and ribs, starting from the tail end, and pull it up to reveal the bottom fillet. Discard the backbone.

4 Slide the spatula underneath the bottom fillet—between the flesh and the skin, if you don't want to serve the skin—and serve.

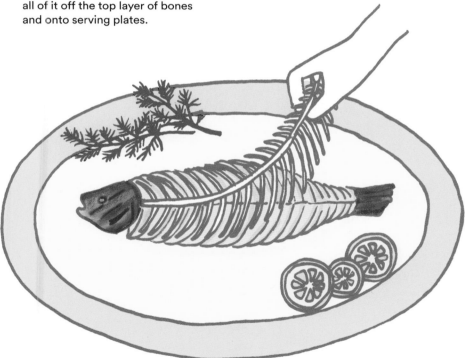

Grilled Whole Fish   Serves 3 or 4

2 large whole trout or red snapper, cleaned and scaled

Kosher salt and freshly ground black pepper

1 lemon, thinly sliced

Vegetable oil

Fresh dill for serving

If you're buying whole fish, look for specimens with clear, bright-looking eyes. Smell the fish too: it should smell like fish, but not weird or "fishy," if that makes sense. We go to Wholey's in the Strip District here in Pittsburgh for live trout from a fishery not too far from here. The fishmonger will pull them gently from the water, stun them with a sharp blow of a mallet, clean them on the counter in front of us, then let them bleed out for a bit in a tub of cold water before wrapping them. We'll scoop some ice into a plastic bag at the front door and set the fish and ice in an insulated bag for the drive home.

Build a hot charcoal fire. Position a well-cleaned grill grate in the grill and let the grate preheat until it's very hot.

Season the fish very lightly with salt and pepper, inside and out. Reserving a couple lemon slices for serving, tuck the rest into the fish cavities.

Grab a paper towel with long tongs, drizzle it with a little oil, and use it to quickly and carefully oil the grill grates. Carefully place the fish, on their sides, on the hot grill. Cook without disturbing the fish for about 8 minutes, then slide a long-handled thin metal spatula under the fish and turn them over onto the other side; the fish should release cleanly from the grate, but if some bits of skin stick or crumple, that's fine, it happens. Cover the grill and cook for another 8 to 10 minutes, until the flesh flakes easily when you prod it with a sharp knife or fork through the skin. Remove to a serving platter and top with the reserved lemon slices and some dill.

Note: You can make this on a stovetop cast-iron grill pan instead of a charcoal grill; it works best with small-ish fish. Preheat the grill pan over one or two burners on medium-high heat, turn on the exhaust fan if you have one, and lightly oil the pan before adding the fish and cooking on both sides until the flesh flakes easily.

Go Bag

Smoking a pork shoulder with me on our back porch in Pittsburgh, my daughter asks whether smoke is an effective preservative of meat. We talk about how it isn't really the smoke that preserves meat but the salt and curing and drying that does it—see salt pork, cured bacon, and dried jerky, for example. She asks how to make jerky.

When we still lived in West Virginia, she had a classmate who lived on a farm a winding forty-five-minute drive into the hills. His mom was a professor of ruminant nutrition, I think. He once brought a tiny bottle lamb to a park in town, and I remember watching him and my daughter sit quietly on the grass holding the lamb between them, very gently—it was unsteady on its feet, and wasn't expected to live very long. My daughter's friend pulled a plastic baggie out of his jacket pocket and offered her some jerky his mom had made from venison he'd harvested himself.

I tell her I'll email her grandmother to ask for the old recipes from Virginia so we can make some. The last time I'd made jerky, she was only five or six.

After a brief pause, she continues, "This is unrelated, but have you ever heard of a 'go bag'?"

Reader, this was not unrelated.

It was the first Tuesday in November 2020. You may remember that day as an especially tense one. I'd walked down the street to vote in the morning, and decided to spend the rest of the day with my daughter tending a fire and monitoring the progress of a large cut of pork, and checking my phone for news only every seven to ten minutes. When my daughter asked about go bags and jerky, I realized I'd been checking the news more like every two and a half minutes and that she was probably picking up on whatever election-related anxiety I'd been feeling.

I ask her what she'd put in a go bag if she made one. Jerky. The portable water filter we'd only used once, to test it out, on a short hike in Coopers Rock State Forest. We'd lain on our stomachs next to a creek and sipped the ice-cold water through the straw. (It worked, I guess—the water tasted like water, and we did not get sick.) Rubbing alcohol? One of those magnesium fire starters you can put on a keychain. The cool crank-operated flashlight Grandpa had given her a while back for fun. A pocket knife for whittling.

"Granola bars?" she asks.

There's always a box of stale ones in the bag I keep in the back of the car in winter along with emergency blankets and waterproof matches and such. "Not good for your braces," I say. "Maybe just dried fruit and nuts."

"How would I get my braces taken off if there's a societal collapse?"

"We'll cross that bridge." I try to reassure her that no collapse is imminent, then change the subject slightly and tell her about the *Twilight Zone* episode in which the last surviving man in the world is thrilled to have all the time to read all the books in the library (as if he couldn't have done that while other people were alive), and then he breaks his glasses.

There's still leftover pulled smoked pork in the fridge and the state of the world outside is still a bit unsettled when we start trying out beef jerky recipes.

As far as I know, she hasn't actually packed a go bag, and I think that's fine.

Lighting a Charcoal Fire in a Grill

There are two easy and reliable methods for lighting lump charcoal in a grill: using natural fire-starter squares (made of sawdust and paraffin), and using a chimney starter. The fire-starter squares are good because they don't create a lot of excess ash and are easier for young people because lighting the fire doesn't involve tipping hot coals out of a chimney; the chimney is good because it lights coals quickly and you don't need anything else other than some newspaper. We only use lump charcoal these days because it doesn't leave any chemical residue on the inside of our grill.

When you're done with the fire, close down all vents completely and put the lid on the grill to starve the fire of oxygen. Don't try to empty the ashes until the next day. The next time you grill, stir the coals remaining in the grill to let the ashes fall through the lower grate; discard the ashes. You can reuse the coals that haven't burned—just add some fresh charcoal over the top.

USING FIRE-STARTER SQUARES

1 Open the lower vent in the bottom of your grill and set the grill grate aside for now. (Scrape the grate clean if it needs it.) Pour lump charcoal into the grill (usually there'll be a small grate in the bottom to allow air to circulate underneath the coals).

2 Tuck two or three fire-starter squares among the coals, evenly spaced in the grill. There should be a piece or two of charcoal extending partly over each square.

3 Using matches or a long lighter, light the torn edges of the squares. The flames rising from the squares will light the coals that extend over the squares, and those coals will in turn ignite the coals around them. When most of the coals on the surface of the pile in the grill are ignited and ashy-looking, set the grill grate over them. When the grate is hot and the fire is strong, partly close the bottom vent to slow down the burn a bit, and you're ready to grill.

USING A CHIMNEY STARTER

1 Open the lower vent in the bottom of your grill and set the grill grate aside for now. (Scrape the grate clean if it needs it.) Pour a layer of lump charcoal into the grill (usually there'll be a small grate in the bottom to allow air to circulate underneath the coals).

2 Lightly crumple up a couple of sheets of newspaper and stuff them in the bottom, smaller section of the chimney. Fill the top section two-thirds full (or less, if you're smoking and want a slow burn) with charcoal.

3 Set the chimney, paper section down, on top of the layer of charcoal in the grill. I like to tilt it back toward the handle at a slight angle to allow more air to flow underneath it, but it's not necessary.

4 Use a match or long lighter to light the paper. The flames from the paper should ignite the charcoal above. When you see that all of the coals in the chimney are lit and most are glowing, use a thick potholder or fireproof mitt to hold the chimney by the handle—it'll be hot!—and carefully dump them onto the layer of coals in the grill. Use a metal poker or tongs to spread them out, then set the grill grate over them. When the grate is hot and the fire is strong, partly close the bottom vent to slow down the burn a bit, and you're ready to grill.

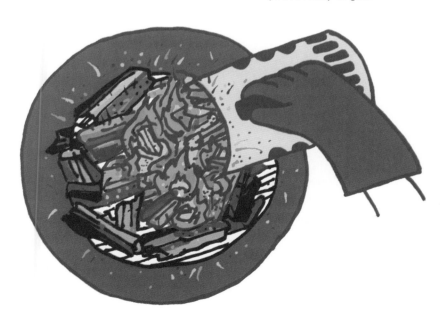

Smoked Pork Shoulder

Makes about 10 cups
(2½ pounds/1.2 kg) pulled pork

PRACTICE SKILLS

Lighting a charcoal fire and maintaining its (very low) temperature

Working with raw meat

Moving a large cut of meat on and off the grill

---

2 tablespoons brown sugar

1 tablespoon kosher salt

1 tablespoon paprika

1 teaspoon onion powder

1 teaspoon garlic powder

½ teaspoon freshly ground black pepper

One 4- to 5-pound (2 to 2.3 kg) bone-in Boston butt pork shoulder

Soft buns

Barbecue sauce of your choice (very optional)

In this recipe I describe how to use a ceramic smoker, but if you're using a kettle grill, here's what to do: Build a small fire on one side of the grill. Put soaked and drained wood chips in an aluminum-foil packet and punch some holes in it to let smoke out, and set it on top of the coals. Put the meat on the grill grate on the side opposite the fire. Put the lid on, with the vent in the lid just barely opened and positioned over the meat side of the grill so the smoke is drawn from the foil packet, around the meat, and out the vent. Every so often, feed a few lumps of charcoal to the fire.

In a large bowl or other container, combine the brown sugar, salt, paprika, onion powder, garlic powder, and pepper. Put the pork in the spice mixture and turn it to coat all sides well, patting the spices into the meat. Cover and refrigerate overnight.

Prepare a charcoal smoker and soak about 1½ cups wood chips (hickory, pecan, or a fruit wood) in water for at least 30 minutes. When the smoker has come up to about 225°F (110°C) and stabilized at that temperature for at least 15 minutes, drain the wood chips and scatter them over the coals, put the grill grate over the coals, and put the pork shoulder, fat side down, on the grate. Cover and cook, maintaining the temperature as close to 225°F as possible and avoiding lifting the smoker lid, for 7 to 8 hours, until the pork is a deep mahogany color, you can pull pieces off the outside fairly easily with tongs, and the internal temperature of the meat is at least 180°F (82°C).

Remove the shoulder to a carving board. When it's cool enough to handle, pull the meat off the bones, discarding large pieces of fat, and shred it with two forks. Serve on its own, or on buns—sauce optional.

Note: This is almost as good simply roasted in the oven: Roast fat side up at 300°F (150°C) for about 5 hours.

258

Jerky   Makes about 11 ounces (310 g)

PRACTICE SKILLS

Trimming and slicing raw meat

Moving baking sheets out of a warm oven

½ cup (120 ml) soy sauce

¼ cup (60 ml) white or red wine

2 tablespoons sugar

1 tablespoon kosher salt

½ teaspoon onion powder

½ teaspoon garlic powder

A few grindings of black pepper

2 pounds (910 g) very lean beef or venison, partially frozen if possible

Chipotle chile powder or ground cayenne (optional)

Choose the leanest meat you can find, as fat goes rancid quickly and will reduce shelf life. The best beef cuts for jerky are round and flank steak. Sirloin is also good, but it's more challenging to slice with the grain into the typically long jerky-like slices—and it's also pretty expensive and better used in other ways, in my opinion. Just about any venison cut will work.

In a small bowl, whisk together the soy sauce, wine, ¼ cup (60 ml) water, the sugar, salt, onion powder, garlic powder, and black pepper until the sugar and salt are dissolved. Set the marinade aside.

With a very sharp knife, trim all bits of visible fat and sinew from the beef and slice it *with the grain* less than ⅛ inch (3 mm) thick; if necessary, use your hand or a wooden mallet to pound thick areas. Put in a gallon-sized resealable plastic bag set inside a bowl or other container and pour in the marinade. Seal the bag, removing as much air as possible, and massage gently to separate the beef slices and distribute the marinade. Refrigerate overnight.

Set the oven to 170°F (77°C). Line two baking sheets with parchment paper.

Lift each slice of meat from the marinade and use your fingers to swipe excess liquid off; arrange the slices on the baking sheets and bake until very dry and stiff but still slightly flexible, about 5 hours. If you'd like, dust the still-warm jerky with chile powder. Let cool completely, then store in airtight (or, preferably, vacuum-sealed) bags in the freezer.

Homemade jerky, in my experience, doesn't last super long at room temperature—moisture always seems to find a way—but well salted, well dried, and tightly sealed, it should be okay for at least a few weeks or a month. If mold forms or if anything seems off about the jerky, just toss it and stock your go bag with dried fruit and nuts.

Building a Campfire

1 Check the fire outlook for your area (weather.gov is a good place to start)—if the weather's been dry, or if it's windy, don't start a fire today. If you're in a state or national park or forest, look for signs indicating the fire threat level and make sure it's green or "low" before you start a fire.

2 Clear a large area of leaves and other flammable materials, and make a circle of stones to keep the fire contained, or use a purpose-built fire ring. Check to see that there are no tree branches hanging low over the area. Have a hose or a bucket of water handy.

3 If you're going to cook over the fire, arrange a grill grate over the area, propped securely on the rocks or fire ring. Set the grate to the side while you build the fire. If you plan to roast marshmallows or hot dogs, find long, still-green sticks (green so they won't ignite) and sharpen one end with a knife.

4 Collect three types of materials: dry grass or leaves for tinder, small dry twigs for kindling, and larger dry logs from deadfall or cut and cured fire-wood for fuel. Don't cut living trees or branches—it's impolite, and they won't burn well anyway.

5 Pile the tinder in a small, tightly packed mound.

6 Arrange the kindling in a rough pyra-mid atop the dry grass.

7 Place a few of the larger logs in a pyramid over the kindling. The logs shouldn't be packed down tightly on the kindling, because you want air to circulate between them—fire needs oxygen.

8 Carefully light the dry grass with a match or flint-type fire starter and blow on it very gently. When the flames reach the twiggy kindling, they'll light it, and the kindling will in turn light the logs.

9 Keep two or three logs on the fire at a time—you need just a small fire for warmth and for cooking over. When the flames have died down and the embers are glowing, carefully set the grill grate over them and let it get hot before you put food on it to cook. (You can also just put a cast-iron skillet on the grate.) Now is the time to roast hot dogs and marshmallows, too—when the embers are sunset-orange and there are no flames.

10 Don't leave the fire unattended. When you're done with the fire, let it die down as much as pos-sible, then pour water over it to completely extinguish it; break up larger coals and distribute the damp ashes in the woods or grass.

Acknowledgments

This odd little book took shape over the course of several years of emails and phone conversations with Holly Dolce, at Abrams, to whom I owe a million thanks for her trust and patience as we figured out just what to do with all my disparate ideas. Thank you for letting me write this book, Holly. Thanks, too, to my editor, Laura Dozier, who, along with Asha Simon, Lisa Silverman, and Kathleen Gaffney, shepherded the manuscript through a complicated design and production process. The book was improved immeasurably by Sarah Scheffel's thoughtful copyedit, and I can't thank her enough for her smart fixes and suggestions. Thank you to Deb Wood, the art director, and Danielle Youngsmith, the designer, for their sensitive work to make the book's many elements both beautiful and functional.

I am so thrilled to have been able to work with the talented photographer Chaunté Vaughn, along with prop stylist Charlotte Havelange and photo tech Paul Yem, in a sunlit studio in Bushwick to produce the photographs you see here. They made the simplest, plainest food look gorgeous without a hint of pretension and were truly a pleasure to spend a few days with besides. I thank them for their good humor, their skill, and their professionalism. Many thanks, too, are due to Amelia Arend, the greatest grocery-shopper and produce-sourcer I could've hoped for.

Thank you to Jenice Kim, whose illustrations are a huge part of why this book looks as charming as it does. She turned a keen eye to my murky photographs and offered artistic interpretations that are both usable and sweetly inspirational.

My good friend Leda Scheintaub gave feedback and encouragement as I wrote and worked on this book, and performed an eagle-eyed proofread of the pages toward the end of the process. Her input at every stage, as always, has been invaluable. Thank you, Leda.

I am immensely grateful to my agent, Leslie Stoker, who has been unfailing in her support of me and my work over many years. Thank you, Leslie, for your understanding, your expertise, and your passion for food writing.

Finally, thank you to my family. My mom and dad taught me to cook and think generously about food, inspiring many of the recipes and stories here. My mom deserves special thanks: She worked the photo shoot like an absolute pro, cooking, prepping, washing pots and pans, and helping make the kinds of in-the-moment decisions I was often too overwhelmed to deal with on my own. And thank you to my husband and our kid, of course, without whose intelligence and companionship and love this book would not have been written.

Sources and Further Reading

INTRODUCTION

Chandler, Adam. "Why Do Americans Move So Much More Than Europeans?" *The Atlantic*, October 21, 2016.

Cronon, William. "'Only Connect . . .': The Goals of a Liberal Education." *The American Scholar* 67, no. 4 (1998): 73–80.

Forster, E.M. *Howards End*. New York and London: G. P. Putnam's Sons, 1910. PDF.

Lustgarten, Abrahm. "Climate Change Will Force a New American Migration." *ProPublica*, September 15, 2020.

Martin, Michael. "Demographer Unpacks Why Fewer Americans Are Moving." NPR, November 23, 2019.

THE CASE FOR A SPOILED APPETITE

Tsakiris, Chloe, Olivia Tsakiris, and Nicholas Tsakiris. *Sea Salt and Honey*. New York: HarperCollins, 2021.

SEMI-CONVENIENCE FOOD

Betty Crocker's Cookbook. New York: Macmillan, 1991 (first ed. published 1969).

Child, Julia, Simone Beck, and Louisette Bertholle. *Mastering the Art of French Cooking, vols. 1 and 2*. New York: Alfred A. Knopf, 1961.

Devi, Yamuna. *Lord Krishna's Cuisine: The Art of Indian Vegetarian Cooking*. New York: Dutton, 1987.

Eliason, Karine, Nevada Harward, and Madeline Westover. *Make-a-Mix Cookery: How to Make Your Own Mixes*. Tucson, AZ: H. P. Books, 1978.

Hughlett, Mike. "General Mills Relaunches Hamburger Helper." *Minneapolis Star Tribune*, July 6, 2013.

Painter, Kristen Leigh. "General Mills' Old El Paso Brand Is a Hit in the U.S. and Is Ready to Expand." *Minneapolis Star Tribune*, September 17, 2016. Park, Michael Y. "A History of the Cake Mix, the Invention That Redefined 'Baking.'" *Bon Appétit*, September 26, 2013.

U.S. Bureau of Labor Statistics. "Women in the Labor Force: A Data Book." *BLS Reports*, December 2014.

MAKE TWO

Berenbaum, Rose Levy. *The Bread Bible*. New York: W. W. Norton, 2003.

Bittman, Mark. *How to Cook Everything: Simple Recipes for Great Food*. New York: Macmillan, 1998.

Brown, Alton. *Good Eats*. Season 7, episode 6, "The Muffin Man." Aired July 23, 2003.

SHE'S GONE ALREADY; SHE'S STILL HERE

Bugialli, Guiliano. *Classic Techniques of Italian Cooking*. New York: Fireside, 1989.

Holbrook, Sharon. "Emptying the Dishwasher Can Improve Kids' Mental Health." *New York Times*, February 11, 2021.

THE HOLY GRAIL

Batra, Neelam. *1,000 Indian Recipes*. New York: Wiley, 2002.

AGE APPROPRIATE

Dobrin, Arnold. *Peter Rabbit's Natural Foods Cookbook*. New York: Frederick Warne, 1977.

AS *YOU* LIKE IT

Jaffrey, Madhur. *Madhur Jaffrey's World Vegetarian*. New York: Clarkson Potter, 1999.

Komolafe, Yewande. "Yewande Komolafe's 10 Essential Nigerian Recipes," *New York Times*, June 24, 2019.

Krishna, Priya. "When Did Recipe Writing Get So . . . Whitewashed?" *Bon Appétit*, July 29, 2020.

Morales, Bonnie. *Kachka: A Return to Russian Cooking*. New York: Flatiron Books, 2017.

Pépin, Claudine. *Kids Cook French*. Beverly, MA: Quarry Books, 2015.

A POT, A POT OF BEANS, AND THEE!

Coleridge, Samuel Taylor. "Constancy to an Ideal Object." Published 1828. Available at PoetryFoundation.org.

Cort, Simon. "Coleridge and the Pantisocratic Pipe-Dream." *Wordsworth Grasmere*, September 2, 2015.

Dragonwagon, Crescent. *Bean by Bean: A Cookbook*. New York: Workman, 2012.

Garrett, Clarke. "Coleridge's Utopia Revisited." *Soundings: An Interdisciplinary Journal* 55, no. 1 (1972): 121–37.

Stott, Andrew McConnell. "Diets of the Romantic Poets." *Wordsworth Grasmere*, August 8, 2016.

TASTES ACQUIRED AND LOST

Alley, Lynn. "The Sour Gene: A Mouth-Puckering Discovery." *Wine Spectator*, October 29, 2019.

Batmanglij, Najmieh. *New Food of Life: Ancient Persian and Modern Iranian Cooking and Ceremonies*, 4th ed. Washington, DC: Mage, 2020.

Callaway, Ewen. "Soapy Taste of Coriander Linked to Genetic Variants." *Nature*, September 12, 2012.

Frontiers. "Supertasters Do Not Have Particularly High Density of Taste Buds on Tongue, Crowdsourcing Shows." *ScienceDaily*, May 27, 2014.

Harries-Rees, Karen. "Tasting Sour Flavours Is Genetic." *Chemistry World*, July 16, 2007.

Liem, Djin Gie. "Heightened Sour Preferences During Childhood." *Chemical Senses* 28, no. 2 (2003): 173–80.

Mennella, Julie A., and Nuala K. Bobowski. "The Sweetness and Bitterness of Childhood: Insights from Basic Research on Taste Preferences." *Physiology & Behavior* 152, part B (2015): 502–7.

Siegel, Bettina Elias. *Kid Food: The Challenge of Feeding Children in a Highly Processed World*. New York: Oxford University Press, 2019.

MAKE DO

Gibbons, Euell. *Stalking the Wild Asparagus*. New York: David McKay Company, 1962.

Martinac, Paula. "The Health Benefits of Eating Dandelion Greens." *SFGate*, December 2, 2018.

Wilson, Bee. "Are We Born Craving a Balanced Diet?" *Discover*, January 20, 2016.

ON SMALL KITCHENS

Wallender, Lee. "The Ever-Changing Average Kitchen Size." *The Spruce*, March 2, 2021.

CULTURE

Katz, Sandor Ellix. *The Art of Fermentation*. White River Junction, VT: Chelsea Green, 2012.

———. *Wild Fermentation*, 2nd ed. White River Junction, VT: Chelsea Green, 2016.

Lohner, Svenja. "A Milk-Curdling Activity." *Scientific American*, February 2, 2017.

McGee, Harold. *On Food and Cooking: The Science and Lore of the Kitchen*. New York: Scribner, 2004.

Patel, Nash, and Leda Scheintaub. *Dosa Kitchen: Recipes for India's Favorite Street Food*. New York: Clarkson Potter, 2018.

Scheintaub, Leda. *Cultured Foods for Your Kitchen: 100 Recipes Featuring the Bold Flavors of Fermentation*. New York: Rizzoli, 2014.

PREFERENCES

LC editors. "Johnnycakes." *Leites Culinaria*, August 19, 2019.

McCarroll, Meredith. "Shall We Gather at Three Rivers?" *Bitter Southerner*, April 22, 2020.

Moss, Robert. "The Real Reason Sugar Has No Place in Cornbread." *Serious Eats*, August 25, 2014.

Pennypacker, Sara. *Pax*. New York: Balzer + Bray, 2016.

Purvis, Kathleen. "Why Does Sugar in Cornbread Divide Races in the South?" *Charlotte Observer*, March 29, 2016.

Tipton-Martin, Toni. *Jubilee: Recipes from Two Centuries of African American Cooking*. New York: Clarkson Potter, 2019.

ORDINARY CHICKEN

Alonzo, Austin. "Inside Costco's New, $450 Million Chicken Operation." *Poultry International*, September 2020.

Bergin, Nicholas. "Chicken Plant Raises Environmental Concerns." *Lincoln Journal Star*, January 1, 2017.

Durham, Sharon. "Chillin' Chickens: Which Method Works Best?" *Agricultural Research*, April 2008.

Finn, S. Margot. *Discriminating Taste: How Class Anxiety Created the American Food Revolution*, esp. ch. 3, "No Culinary Enlightenment." New Brunswick, NJ: Rutgers University Press, 2017.

Georgia Ports. "Savannah Now the Top US Port for Ag Exports." Press release, June 25, 2020.

Gray, Margaret. *Labor and the Locavore: The Making of a Comprehensive Food Ethic*. Berkeley: University of California Press, 2014.

Kristof, Nicholas. "The Ugly Secrets Behind the Costco Chicken." *New York Times*, February 6, 2021.

Mishan, Ligaya. "The Activists Working to Remake the Food System." *T: The New York Times Style Magazine*, February 19, 2021.

Neuman, William. "New Way to Help Chickens Cross to Other Side." *New York Times*, October 22, 2010.

Nosrin, Samin. *Salt, Fat, Acid, Heat: Mastering the Elements of Good Cooking*. New York: Simon & Schuster, 2017.

Stuesse, Angela, and Nathan T. Dollar. "Who Are America's Meat and Poultry Workers?" *Working Economics Blog, Economic Policy Institute*, September 24, 2020.

BLISS POINT

Moss, Michael. "The Extraordinary Science of Junk Food." *New York Times Magazine*, February 20, 2013.

GROCERIES IN A SMALL TOWN

Friends of Deckers Creek. "History," Deckerscreek.org.

Mellett, Julia. "St. Mary's Byzantine Catholic Church." YouTube, December 10, 2018.

Taylor, Beth Kurtz. "Halushki Power!" *Pittsburgh Post-Gazette*, March 11, 2015.

Venham, Christy, and Jeanne Grimm. "The Morgan Shirt Factory." West Virginia Department of Arts, Culture, and History, wvculture.org.

PATIENCE

Schulze, Eric. "An Introduction to the Maillard Reaction: The Science of Browning, Aroma, and Flavor." *Serious Eats*, April 13, 2017.

A FORTNIGHT OF CAKE

Gampp, Yolanda. *How to Cake It! A Cookbook*. New York: William Morrow, 2017.

Kassem, Amirah. *The Power of Sprinkles: A Cake Book by the Founder of the Flour Shop*. New York: Abrams, 2019.

NO RECIPES, NO MASTERS

Child, Julia, Simone Beck, and Louisette Bertholle. *Mastering the Art of French Cooking*, vol. 1. New York: Alfred A. Knopf, 1961.

Fisher, M. F. K. *With Bold Knife and Fork*. New York: Smithmark, 1968.

Gunther, Caitlin Raux. "The Story of France's Most Extraordinary Pastry." *Food52*, October 17, 2019.

Shapiro, Laura. "When Did Following Recipes Become a Personal Failure?" *The Atlantic*, April 2021.

TO CATCH AND RELEASE

Anderson, Sheridan. *The Curtis Creek Manifesto: A Fully Illustrated Guide to the Strategy, Finesse, Tactics, and Paraphernalia of Fly Fishing*. Portland, OR: Frank Amato Publications, 1978.

Strike, Karen. "Walter Molino's Amazing True Story Death Scenes: Italian Illustrator's Mid-Century Art Must Be Seen to Be Believed." *Flashbak*, December 7, 2020.

Recipe Index

Index

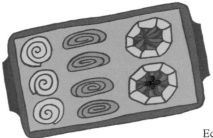

Editor: Laura Dozier
Designer: Danielle Youngsmith
Managing Editor: Lisa Silverman
Production Manager: Kathleen Gaffney

Library of Congress Control Number: 2022942356

ISBN: 978-1-4197-4938-4
eISBN: 978-1-64700-996-0

Printed and bound in China
10 9 8 7 6 5 4 3 2 1

When foraging and using wild plants it is essential that readers use extreme
caution and consult physicians or other medical professionals as needed.
The Author and Publisher disclaim any and all liability in connection with
information in this book about the foraging and use of wild plants.

Abrams books are available at special discounts when purchased in quantity
for premiums and promotions as well as fundraising or educational use.
Special editions can also be created to specification. For details, contact
specialsales@abramsbooks.com or the address below.

ABRAMS The Art of Books
195 Broadway, New York, NY 10007
abramsbooks.com